Found Theology

Found Theology

History, Imagination and the Holy Spirit

Ben Quash

B L O O M S B U R Y

LONDON • NEW DELHI • NEW YORK • SYDNEY

Bloomsbury T&T Clark

An imprint of Bloomsbury Publishing Plc

50 Bedford Square
London
WC1B 3DP
UK

1385 Broadway
New York
NY 10018
USA

www.bloomsbury.com

Bloomsbury is a registered trade mark of Bloomsbury Publishing Plc

First published 2013

British Library Cataloguing-in-Publication Data
A catalogue record for this book is available from the British Library.

ISBN: HB: 978-0-5672-9560-6
PB: 978-0-5675-1792-0
ePDF: 978-0-5672-2064-6
ePub: 978-0-5671-1165-4

Library of Congress Cataloging-in-Publication Data
Quash, Ben
Found Theology/Ben Quash p.cm
Includes bibliographical references and index.
ISBN 978-0-5672-9560-6 (hardcover) – ISBN 978-0-5675-1792-0 (pbk.)

Typeset by Deanta Global Publishing Services, Chennai, India
Printed and bound in Great Britain

For Zanz
My Found One

CONTENTS

ACKNOWLEDGEMENTS

The title and the theme of this book owe themselves to two remarkable thinkers and friends: the late Dan Hardy and Peter Ochs. Hardy was an inspiring exemplar of the kind of Found Theology to which I try to do justice here, and Ochs, in his deeply appreciative and perceptive interpretations of Hardy's thought, is the originator of the term itself. I am grateful to him for his generosity in letting me appropriate it as the title of this book.

Dan was part of a small group I was privileged to meet with – roughly once a month – for over 10 years between 1996 and 2007, a group that also included David Ford and Tim Jenkins. The theology here would never have developed as it did without the benefit of those discussions, and my debts to that group are incalculable. Bob Gibbs and Deirdre Baker were wonderful companions in a series of adventures into Collingwood and other writers on fantasy, folklore and imagination as I was hatching the outline for this book. My colleagues at King's College London have been a thoroughly congenial and intellectually stimulating body of people among whom to work.

As this book has gone through the final stages of gestation and has – finally – reached the point of delivery, my wife Susannah and I have had a baby on the way too. He is due in just 6 days' time as I write this. My research assistant, Chloë Reddaway, has observed certain analogies as she has helped me get the book out, and now that it is done, my response is that she is as good a midwife as one could ever wish for. I am immensely grateful to her for the hours she has put into preparing the manuscript. Throughout, she has been collected, constructive, quietly encouraging and immaculately efficient.

I should like to thank Elizabeth and Michael Middleton, who in a deeply generous but unassuming way gave us a roof over our heads for seven months while our own house was being stripped back to its barest bones and rebuilt. It was under that peaceful roof that much of this book was written.

Anna Turton, Caitlin Flynn, Grishma Fredric and their colleagues at T&T Clark have been heroically committed to turning this manuscript around in an exceptionally short time.

My dear sons William and Joseph have made sure I knew life was more than writing (or house building).

And to Susannah I say thank you for being my best-ever finding, and for finding me in ways I could never have imagined possible. Your companionship in theology as in every area of life involves daily and dizzying discovery, as well as an unshakeable sense of home.

Ben Quash
Feast of St Edith Stein, 2013

PREFACE

*I still have many things to say to you,
but you cannot bear them now.*

(JN 16.12)

*To know Him means to know Him again and again,
in ever new ways.*

(KARL BARTH, *CHURCH DOGMATICS* II.1, 322)

'Myself, I believe in God', wrote D. H. Lawrence. The God he goes on to discuss, however, is a God he wants to contrast with the 'owned' God of the established religion of his day. '[W]e, being creatures of obstinacy and will, we insist that He cannot move . . .', observes Lawrence disparagingly. But such an immobile God can only be an idol: a possession and not a constant, transforming discovery. The God he wants to evoke is fierce, free, impalpable and elusive. This God can only be found, and found again, for this God is 'forever departing from us'. And it is the activity of the third person of the Trinity with which Lawrence most associates this summons to a life of constant finding:

> Only the Holy Ghost within you can scent the new tracks of the Great God across the Cosmos of Creation. The Holy Ghost is the dark hound of Heaven, whose baying we ought to listen to, as he runs ahead into the unknown, tracking the mysterious, everlasting departing of the Lord God, who . . . has gone over our horizon. . . . We go in search of God, following the Holy Ghost, and depending on the Holy Ghost. . . . [W]e hear his strange

calling, the strange calling like a hound on the scent, away in unmapped wilderness.[1]

Hans Urs von Balthasar may seem an unlikely ally of Lawrence here, yet he can be invoked as such – even though he too infrequently practises in his later theology what he preached in his earlier days. At his best, he describes the disruptions and novelties of history as things to which the Church can only respond adequately if it has a suitably developed account of the work of the Holy Spirit. He points out in *Razing the Bastions*,[2] for example, how in the fifteenth and sixteenth centuries one external and another internal shift took place in Western history: the voyages of discovery of new worlds and the Protestant Reformation. They were two vast new historical eventualities, or 'findings', and they required of the Church an interaction with the non-Christian world on an entirely new basis, because:

> [the] geographical-political inner room and the spiritual-intellectual inner room of Christianity [had found] themselves unexpectedly brought into a continuity[3] with the surrounding world, and this situation demanded (and still demands) that all the instincts be newly attuned and the interior organs of balance be differently disposed.[4]

Balthasar sees this shift continuing to require an 'immense transformation in [Roman Catholic] Christian consciousness'.[5] It is a matter of the Church coming out of 'a splendid isolation' and being part of 'the tumult of the age' in solidarity with humanity as a whole.[6] His 1952 assertion is that a 'Baroque theology' has been over-committed to a backward-looking attempt to perpetuate tradition for its own sake: 'its relationship to its own past leaps to

---

[1]Lawrence 1988, 191. I am most grateful to Gregory Seach for introducing this passage to me, and so helping me at a crucial stage to understand something of the book I was trying to write.
[2]Balthasar 1993.
[3]That is, 'a horizontal (and no longer hierarchical) solidarity'. Balthasar 1993, 50.
[4]Balthasar 1993, 49.
[5]Ibid., 58.
[6]Ibid., 93.

the eye, but not its relation to its future'.[7] Balthasar saw this risky task as evidence of the movement of the Holy Spirit. It required a theology of the Holy Spirit as what Balthasar calls *Ausleger* – the layer-out (or expositor) in historical process of the knowledge of God into which creatures are never-endingly invited.[8]

Found Theology will argue that the perfection of God's revelation in Christ is not compromised by – indeed, precisely implies – an ongoing historical dynamic whereby, in God, human beings are constantly invited to *relate the given to the found*. The givens come alive only in this indefinitely extended series of encounters with new circumstances, and the Christian assumption ought to be that no new found thing need be construed as a threat to what has been given, for we have to do with the same God both in the given and in the found. The God who has 'stocked our backpack for the journey', so to speak, also 'places things in our path', up ahead of us. The presumption that the givens of Christian faith will help to order and illuminate newly encountered experiences or challenges can work the other way too: found things, conceived as gifts of the Holy Spirit who unfolds all the riches that are in Christ, can and must reconfigure, unlock and amplify what is already held true by the Church.

A characteristic feature of theology in this vein will be that it is *patient*, in a 'theologically informed and spiritually sustained' way.[9] It will be provisional by instinct, refusing the idea that the efforts of the ordering intellect can achieve the reconciliation of all historical experience in a definitive formulation or scheme. Moreover, it will be inclined to correlate this humility of the intellect with the awareness that we cannot lay claim to complete *holiness* this side of the eschaton; in other words, the intellectual humility of its approach will express a determinedly anti-Pelagian stance. Both those 'conservatives' concerned with a sub-Calvinist 'purity' of doctrine delivered by a cadre of sound knowers to an audience of obedient recipients, and those 'liberals' confident that they know better than the tradition because of their superior intellectual and analytical resources are thereby challenged, as they are by the examples of their forebears, to beware of selling short

---

[7]Ibid., 18. See also p. 51 and note 1.
[8]For example, in Balthasar 2000, 13.
[9]Williams 2003, 7.

the principle of the free, prevenient grace of God; the priority of the divine initiative, and our dependence on it at every point, whether in our growth in sanctity or in our growth in knowledge. It is a commitment to this that makes us ready both to find and *be found* by the Holy Spirit.

The doctrine of the Holy Spirit that is closest to this in recent theology is, perhaps, the one articulated by Rowan Williams in his essay 'Trinity and Revelation' in *On Christian Theology* (Blackwell, 2000), in which the Spirit is conceived as spiralling generatively forward in history, helping the Church to think ever more deeply about the meaning of its own thought and practice. I will spend some considerable time in dialogue with this essay in Chapter 1, and ideas from it will recur at various points in the book.

The key theoretical resources that will be turned to in exploring this argument, however, are (i) theories about the resistance of texts – especially scriptural texts – to definitive interpretative closure, and this will involve an adaptation of the concept of 'maculation' developed by the Jewish scholar David Weiss Halivni in recent years; (ii) reception aesthetics (first developed by Hans Robert Jauss in the 1960s and 1970s); and (iii) theories of abductive reasoning (especially as articulated by C. S. Peirce, and – in an earlier age, but in an English, 'Platonic-empiricist' tradition of thought that will be important for my purposes – by Samuel Taylor Coleridge). An affirmative appropriation of the benefits (or 'generosity') of maculation frees the theological interpretation of Scripture from pretensions to timelessness or ahistoricity. Jaussian reception theory relates the *past* to the *present* by insisting on the importance of the historical series of interpretations that binds them. Abduction relates both past and present to the *future* in a way that insists on the centrality of imagination (creative and energetic conjecture) as an unfinalizable process oriented to making the best sense of old and new data together, in ever-changing historical circumstances. Theories of maculation, reception and abduction are fundamentally committed to the inescapability of historical process as the medium of human interpretation, and indeed are largely celebratory of it. All three theories advocate the constant relating of the given to the found.

This book will be original in the extent to which, by appropriating these theories theologically, it represents them in the context of an historicizing pneumatology, claiming that history, which is a central focus for all three theories, is *the gift and the medium of the Holy Spirit*. It starts where my first book – *Theology and the Drama of History*[10] – left off: the last chapter of that book was a meditation on Hopkins's poem *The Wreck of the* 'Deutschland', read as a quest to reconcile with maximum integrity a traumatic new historical event with a belief in a providential God. Hopkins's line 'Over again I feel thy finger and find thee' stands as an invitation to a pneumatology; the Spirit is the one to be 'found' over and over again, and in the finding of the Spirit one realizes oneself as, in fact, caught up in a trinitarian dynamic, in which the Son who shows us the Father is redelivered to the Church by way of its active, imaginative engagement with the events of history. The provisionality and risk of error that attends this process is part of life in the Spirit; part of the call to responsibility that marks the human vocation.

As a paradigm for the working of pneumatological receptions and abductions in history, the book will devote certain chapters to looking closely at Christian artistic traditions, via a number of case studies. These represent a rich source of examples of the way that new times (new found things, or 'findings') properly stimulate new expressions of known and loved things, and sometimes change the way they are understood. The arts display in a singularly unapologetic way the centrality of the human faculty of imagination to the task of relating found to given, but in doing so they offer resources for analogous activities of reasoning in the life of the Church – for example, when the Church finds itself invited to interpret Scripture in new contexts, or when required to make ethical judgements about complex new issues (in a way that shares the English common law tradition's eschewal of ahistorical appeals to timeless principles in favour of a commitment to a 'sapiential' coming to judgement on the basis of close attention to historical precedent).

Among other things, therefore, this book hopes to be an unusual and groundbreaking exercise in the interdisciplinary discussion of theology and the arts. It is sometimes remarked that scholarship in the arena of theology and the arts is frequently shallow because its practitioners employ relatively few critical tools, and because it is prone to the deployment of examples from the arts only when they are deemed useful for the illustration of a preconceived

---

[10]Quash 2005.

theological point. This book will bring distinctive critical resources
(from Halivni, Jauss, Peirce and others) to make the discourse more
disciplined and more ambitious. It will also aim to show that looking
at how the arts have functioned within Christianity does far more
than simply resource a specialized discourse about Christian art; it
discloses profound insights about the functioning of historical and
imaginative ('receptive and abductive') Christian reasoning *per se*.

A brief look at the contents page will show how it is intended
that some of the chapters will use reflection on a particular work
of art (or body of work) – visual or literary – as an entry point into
some aspect of 'foundness' or 'finding', and the forms of reason it
generates.

D. H. Lawrence, therefore, sets the tone for the present book's
intention to remain in constant dialogue with the arts – and the
arts in various strands. The vision these dialogues are intended to
serve and enrich, meanwhile, is one that both shares Lawrence's
thrill of excitement at the God who takes us over new horizons, but
also wants to supplement his vision of God as a God of constant
recession with a vision of the God who is also always approaching.
This is the God Dietrich Bonhoeffer construes in *Act and Being*
as perpetual Advent.[11] The life-giving Spirit is a Spirit of continual
donation. Such a God is manifest in an otherness from us, an
independence of us, that breaks our idolatrous hold on God – and
will often, therefore, feel like 'departure'. But this thrill is also, in
Christian terms, the thrill of the lover's approach:

> God's silent, searching flight:
> When my Lord's head is filled with dew, and all
> His locks are wet with the clear drops of night;
>   His still, soft call;
>   His knocking time . . .[12]

---

[11]Bonhoeffer 1996.
[12]Henry Vaughan, *The Night*, ll. 31–4. See H. Vaughan 1976.

1

Historical finding

Introduction

The theology advanced in this book understands ongoing history as a gift of the Holy Spirit, to relate us to God in Christ, and it is energetically opposed to models of doctrine that assume for it any sort of ahistorical completeness; that assume it to be a set of securely held propositions from which all necessary implications for Christian belief and practice can then be deduced in any time and place.

While recognizing that there is a whole set of 'givens' with which Christian theology can work – and most especially the fact of Christ's incarnation as witnessed to in Scripture, and the fact of the Church with its practices of worship – I will argue that an excessive emphasis on such 'givens' (i) risks insulating us from new historical experiences and what can be learnt from them; (ii) supposes that we already have a sufficient grasp of just what those givens really are and mean; and (iii) can imply a view of God's detachment or absence from the ongoing world of apparently contingent historical events, and those bits of our experience of the world that do not immediately seem to fit the 'story' we have inherited.

It is in service of a countervailing exercise in Found Theology that I reassert the importance of *historical process* to the development of humans in their knowledge and enactment of truth. As will emerge, I also happen to believe that there is something very profound in a specifically English tradition of theology – by which I mean largely, but not exclusively, an Anglican tradition of theology – that seeks to make a theological virtue of this historicality. The adoption of theological methods that were so highly attuned to the effects of historical process may in part have been a way of dealing theologically with the peculiar impact of historical circumstances on the English Church in the sixteenth and seventeenth centuries.[1] But imposed conditions can be turned to good advantage. One of the fruits of a heightened historical sensibility is an enriched (and enriching) doctrine of the Spirit. Assuming that the virtues and efficacy of *any* theological method must in the end be attributed to the work of the Holy Spirit, then the efficacy found to reside in historically sensitive methods like those fuelled by the turbulent search for ecclesiastical settlement in the sixteenth- and seventeenth-century English Church pressed (and still presses) for a pneumatology in which history will also be a central theme. And another significant fruit of the English turn to history (one which will equally occupy this book) is the role it has played in generating a theology that works in artistic media, and above all in poetry, as well as in more conventional media to express what it wants to say. There will be more on this in due course.

That an English tradition is the focus of sustained attention at various points in the chapters that follow is not intended to exclude or denigrate other theological approaches in other contexts. This book is not meant to be an exercise in Anglican self-congratulation (although these days, Anglican self-confidence is encountered rarely enough). The intention is to highlight a set of theological experiments and habits of mind that should be seen as part of the inheritance of the whole Church, and not the preserve of one part of it alone. These habits of mind will have many affinities with traditions of theological thought and practice that have grown in different intellectual and ecclesiastical climates; they will permit analogies to be drawn with some others; and they will generate productive contrasts with yet others. My assumption is simply that if one is ever to be properly catholic, one must also be particular, and that what is worthy of general use must once have proved itself of specific use too.

Found Theology and found objects

Talking of Found Theology permits a useful contrast to be drawn between the found and the made. This book's title – *Found*

---

[1] It may have older roots too, in a tradition of English thought that is congenitally suspicious of universals.

Theology – deliberately echoes those movements in modern art that have concerned themselves with 'found objects'. We might highlight here the instructive way in which artists who use found objects have been both reformers of the artistic assumptions and canons of value they inherited at the start of the twentieth century, and respecters of the material forms that present themselves in the world – forms which such artists incorporate rather than claim to create *ex nihilo*; forms over which they do not try to exercise total mastery.

Of course, in some of its forms this art of the found is simply renewing a claim that was central to the cult of the Romantic genius: I can take any mundane thing, add a single drop of my own godlike inspiration, and – lo! – declare that it is now *art*. Base metal is now gold; the artist a new alchemist. Marcel Duchamp's celebrated *Fountain*[2] is both the fountain*head* of a new set of artistic practices and experiments in the modern period, and, at the same time, the rather delayed outworking of a Schopenhauerian argument that the artist's job is to 'lift' an object out of the immanent system of mundane causality (governed by the principle of sufficient reason that Schopenhauer so disliked) and allow it to stand apart from it, as somehow absolute in its own terms; successful or unsuccessful in its claim to be 'pure' art to the extent to which it extravagantly jettisons any relation to the utile and the preconceived.

But in other forms, the modern art of the found is art in more fully responsive mode. It can be seen, for example, in the delicate sacramentality of Jim Ede's assembly of found objects in Kettle's Yard in Cambridge. The questions about randomness and pattern that some artists were exploring through experiments in Dada, or other kinds of radical abstraction, were, in the hands of Ede (and many of the artists whose work he patronized), explored through natural objects arranged to express human pleasure and test the affinities and sympathies that seemed often to present themselves unbidden in the conjunctions of things. The arrangements emerge from human contemplation yet remain an honouring of qualities discerned in the objects themselves – and their relations – whereas the inversion of a lavatory bowl seems by contrast to be a noisy

---

[2]Duchamp's 1917 *Fountain* was photographed by Alfred Stieglitz and can be viewed online via the MoMA website (accessed 15 August 2013) at: http://www.moma.org/interactives/exhibitions/2010/originalcopy/intro05.html

claim to attention that principally honours the act of the artist.[3] The art of the found that can be refound by visitors to Kettle's Yard is non-didactically optimistic that there are meaningful depths and rewarding pleasures in the way the world coheres, and that artists and viewers-of-art (who are likewise part of this interconnected world) add more to its fullness and self-actualization by their participation in it; their creative yet faithful interaction with it.

The art which displays this second type of relation to found-ness (the 'Ede-type' rather than the 'Duchamp-type') is no less revolutionary than Duchamp, Arp or Mondrian: its break from the imitative realism of nineteenth-century 'drawing room' art, whose rules and expectations had atrophied and become self-referential, is comparably stark. But, on the other hand, it is more modest in its claim that, to a very significant degree, the creation of art is to be understood as a mode of reception, like the reception of a new discovery or idea that comes from someone or somewhere unexpected. It is not all about the artist's Promethean powers, or even his or her technical brilliance.

The examples and arguments of this book are theologically related to Ede's aesthetic. A theological practice or disposition that is constantly ready to find will have good reasons to regard the theology that emerges (and is bequeathed to the Church) as itself found, rather than as cleverly concocted. This commitment to the development and transmission of theology that is found and not

---

[3]There are analogies here with the difference (a *moral* difference in at least some respects) that John Ruskin was keen to assert in *Modern Painters* between landscape artists who really contemplated and responded to what they saw (principally, Turner) and those who vaunted themselves at the expense of the integrity of their subject matter:

> I assert with sorrow, that all hitherto done in landscape, by those commonly conceived its masters, has never prompted one holy thought in the minds of nations. It has begun and ended in exhibiting the dexterities of individuals, and conventionalities of systems. . . . The sense of artificialness, the absence of all appearance of reality, the clumsiness of combination by which the meddling of man is made evident, and the feebleness of his hand branded on the inorganization of his monstrous creature, are advanced as a proof of inventive power, as an evidence of abstracted conception; nay, the violation of specific form, the utter abandonment of all organic and individual character of object . . . is constantly held up by the unthinking critic as the foundation of the grand or historical style, and the first step to the attainment of a pure ideal. (Finberg 1927, 135–7)

simply made – because it arises from a theological approach that is open and responsive to findings – is captured well by Daniel W. Hardy, one of the key conversation partners of this book:

> [T]he Church moves, the theology moves, church movement becomes new theology and the theology's movement contributes to the new Church.[4]

The found and the given

The choice of *Found Theology* as a title will quite properly raise questions as well as suggest analogies, however. In particular, it will raise questions, first, about what sorts of 'givenness' the book's discussions of 'foundness' are being contrasted with; and, second, about whether 'foundness' and 'givenness' can be all that neatly contrasted with one another anyway.

At the outset of this undertaking, we need at the very least to acknowledge a distinction between the everyday, non-theological uses of the language of givenness to mean brute 'thereness' – perhaps best illustrated in the German *es gibt*, which English translates as 'there is' – and, more explicitly, the theological uses of the language to imply in every reference to a given thing the divine Giver as well. This distinction between two ways of talking about givenness cannot, of course, become a straightforward contrast for theology. Although the distinction finds itself accentuated in the gulf between modern theological and philosophical discourses – between, for example, a trinitarian defence of human gift-giving as participation in the divine generosity, and a variety of philosophical alternatives (a phenomenological method, for instance, which brackets metaphysical truth claims and concentrates solely on what presents itself to the human consciousness; or a Derridean tradition that argues that gift language marks the site of something infinitely regressive and tauntingly elusive) – nevertheless, a Christian theological account will want to propose that every existent thing (everything of which one can say *es gibt*) is a sign of its Creator (a gift). It is not to be related to as an end in itself (*enjoyed* as a mere

---

[4]Daniel W. Hardy (as told to Peter Ochs), in Hardy, Hardy Ford, Ochs, and Ford 2010, 89.

thing), but used as an occasion for growth in relationship with God (*used* as a *sign*), which is to safeguard it from possessive, idolatrous appropriation, and, paradoxically therefore, to enable it actually to be delighted in (i.e. enjoyed properly) as well. The givenness-as-thereness, which is a feature of the objects of daily encounter, is to be seen as opening onto their givenness-as-createdness; our perception of what is there is always to be in motion towards a fuller (but not a wholly other) perception of their origin in divine grace.

It may also be helpful to state here that the opening contrast I have already begun to draw between 'givens' and 'founds' is probably not ultimately sustainable. In many ways it might have been more appropriate to call this book *Finding Theology*, inasmuch as the continual activity of finding concerns it a good deal, and because the moment that something is 'found', it often quickly becomes in itself a 'given': something we *once* found, and now possess. But, apart from the fact that it is satisfying to break the trend which leads so many theological publications to have titles with '-ing' in them,[5] I think there are ways in which an object's (or an event's) quality of 'foundness' can continue to cling instructively to it even when it is incorporated, canonized and revisited – so it does not always become *taken for granted* (as some past things do when they become 'givens') just because it is *past*. The baptism of the Gentile centurion, Cornelius, and his household under the guidance of the Holy Spirit in Acts 10 shows how a new theology had to be found then, and yet it is a story that continues to suggest the possibility of discoveries and surprises close at hand now. Such examples of Found Theology at work powerfully heighten our sense that in the age of the pouring out of the Spirit, we must live in the expectation of more findings still to come.

A fully theological account, of course, of how it is that all things in creation – past, present and future – have their origin in God will need to affirm that at some level (the most important level) *everything* is 'given', and *everything* is 'found'. So, my contrast between givens and founds is best understood as a heuristic device, intended to help bring a set of issues into focus. For now, therefore, I retain the contrast – and in doing so, I am in company with the Jewish theologian Peter Ochs, who undertakes to describe what is at work in the thought of a number of 'post-liberal' Christian theologies

---

[5] I include my own.

of recent decades, and identifies a contrasting set of tendencies in the respective American and English adaptations of this post-liberal agenda. They fall, for him, into a more christocentrically weighted concern with the given, on the one side, and a more pneumatocentrically weighted emphasis on the found, on the other. Ochs will be a key conversation partner throughout this book – along (as I have said) with the Christian theologian of whom he is one of the best expositors: Dan Hardy. This is a useful moment to introduce some of the key aspects of Ochs's description.

'Another Reformation': Peter Ochs on Christian post-liberalism

In twentieth-century and now twenty-first-century English-speaking theologies – and especially those shaped to a significant extent by the thought of Karl Barth – there has been a developing emphasis on how theology must unfold in history, narrative and practice. Associated with the so-called Yale School, these theologies are often called post-liberal:

> Postliberals often attempt . . . to reclaim what they consider prototypical sources and norms of the church or synagogue and of the university (or seculum) and to offer their criticisms from out of these sources and norms.[6]

Ochs describes how a largely North American post-liberalism has achieved important ends for theology by its emphasis on the givens that inform Christian life in community. This emphasis on givens may focus variously on scriptural narratives, sacramental forms or all practices of worship (whether sacramental in character or not), but it is largely christocentric in character – Jesus Christ being the already given and perfect revelation of God's loving will and purpose, and Scripture, sacrament and liturgy being part of Christ's legacy. In Ochs's words:

> The reformational process of doctrinal formation [in this largely North American tradition] is an ecclesial process of rereading

---

[6]Ochs 2011, 6.

the Gospels' witness to the life of Christ. This rereading uncovers historically specific guidelines for doctrinal reformation.[7]

Of the figures that Ochs examines, in this North American tradition, two fit his description especially well: George Lindbeck and Robert W. Jenson. Lindbeck, as Ochs interprets him, reaffirms in a certain way 'the Reformational doctrine of *sola scriptura*'.[8] He does so with an ecumenical agenda, wanting to '[repair] the fissures (the errors, heresies or sins) that periodically threaten [the Church's] unity', and this is what leads him to re-examine how the Church should be guided by its reading of the Gospel witness.[9] '[T]he redemptive reading of Scripture provides *the* definitive criterion for ecclesial repair.'[10] Jenson, likewise, '[adopts] the gospel as a reformational guide', and is wedded to '*the particularity* of that gospel witness' (which, importantly, makes his, like Lindbeck's, a theology resistant to adopting a supersessionist attitude to the Jews).[11] Lindbeck's and Jenson's American brand of post-liberalism[12] is recognized by Ochs as a valuable and principled corrective to 'modern movements in the American church' that they judge to be neglecting the person of Christ. These movements seem to them to be 'liberal or universalizing, naturalist, overly politicized, and wary of the scriptural canon and doctrine'.[13]

But Ochs then goes on to propose another model of 'reformational practice' ('another Reformation'), which he identifies especially with a strand of British-based theology, all of whose main proponents are Anglican. Dan Hardy is offered as perhaps the fullest exemplar of this tradition.[14] If the North American variety of post-liberalism can be understood (in parallel with developments in twentieth-century Roman Catholic theology that were in their own way a 'reformation'

---

[7]Ibid., 125, 259.
[8]Ibid., 39.
[9]Ibid., 36.
[10]Ibid., 47.
[11]Ibid., 68.
[12]The other American post-liberals whom Ochs examines, by his own admission, do not quite so neatly fit the mould: Stanley Hauerwas, in particular, has a pneumatological bent which means he has a good deal in common with the Anglicans who are looked at in the second half of the book.
[13]Ochs 2011, 28.
[14]See, for example, Hardy 2001.

of an atrophying paradigm) as *ressourcement* – a going back to early sources for the sake of present renewal – then the British-based alternative can, says Ochs, be seen as more like *aggiornamento* – the opening up of Christian thought and tradition to new currents of thought in its intellectual and cultural environment, including new forms of political and social life.[15]

Scripture remains profoundly important here as a locus for finding and knowing God, but just as important are 'the things of the world, and the persons and events of history', for the assumption of this second type of post-liberalism is that God will be found and known in these things too:

> To live in the Spirit of wisdom is to inhabit God where one finds him – where one finds God in Scripture and where one finds him in the world and in history.

Attentive reading of *Scripture*, of the *world* and of *history* constitutes and sustains a certain sort of wisdom (suggesting that the study of the Bible, ethnographic enquiry and an informed historical sense are all essential features of a wise theology). Scripture might seem to be the most 'given' of the three, in the sense that it stands as a relatively clear and authoritative reference point for Christian self-orientation or community-orientation, but – as we will have occasion to explore at greater length in Chapters 2 and 3 – Scripture too is something that will elude any possessive appropriation, and it is constantly liable to be discovered somewhere other than where we thought we had put it for safekeeping. There is a complex interplay between these three loci of discovery, and all of them – even the Christian use of Scripture – require the recognition that a high degree of contingency is operative whenever God is 'found' by means of them. The British-based variety of post-liberalism, Ochs argues, is better adapted to recognizing this fact than the North American.

The British variety of post-liberalism is underpinned by a thoroughly non-dualist view that 'all creatures, nations, and denominations come under the mystery of Christ's care and thus merit care by Christ's disciples . . .'.[16] Or, to put it in other words, a view

[15]Ochs 2011, 190.
[16]Ibid., 169.

that nothing is mere rubble, however much it might seem that the
Church's best option is to police a small area of meaningful order
as the detritus of history mounts up around it. This very positive
account of the divine as the source and ground of the historical
world in all its aspects can also permit an affirmation of politics,
the non-human natural world, sex, art and other aspects of social
life as parts of the medium in which we relate to the truth of Christ.
This underwrites an Anglican theological style that John Milbank
has characterized as 'ultramediatory'.[17] Or, in Ochs's words, a trust
(which is 'one of the wisdoms of Anglicanism') that:

> Christ's work begins with whatever one finds in the world, rather
> than beginning with theological concepts that precede the world
> and require the world to reshape itself in order for Christ's work
> to begin to be done.[18]

It will matter to such a Church 'where it has been in the world and
what has actually happened to its members in history'.[19] History is
the God-given medium of encounter with God, and only a historical
sort of finding (a historical finding which thematizes and embraces
its historicality rather than seeking to compensate for or to suppress
it) is properly equipped to resist the abstractly universalizing claims
that frequently tempt Christian discourse about God and the nature
of the Church – hence the title of the present chapter.

   This, it can plausibly be claimed, is one beneficial consequence
of something for which the Church of England is often fiercely
criticized: its close identification with the powers of government
vested in the monarch and Parliament. Stanley Hauerwas, for
example, distrusts the Constantinian nature of this alliance, seeing
it as profoundly compromising of the Church,[20] and there is no
doubt that it can be, and at times has been. What Ochs discerns
in this proximity, however, is a framework that is also capable
of sustaining responsible attention to the world and to history

[17]For some of Milbank's discussion of the importance of the mediatory in Christianity
(and monotheistic religion) more generally, see Milbank 2010 (accessed 13 August
2013) at http://blogs.ssrc.org/tif/2010/12/01/culture-nature-mediation/
[18]Ochs 2011, 168.
[19]Ibid., 167.
[20]Hauerwas 1991.

(i.e. to what must continually be found if the Church is to fulfil its task):

> [T]he Church of England attaches itself to a worldly polity and . . . shares responsibility for the welfare of all citizens of that polity. . . . The subjects to whom the church is responsible are not determined a priori; they come as history has led them. . . . [T]here is no predicting whom history may lead to the polity's – and the church's – doorstep.[21]

The naming of cats

'The naming of cats is a difficult matter,' wrote T. S. Eliot.[22] He was talking playfully about the difficulty of doing justice to the unique and particular properties of each created, feline nature; the ineffability of the individual instance. As it happens, this emphasis on the challenges of doing justice to particularity is one of the dominating themes of the present book – but it is not the immediate concern of this excursus. Instead, being playful in our turn, we will here say that the naming of cats has another difficulty about it; the naming of cats is a difficult matter not just because it is hard to get right, but also because naming carries demands and obligations with it.

To give a cat a name is to be in relationship with it, and from that point on, it is not merely an anonymous cat; you cannot overlook its needs in the same way as you might have done before. It cannot ever again be invisible to you. If it is hungry, it will be harder for you not to feed it once it has a name. And yet, its arrival in your life may not have been something you especially chose. Maybe it was a stray cat that adopted *you*. There are countless millions of stray cats across the globe – and most people will not usually give them a second thought. But of all the cats in all the towns in all the world, a particular one walks into yours: into your town, up to your doorstep – and then things have somehow got particular, and that is a bit more difficult to extricate yourself from.

---

[21]Ochs 2011, 173.
[22]Eliot 1974, 9–10.

What is true for cats is true all the more for human persons. In Isaiah 40, God's people in exile experience themselves 'found' by God, and this experience of being found takes the form – among other things – of the knowledge that they are named. '[The Holy One] brings out their host by number, calling them all by name' (Isa. 40.26). The sudden permission to return from exile in Babylon to their own land bursts upon them as a miracle of unexpected and decisive deliverance, and they are reminded again of the Exodus because this return is like a second Exodus, and that in turn looks to them like a sort of recapitulation of creation itself, when God drew the world into being from what was just void. This section of the Book of Isaiah rejoices in drawing those connections. 'Out of a situation where there was no identity, where there were no names, only the anonymity of slavery and the powerlessness of the ghetto, God makes a human community; . . . gives it or restores to it a territory'; calls it by name.[23]

The naming here is a sign of covenant obligation: the confirmation of a commitment. It is not just that the returning exiles happen to be in the area as God's mighty action takes place – like anonymous bystanders or bit players. They are not just 'found to be there', as though by chance. They are really *found*, which is to say they are known and affirmed intimately; their election reasserted by God and felt powerfully by them. To put it in terms of our analogy, these lost cats coming back from Babylon find themselves named, and there is a promise that goes with that naming; a renewed promise to maintain relationship with them; to care for them: 'Why do you say, O Jacob, and speak, O Israel . . . "My way is hidden from the LORD, and my right is disregarded by my God"? Have you not known? Have you not heard? The LORD is the everlasting God, the Creator of the ends of the earth . . . He gives power to the faint, and to him who has no might he increases strength' (Isa. 40.27-29). Their being called by name is the manifestation of an assurance that God will continue to accompany them and defend them.

Are there ways in which these insights derived from a reading of Isaiah 40 might in turn resource the practices of the Church? I believe that one could do a lot worse than to let them promote a sense of ecclesial obligation to those that the Church finds 'on

---

[23]Williams 2000, 67–8.

its doorstep'. Such a sense of obligation is one form of that more general pneumatological openness to meeting Christ 'wherever and however he appears',[24] which Ochs identifies as a general mark of an Anglican ecclesiology. This pneumatological openness takes a particular political as well as ecclesial form in the Anglican settlement. The Church of England in its established form is committed by its parish structure to minister to all those who live in England. Every area of land is covered by a parish, and every resident of every parish – whether he or she is an Anglican or not, whether he or she is a Christian or not – is someone to whom the Church has an obligation. They are 'souls' for whom the parish understands itself to have 'curatorial responsibility'. The parish and its priest enact a 'chaplaincy to place',[25] not just a targeted ministry to those individuals who are signed up members of the institution. In these terms, no one ought to be regarded as just 'happening to be in the area'. Each person is to be treated as a significant 'finding'. With such foundness comes a right to be acknowledged, recognized, named (and indeed – though this is sometimes a source of controversy in the Church – Anglican churches in England are literally obliged to baptize, and thus also ritually name, all those in their parish who request it).[26]

It is important to acknowledge that the analogy between the finding-and-naming that God does in Isaiah 40 does not entirely map onto the finding-and-naming that the Church might do. God's finding is better described – in the way that the language of election sometimes seeks to do – as wholly proactive: making a people where there was once not a people (and this is why Isaiah 40 so naturally also evokes the fundamental language of divine creation). The Church's finding is always responsive; understood, as we have seen, as a form of openness to the Spirit. Nevertheless, the Church's finding is an imitation of the divine finding in the key respect that

[24]Ochs 2011, 169.
[25]I owe this concept to Timothy Jenkins; see, Jenkins 2006.
[26]Admittedly, the Church-State relation has taken markedly different forms in other manifestations of Anglicanism worldwide, and the Church of England is by no means a typical province of the Communion as a whole, but my own experience of hearing the Primates of the Communion describe what their churches do at their conference in Oporto in 2000 is that there is a recognizable family resemblance between them in the degree to which (even when they are minority churches) they take on a high degree of social responsibility.

it says 'what I have found I will relate to' (as God says 'what I have elected I will covenant with'). Naming is the Church's affirmative response to finding.

In the particular circumstances of his incarnate, historical life, Jesus Christ can be seen to enact a finding that is at once responsive *and* creative. In this regard, Christ's way of finding is an intimation of the union of divine and human natures that is uniquely his. The *divine* power in this activity of finding is evident in Christ's healings, the restorations to life, the summonses to discipleship whose effectiveness otherwise seems humanly inexplicable. It is significant, for our purposes, that the *human* mode of finding is meanwhile described by the Gospels as a mode of submission, or openness, to the Spirit. It is a 'being led by' the Spirit (Mt. 4.1; Lk. 4.1).[27] Jesus Christ in his earthly ministry genuinely seems to 'come across' things: people and situations that are neither sought nor chosen by him, but to whom he responds in the assumption that he has been led to them by the Spirit, the Spirit who (as the New Testament suggests) directs Christ as a sort of 'necessity'. Hans Urs von Balthasar, in particular, has made a great deal of the pneumatological significance of the divine *mandatum* that defines and shapes Christ's mission on earth.[28] Christ's task is to stand in relation to this direction as one ready to be a creative finder.

From a great many possible examples in the narratives of Jesus's ministry, we may take just one to illustrate the point: the intriguing encounter he has with Simon Peter's mother-in-law in the Gospel of Mark (Mk 1.29-31). She perhaps more than most other figures in the Gospels is like a stray cat whom Jesus unpredictably encounters at a particular place at a particular time. She finds herself under Jesus's nose, so to say (and he finds her); it does not seem as though either of them sought the other out.

A friend of mine who is a distinguished New Testament scholar said of this little scene (in a way very typical of that academic discipline): 'Well, it's so inconsequential it's almost bound to be

---

[27]That Jesus shares this condition of being led by, or guided by, the Spirit with other human beings is evident in, for example, Lk. 2.27 ('Guided by the Spirit, Simeon came into the temple') and Jn 16.13 ('When the Spirit of truth comes, he will guide you into all the truth').
[28]This is in the context of Balthasar's discussion of the 'trinitarian inversion'; see Balthasar 1992, 188ff.

genuine – why else include it in the Gospel? It's not a dramatic or exciting miracle, like the multiple healings of the demoniacs that follow. It's just Simon Peter's mother-in-law, with a fever'. In one way, he was right: it *is* inconsequential. But in another way, the whole particularizing miracle of the Christian Gospel is displayed in this little scene. It is, after all, deeply personal. Simon Peter's mother-in-law is not a representative figure. She does not stand for anything. She is not a symbol or a concept or a type. She is Simon Peter's mother-in-law; she is ill; and she finds herself in Jesus's presence, whereupon he takes her by the hand and raises her up. It is perhaps rather melodramatic to describe this as her re-creation, her exodus or her return from Babylon, but there is a wonder to it nonetheless, and that is that Jesus has related to her wholly as herself, as the unique and irreplaceable person that she is. She was not just 'found to be there'; she was *found* there.

In bringing this excursus to a close, I want to re-emphasize the pneumatological claim at its heart. It is one that will remain important in the book's argument as a whole. It is the claim that Christ's active ministry discloses a Holy Spirit who works by placing things to be found. To put it more strongly, Christ's story in the Gospels legitimizes the theological assertion that the Holy Spirit's communication of the divine will take the form of foundness. This is, I believe, what Peter Ochs means when he states that '"foundness" is a pneumatologically valid criterion for measuring the divine will'.[29]

Challenges to the model

A range of further questions is, of course, raised by this claim, the most substantial of which is whether it entails the uncritical acceptance of everything that one encounters as *meant to be*. Two potential objections might be hidden in this question.

The first is that Found Theology in an Anglican (or British post-liberal) style is (in weak form) disablingly relativistic, and (in strong form) positively anti-traditional. At the very least, it can seem to deny one any criteria for deciding whether a new discovery or encounter

---

[29]Ochs 2011, 169.

should be allowed to override a principle previously held dear. In a stronger form, it may lead to the claim that the meaning discerned by some individual or group in a new discovery or encounter is always to be privileged over inherited understandings whenever they seem to conflict. Oliver O'Donovan is a fierce critic of this second tendency when describing what he calls 'historicism' in theological and ethical debates within the churches: such historicism 'consists in confusing the good with the future',[30] with the corollary that the present is always preferred to the past (because the present is one step nearer 'the good'). The 'immediacy of [an] insight' is asserted to have a persuasive power that obviates the need to engage with and learn from one's traditional authorities; this perspective tends to make even the interpretation of Scripture seem 'superfluous'.[31]

The second objection is that bad things – including tragic experiences – must simply be accepted uncomplainingly and without protest. Found Theology threatens to underwrite a 'quietist' response, inasmuch as it seems to require no interrogation and no resistance to the way the world is. These are both concerns to which we will return at intervals as the book develops.

For now, in response to the concern about relativism, we might turn back to Ochs and note that he is fully aware of the issue. He does not think it can, or should, be denied outright. 'To know in the

---

[30]O'Donovan 2009, 88.

[31]Ibid., 26. O'Donovan makes the authority of canonical Scripture his key 'given' in this context. He is quite confident of the ability of the Holy Spirit to 'open up perspectives that are not immediately apparent' in any situation of moral or doctrinal argument between opposed parties faced with new issues, but he insists that such moments of finding will depend on the opponents being 'sincerely committed to the church's authorities, Scripture chief among them'. Only for one 'determined to be taught by Scripture' are there 'things still to be learned' about how to read 'the age in which we live' (O'Donovan 2009, 33). My model of finding is very sympathetic to this one. Although the present book will not make it its business to adjudicate specific debates with the contemporary Church about things that the Spirit may or may not have helped it to *find* through recent historical experience – the endorsement of gay marriage, or the consecration of women as bishops, for example – I am convinced that a serious determination to be taught by Scripture must surely be a central feature of such debates. However, for good or ill, the pages that follow offer a rather less manageable and tidy account of how various 'authorities' interact in the business of coming to (and communicating) a theological understanding than can be discerned in O'Donovan's suggestion of a sort of neat pyramid of authorities at whose summit Scripture is enthroned.

Spirit is to know contingently', he says. It is 'to know in relation to one's found history and thus contingently and fallibly'.[32] But this does not entail a complete relativism – here is where the tradition-specific aspects of the post-liberal enterprise are also at work, articulating that whenever one meets some found thing, one meets it in the light of a tradition of thought and practice, which shapes one's interpretation and response. One might even say that without any *givens*, one would not be able to *find* anything either: certain givens are a *condition* of finding. Specifically – for Christians – the example and teaching of Christ are a constant touchstone.

> [The temptation on this side is,] swept into the Spirit's movement, to forget or neglect the Logos, as if the way of renewal were not also the way of the Son, nourished by his Word.[33]

In a specific discussion of Hardy's work, Ochs sees here a christo-logical resource for defending against some sort of capitulation to the powers of this world (of the 'Constantinian' sort that Hauerwas and others have worried about, perhaps) while not yet sacrificing an openness to the found.

> Hardy places loyalty to Christ first, so that his engagement with worldly powers comes not by compromise, but by way of God's presence in the world.[34]

Then, in a discussion that extends to the work of Hardy's close colleague and son-in-law, David Ford, he expounds this further. It is not that 'foundness' should simply trump 'givenness'. Each must be in a mutual and dynamic relationship with the other, which will, at the same time, require vigilance in the Christian to ensure that one does not adversely distort or deny the other. What seems to be found in the Spirit needs testing against what has been given in the Son: it is only in the interaction of both that revelation is constituted.

There is a risk in thinking that this 'testing' of what seems to be found in the Spirit against what has been given in the Son will

---

[32]Ochs 2011, 167.
[33]Ibid., 213.
[34]Ibid., 167.

never make any difference whatsoever to the latter. To adopt the paradigm that Ochs uses in his discussion of Ford, this would be to take the role of Job's comforters, whose givens include, so they think, all the answers to what they find before them in Job's traumatic situation. Given representations like this too easily 'freeze into idols'.[35] The *dynamic* relation between found and given must be genuinely *mutual* too. There is always a temptation 'to fear the Spirit's freedom and hold fast only to trusted images of Christ':

> In Ford's reading this is, in the face of severe trauma, to cling to an established knowledge of God rather than risk an encounter with God in the unknown.[36]

The more desirable option, however, is not to rush to the other extreme, and abandon all hope in one's tried and tested reference points as one rounds each new bend in the river of history. It is to seek the deepest integration of both found and given that one is able to at any particular moment, in the light of a faith in God who is 'agent as well as source of redemption';[37] at work in the world and in history as well as in Scripture and liturgical rite.

The objection that an excessive emphasis on the found entails not only relativism but also quietism is a challenging one that ought not to be made light of. We might simply note, for now, that the Joban example, developed by Ford and highlighted by Ochs,[38] is very far from offering a romanticized notion of what forms the found may take. What is important here is that suffering experience, traumatic experience, in its resistance to easy assimilation, is in fact one of the key arguments in *favour* of a theology of the found. The premise that each new encounter is to be taken with utter seriousness in its own unique particularity, and not prematurely universalized or made illustrative of something already familiar, is a warrant both for theological responsibility in the face of trauma and (in another but related discourse) for pastoral sensitivity.

---

[35]Ibid., 217.
[36]Ibid., 212.
[37]Ibid., 189.
[38]And informed in both cases by an extended engagement with the thought of Susannah Ticciati. See Ticciati 2005.

That said, there are often reasons to interrogate instances of trauma (which, as Ochs makes clear, can as well include the sufferings of Jews as a result of Christian supersessionism as they can the misery of Job) in the expectation that they may be pointing to 'the emergence of a new world'. A cry can be the first signal that something is in need of repair, and *may* therefore be the first portent of that repair. Even 'found suffering', in other words, may need to be embraced and learned from in order that the given may remain healthy. On these terms, as Ochs says, 'Israel's suffering' can be seen as 'a corrective to excessive criticisms of the British for following the Spirit where it will'. On the other hand, the newness that may emerge in a reordered understanding of one's givens, after a new finding has taken place, 'will not be altogether new but will remain in relation to the old, a corrective to excessive criticisms of the Americans for turning to the Word as trusted guide in times of upheaval'.[39] In these remarks, Ochs displays in concise fashion that the need for given and found to be in dynamic and mutual relationship also implies the need for North American and British-based Christian post-liberalism to be in dynamic and mutual relationship – which is one of his main objectives in writing his book.

The indefinite series: Analogies not universals

Before closing this chapter, I want to remain close to Peter Ochs's thought in one more aspect, because of its relevance to the emphasis on historicality that will mark my own book in its entirety. The emphasis on historicality is accompanied by, and strengthens, an emphasis on creaturely particularity in a way that has also begun to emerge as important.

Ochs insists that one of the great virtues and opportunities of Christian post-liberalism is its recovery of confidence in traditioned practice. Jews, Christians (and other religious people) can make common cause in this area because many religious traditions have been harmed by the universalizing accounts of meaning that have achieved such dominance in the modern period. These accounts,

---

[39]Ochs 2011, 213.

as the social anthropologist Timothy Jenkins and I have argued in another context,[40] have emerged in a way that echoes how, under the influence of Greek ideas, the Roman 'law of nations' developed into the idea of a Natural Law.[41] This Natural Law was allegedly superior to all local custom and practice, was held to exhibit universal principles (although these could not readily be given a content), to be capable of being applied everywhere, and therefore to be above any tribal or religious particularity. In this way, a pragmatic supplement to civil law became a universal (though fictitious) truth, above or behind all empirical laws. Embracing the concept of a universal law of nature became a means of ceasing to pay attention to local settlements, and made it less easy to do justice to a certain body of complex material.

The advance of Enlightenment ideas of 'secularity' and 'religion' has effected a similar process in relation to specific religious traditions, helped indeed by the Natural Law model. These ideas have been aided by the model of science as objective truth; yet, in this form, universalizing ideas about 'religion' and 'the secular' arguably become a mask for the power of the State to expand its claims and responsibilities over and against civil society in general, and religious communities in particular, and equally (when it suits them to adopt the categories in particular circumstances) a cloak for commercial and other interests too. These other interests, to confuse the issue, may opportunistically include religious and ethnic interests on occasion. But ultimately, as in the case of Natural Law, we witness here the deployment of a general category (in this case, 'religion') to deal with highly diverse and complex material in a way that, while presuming to clarify it, often renders it opaque. Vital elements of what make religious traditions meaningful to their adherents, socially fruitful and significant, and different from one another, are lost to view. There is a move towards highly theorized synthetic categories with relatively little descriptive or critical purchase.

---

[40]Jenkins and Quash 2009. I reproduce some of the document's arguments in this paragraph and in the one that follows it.
[41]The Roman 'law of nations' was originally conceived of as some sort of lowest common denominator, inferior to Roman civil law, which allowed settlement of disputes between the (non-Latin) 'nations' resident in Rome, and permitted trade between Romans and these other populations.

Ochs's own distrust of such universalizing tendencies leads him to endorse an analogically structured form of thought which, as he outlines in a further chapter on the thought of John Milbank (the third and most ambiguous of his triad of British-based post-liberals) is 'pleonasm in reasoning'.[42] He is referring to Milbank's 1997 essay 'Pleonasm, Speech and Writing'.[43] Pleonasm, in the sense of the word that Milbank deploys and that Ochs takes up, is not so much *excess verbiage* as *non-identical repetition*, a creative repetition that is at the heart of generative, historical language use. It has parallels in the forms of life – texts, beliefs and practices – that sustain and shape religious traditions. Each in its particularity can hope to find insights in its own tradition non-identically repeated in others – insights that will prove themselves capable of being brought into relation with one another – thereby bringing the different religionists into relation too. But this will not mean identifying a universal concept in reason as the necessary *tertium quid* for relation; rather, it will involve identifying a *significant form* of some kind – one that emerges within a religious tradition and is situated in its practice. The example that Ochs takes as most significant for Christians, with good reason, is the Eucharist. He works this out at greatest length when he is discussing Dan Hardy's theology. In the Eucharist, according to Hardy, Christians find the Spirit (and find Christ *in* the Spirit). This becomes the condition for their sociality. Eucharistic participation then becomes a particular resource for understanding all other dimensions of the Church's life and practice, and *other extra-ecclesial forms of sociality as well.* For Hardy:

[What is recognizable] within his denomination's experience of communion must, he believes, have an analogue in the way that the Spirit visits each human community, however differently each community may name and recognize these visitations.[44]

Notably, Ochs regards the Anglican aspects of Hardy's eucharistic theology as especially accommodating of this pleonastic extension, and this is because an Anglican doctrine of the real presence does

---

[42]Ochs 2011, 240.
[43]Milbank 1997, 55–83.
[44]Ochs 2011, 188.

not depend on a model in which an ideal eucharistic form is subsequently distributed but only validated with reference to an immaculate prototype ('from the centre', so to speak, by virtue of its being licensed by a magisterial authority that also licenses that doctrine – transubstantiation – an adherence to which guarantees the efficacy of the rite). Rather, the eucharistic form is sustained (and thus 'found') precisely within 'historically and spatiotemporally particular' contexts.[45] It is real, but only as locally and temporally situated.

Another way of putting this is to say that the sacramental form of Christ is 'everywhere in particular' by the work of the Spirit. This is a point which the Baptist theologian Paul Fiddes has echoed when arguing that an English tendency to see nature itself as sacramental is a tendency to which Anglicanism has been crucial: real presence without a special metaphysics of transubstantiation makes that presence 'infinitely extendable' (or, in a formulation I will prefer here, 'indefinitely extendable').[46] At this point, the category of the *general* comes clearly into view, both in its importance and in its riskiness. For Hardy and Ochs do indeed want to say that a certain sort of generalization is legitimate – and indeed essential if any of their optimism about the possibility of recognition across religious traditions is to be justified. But this cannot be a generality that is really supposed universality by another name. It is a generality that may *only* be approached by way of the particular in a series of specific analogical connections; a generality which may never leave the particular behind:

> Hardy is for this reason willing to draw analogies beyond his specific eucharistic examples, but he is not willing to do so by way of a universal concept. Or to put it another way, his ecclesiology is "always local to his account of a particular church in the Anglican Communion", even if, at the same time, "always general" – both in its claim to illuminate a wider account of the church and also to yield a description of the dynamics of human sociality.[47]

---

[45]Ibid., 252.
[46]Paul Fiddes, in a point made in a discussion at the Oxford Theological Society in May 2008.
[47]Ochs 2011, 183.

For Ochs, this is reminiscent of Talmudic thinking, even as it is typical, arguably, of a figural tradition of reading within the Church:

> [Hardy's] kind of generalization displays what the philosopher Charles Peirce calls "indefinite growth," as opposed to abstract "universalization." This means that the type will reappear in various analogous ways, but not in ways that we individual thinkers can anticipate.[48]

In Christian terms, this sort of generalization is, says Ochs, *pneumatological*.

To take this to be true is to find resources to allay what might have been a gnawing worry in the wake of this chapter's earlier excursus into the 'naming of cats'. The claim made in that excursus was that human beings are utterly precious to God; they are cats with names. God is not just interested in achieving his goals in a sort of abstract way, regardless of who helps or hinders him. Rather, he is interested in the persons for their own sake. A god for whom the question 'Who?' doesn't matter is, we might say, not the Christian God. God is the creator, redeemer and lover of persons.

The personalizing love Jesus shows to those whom he encounters, Simon Peter's mother-in-law included, both testifies to this divine regard for persons and, at the same time, operates in a responsive mode: receptive to those particular persons he is given to find. It is in the mode of this human and responsive finding that the Church's care for persons seems properly to unfold.

But the gnawing question presents itself precisely here: it is all very well that Simon Peter's mother-in-law is healed, but what is to be done about all the other mothers-in-law who never found themselves lucky enough to have Jesus cross their path? Let alone all the other sick people in the world? Or, a comparable question, what about all the other stray cats in the world? Feeding the one who turns up on your doorstep does not help the rest of them.

These are good questions, to which the account of analogical reasoning (and a corresponding 'indefinite growth' that has practical and ethical forms) can suggest some sort of response.

---

[48]Ibid., 189.

Where the Church is concerned, the proper response could begin with something like St Paul's account of his own ministry in 1 Cor. 9.16-23. In this passage, Paul declares himself to be seeking the unique particularity of all those to whom he hopes to bring the Gospel, and trying to come into a new and closer relationship with them in the name of that Gospel. He is, we might say, naming cats – left, right and centre – and that is changing him, too, as relationships always do. It is stretching him in all kinds of new ways towards a fuller comprehension of the limitless love of God in Christ – not limitless in a bland, abstract way, but limitless in its reaching towards each particular person: limitlessly particular. Paul is the servant of the Gospel, and his understanding of what this entails leads him to the work of providing for all people by meeting them in their particularity. He is striving to feed the stray cats of the Gentiles, whom he has found turning up at his door asking to be fed, along with the Jewish house cats to which he already had obligations. To the Jews, he is a Jew; to those outside the law, he becomes like one outside the law; to the weak, weak; and so on. This is not some sort of chameleon-like behaviour, though it could easily be read like that. Paul is not saying whatever his audience at the time might want to hear; pandering to them; trimming his sail to the wind. He is, on the contrary, conforming himself to Christ. He is pouring himself out, setting himself and his rights and his inheritance aside, in order to really encounter the others he is confronted with in all the particularity that is theirs, because that is what Christ did. Paul did not ask these cats to come to his door (as he says: 'necessity is laid upon me' [1 Cor. 9.16]), but his life is now Christ's. That is a life in which love is always concretely and particularly taught and learnt – not in universal, abstract principles – and it requires a response to what is found in front of you, under your nose, here and now.

The Church's imitation of the one who was supremely there for the world, by being for it too, will also be an imitation of Paul, who initiates a chain of transmission of the kind that characterizes the life of any religious tradition. Collectively, Christians learn in the Church that they are to do what they can to widen the range of their encounters in Christ's name, with the power that is in them, trusting to God that he will graciously provide them with the resources they need for the task. But, they are not to think there is some other route to doing God's work than being particular and personal. Formulating universal principles for the care of cats and the healing of mothers-in-law all too easily becomes an alternative to feeding the cat that came to your door and invited you to name it, or helping the mother-in-law of the friend whose house you went to visit.

There is, in other words, no substitute for face-to-face encounters in service of the Kingdom of God. It is never served by escape from the particularity of the here and now, the you and me or by retreat into universal principles. If Christians are worried that they cannot do it all themselves, cannot make the whole difference or solve the whole problem, then that is probably a good lesson for them to learn. For in God's providence, Christians must trust that other agencies than theirs are working together for good, that others will be feeding other cats, and that it is not all just down to them.

A second and related answer to that question – 'what about all the rest?' – returns us to the Gospels – and specifically to Mark 1 and the episode at Simon Peter's house. In the scene that follows that healing, Simon and his companions find Jesus praying in a desolate place, before sunrise, and they say to him 'Everyone is searching for you.' And he says to them, 'Let us go on to the neighbouring towns, so that I may proclaim the message there also, for that is what I came out to do' (Mk 1.37-38). And they go.

The healing of Simon's mother-in-law is thus shown only to be a beginning. It is the beginning not of a universal proclamation to the whole world, nor of a standardized care package for issue in all cases of need. It is the beginning of an indefinite series of particular encounters, particular facings, particular renewals, particular givings of names. Jesus sets off to begin the process of going from town to town. The miracle of his resurrection means that he can still do it in the power of the Holy Spirit who continually makes him findable again – for he is alive; he is the risen one. In the Spirit, he is still making his way to towns and homes, still pronouncing names. There ought to be no fear that he will overlook anyone, or fail to reach some. 'Everyone is searching for you,' say the disciples. 'Each will find me' is the Gospel message, for he is the Lord, the saviour of all, who numbers the hairs of our heads, and knows us more intimately than we know ourselves.

The Spirit spiral

The danger of glib talk about "authorization" and the authority
linked with it is of theologizing what is "given" as if the given
represented the finished, the fixed.[49]

I will conclude this chapter in conversation with Rowan Williams's
seminal essay 'Trinity and Revelation'[50] by showing how his account
there of the generativity of the Holy Spirit might relate to some of
the themes of finding, foundness and historicality that are central
to this book.

Williams makes radical generativity the mark of divinity in this
chapter; the radicality is marked by what a traditional doctrinal
formulation has called its *ex nihilo* quality. It is absolutely
uncalled for; non-necessary; gracious. It is relatively easy to
attribute this radical generativity to the first person of the Trinity,
in the context of a doctrine of creation. The interesting challenge
Williams faces, theologically, is how to maintain a comparable
generativity – one that is in some analogous way *ex nihilo* – when
speaking of the second and third persons of the Trinity, who are
understood in the context of their processions as 'begotten' and
'spirated', respectively, and therefore, in some more obvious sense,
are *responsive* to a source that begets and breathes them. To put
it baldly, how can what is responsive also be generative *ex nihilo*?
Does the mode of response inevitably compromise radical creative
freedom?

Williams's response begins, confidently, with the second person
of the Trinity. He affirms of Jesus Christ that 'the "generative"
character of his story is as radical as the generative significance
of our language about the world's source and context, God'. How
is this so? Because, argues Williams, his life and teaching open
up completely, radically new possibilities in human thought and
practice (and the very inseparability of thought and practice in
this context is part of his gift). In a way that may seem superfi-
cially paradoxical, these new possibilities are the result of Jesus's

---

[49]Williams 2000, 132.
[50]Ibid., 131–47.

introducing ambiguities and conflicts into the task of following God faithfully:

> The revelatory nature of the life, death and resurrection of Jesus is manifest in [an] "initiation of debate" at an unprecedentedly comprehensive level.[51]

One of the liberating effects of this debate and ambiguity is precisely that there can be a glorious, theophanic release of overly tidy and sometimes self-serving human constructions of God:

> Jesus' reconstruction of humanity, liberating men and women from the dominance of past patterns, is Godlike.[52]

The experience of this Godlike liberation in an encounter with Jesus Christ compels the Christian to say that radical generativity is compatible with dependence. It is a 'creativity which is *responsive* rather than simply initiatory'. Jesus Christ is 'God *as* dependent'.[53]

Williams's account of the creative disturbance bequeathed by the incarnate Logos is already a theological counter to any neat account of what is made 'possessable' in Christ – and shows that it can be too easy to align christocentrism too neatly with 'givenness' and pneumatocentrism too neatly with 'foundness' (or novelty). Peter Ochs may at times overplay the way that theologies of givenness and theologies of foundness map onto different patterns of trinitarian allegiance, even though his critical approach is heuristically so useful. Moreover, in Chapter 3, Williams's account of the ambiguity that is introduced by Christ (i.e. the second person of the Trinity, not only the third) will prove highly useful in relation to one of the three key theoretical concepts that I want to deploy in service of Found Theology.

As any trinitarian doctrine rooted in a classical account of the coinherence and indivisibility of the 'persons' ought to do, Williams works with a model in which what is said most properly of one may also be said of the others. Nevertheless, he then turns to the

---

[51]Ibid., 138.
[52]Ibid., 139.
[53]Ibid., 140.

question of what seems distinctive about the divinity of the Holy
Spirit – and the answer here is far more centred on a generativity-in-
historical-extension that is the mark of the fellowship of the Holy
Spirit:

> Radical generative power is ascribed to the life of Jesus, but it
> is also ascribed to those events in which, through the ages, the
> community learns and re-learns to interpret itself by means of
> Jesus (and nothing else and nothing less).[54]

The Spirit's characteristic way of being generative, with its own
analogies to the absolute creative power that brought the world
into being from nothing, is a power of continual 're-formation' in
the lives of believers, both as individuals and as communities. The
form that is continually 're-formed' is, of course, Christlike, and
the process of re-formation happens participatively, as creatures
find Christ taking shape within and among them by virtue of their
sharing in and with his living example. The Spirit is the medium of
this participation.

The historical work of the Spirit is a constant proving of the
fundamental Christian wager, namely, that the 'foundational
story' of Jesus Christ, with all its particularities of place, time
and religious context, can be shown to be '"at home" with all the
varying enterprises of giving meaning to the human condition'. In
other words, and in line with Ochs's emphasis, the relevance and
meaningfulness of Christ for all people in all times will display itself
not through an abstract, universal principle, but by its limitless
power to reach across (and to bind) time and circumstance:

> Thus the "hermeneutical spiral" never reaches a plateau. For the
> event of Christ to be authentically revelatory, it must be capable
> of both "fitting" and "extending" any human circumstance; it
> must be re-presentable, and the form and character of its re-
> presentation are not necessarily describable in advance.[55]

Here, Williams captures the way in which the relations of the
trinitarian persons are not well described as outside or beyond
history, but as encompassing history. The unending business of
testing for Christlikeness, and of rediscovering and being, once

---

[54]Ibid., 140–1.
[55]Ibid., 142–3.

again, incorporated into Christ, is 'what we mean by the illuminating or transforming operation of the Spirit'[56]:

He will take what is mine and give it to you. (Jn 16.15)

And this is a process – or what Williams here calls an 'enterprise' – that is an intrinsic part of the trinitarian life itself. It is quite compatible with the perfection (or to use an equally good New Testament term, the fullness) of God. But the extendedness, the 'spirality', of the Holy Spirit's activity marks what Williams calls 'the necessary distinction' between the second and third persons. At some level, and taking into account all the caveats that have been entered so far, this is a distinction between given and found: 'between the event that defines the field and the terms of the interpretative enterprise, and the enterprise itself'.[57]

One concluding remark, whose intention is to mark the site of a discussion which will be developed further in the final chapters of this book: for Williams, the human faculty most expressive of the *imago Christi* – which is to say, of creativity in the mode of dependence – is that of imagination. Imagination does not need to pretend to have no debts in order to be genuinely and radically creative. It does not make itself subject to some alien law (to 'heteronomy') by being receptive. In relation to Christian thought, speech and action – which are inspired by the Holy Spirit in history – it is possible to say two things at once. First:

We speak because we are called, invited and authorized to speak, we speak what we have been *given*, out of our new "belonging", and this is a "dependent" kind of utterance, a responsive speech.[58]

But second:

[I]t is not a dictated or determined utterance: revelation is addressed not so much to a will called upon to submit as to an imagination called upon to "open itself".[59]

---

[56]Ibid., 143.
[57]Ibid., 144.
[58]Ibid., 146–7.
[59]Ibid., 147; the reference to imagination 'opening itself' is a reference to Ricoeur 1980, 117.

The receipt of God's self-communication in the mode of revelation is itself the work of God, who is radically creative both in
initiatory and in responsive ways. In human terms, the receipt of
God's self-communication in the mode of revelation – which is a
working of God in us – is fruitfully explored as imagination, or
(at the very least) as something very like imagination. Imagination
works in history, and with the particularities of material creatures,
to make analogical connections between things and to disclose the
binding of the world which is its God-given state.

In this spirit, we turn to the first of three sections which constitute
the backbone of the book's enquiry, each of them beginning with
a case study that examines the creative work of the Christian
imagination.

PART ONE

2

'I will happen as I will happen'

(EXOD. 3.14)

Introduction

This chapter's arguments are indebted to an extraordinary book by Brian Cummings (as sensitive to literary as it is to theological nuance, and masterly in showing the interplay of both).[1] Its arguments and its examples will likewise be both theological and literary, and centre on two intellectual challenges that were faced in England during the Protestant Reformation.

One of these challenges belongs to the early stages of the English Reformation, to a time in which a certain sort of 'conservative' loyalty to the Latin of the *Vulgate* as the shared Scripture of the universal Church (which is to say, of the Church of Western medieval Christendom) engendered a stubborn refusal to see in its translation into a new and very different language the possibility that new and potentially enriching meanings might emerge. Such meanings – though new – did not need to be regarded as substituting for or contradicting older ones (though it seems that they *were* regarded in this way by many). An 'additive' rather than a 'substitutionary' logic with a high view of historical development as part of God's will for the Church would not have been so defensive. But a

---

[1]Cummings 2002.

great deal of intellectual effort went into the forcible conforming
of English grammar to Latin, perhaps (partly) out of a concern
to preserve a timeless and universal *signifié* behind the variable
signifiants of scriptural words. (This happened despite the –
apparently forgettable – fact that the Latin of the *Vulgate* was itself
a translation from Greek and Hebrew.)

If the first sort of betrayal has something distinctly Catholic-
leaning about it, in its attachment to a Latin text which stands for
universal, suprahistorical, suprageographical meaning (a correlate
to a scholastic and then a neoscholastic understanding of doctrine
itself which remained powerful in Roman Catholic thought after
the Reformation), then the second is uniquely Protestant and
perhaps most quintessentially embodied in Calvinism.

Calvinist scruples about the theological risks of claiming any role
for human activity in earning divine grace led to a radical account of
the utter gratuity of divine favour. Yet, this account was accompanied
by an account of the assurance – the experienced certainty – of
the elected believer, which in its own way entailed a disregard of
historical discovery. Assurance of election was suprahistorical in
the sense that nothing that history might subsequently throw into
one's path could make any difference to it – not even the actions
of the elect themselves (however morally disordered they might
be in their living). An eternal decision of the Godhead that was
unaffectable by any merit on the part of the believer, made its effects
felt epistemologically in the believer's own assurance of salvation.
There was no need for anything more to be *found*; all was already
given – both the grace of election itself, and also the knowledge of
that election.

Both the Catholic-leaning concerns of those who would translate
the Bible only on the assumption that English could add nothing
new whatsoever to Latin, and the Calvinist concerns of those
who thought that historical experience could add nothing new
whatsoever to one's confidence of election (let alone to one's election
itself) share this key thing in common: they are wholly focused on
some given of the Christian faith. Whether this is the objective form
of a given text in a given language, or the subjective form of a given
assurance of personal salvation, neither position is constructed with
any kind of intrinsic openness to the *found*.

My bolder claim in this context is that in this key respect they
are not constructed with any really significant theological account

of the work of the Holy Spirit in history, delivering again and again to the Church (often through 'additive' surprise) the full riches of the meaning and gifts of Jesus Christ.

We will look at each of these intellectual challenges in turn.

An English Bible: The *Vulgate* and the vernacular

England in the sixteenth century found itself under the pressures of the rising forces of the Protestant Reformation. In a way that paralleled developments elsewhere on the Continent, the native language of England was – by some – being asked to take on the task of carrying religious meanings (including the very words of the Lord) that had for centuries been transmitted by Latin alone. In an unprecedented set of historical developments, the English language was being tested, experimented with, to see if it was up to becoming the bearer of a national religious culture. As Brian Cummings has pointed out, this was to invest it with 'a peculiarly heavy charge'.[2]

The experience that Western Christendom underwent in taking on the task of translating the Bible into the vernacular (indeed, into many vernaculars – though our focus here will be on English in particular) is a paradigmatic case of theology confronted with 'findings'. Translating the Bible into versions that sit alongside the long-established Latin causes theology to *find* things that press it towards new insights, new styles, new capacities. In cases where it refuses to accept that it is finding anything new at all, it displays odd contortions.

The fear that drives these contortions can be interpreted as a fear that the pressure towards new insights, styles and capacities must necessarily entail a betrayal of the original ('given') subject matter. Yet, at the same time, this same subject matter could be said to be betrayed by refusing the 'foundness' of a vernacular medium and its idioms. There might be a betrayal involved in imposing falsely, and perhaps even violently, on the medium itself, to make it conform to something it is not, and thereby making the speech of Scripture itself unwieldy, stilted or artificial. But beyond that, keeping it Latinate

---

[2]Ibid., 187.

might be a betrayal of the very *content* of Christian Scripture, and
especially its communication of how to live faithfully and creatively
in history; how to 'find' well. (My argument in this book is that this
guidance in 'how to find well' is particularly clearly articulated in
the context of a scriptural pneumatology[3] – and this is a theme to
which we will return periodically.) In this second sort of betrayal,
what is done to the medium performatively contradicts what seeks
to find *expression* in that medium.

William Tyndale himself, of course, was not translating from
Latin, but from Hebrew and Greek. A facility in these languages –
and especially the former – was still a relatively new and rare thing
in post-medieval Europe, and herein lay the beginnings of that
anxiety about Latin's deposition as *lingua sacra* that would be so
acutely compounded by the subsequent proliferation of translations
of the Bible. Cummings writes:

> The study of Greek and Hebrew raised a conflict in grammatical
> studies not because of the stylistic beauties or erotic paganism
> of classical Greek but because of *the problem of comparative
> grammar* [my emphasis]. The ancient languages exposed an
> *aporia* in medieval grammatical theory by having a grammatical
> structure which could not be rationalized fully by the terminology
> developed in relation to Latin. This was particularly true of
> Hebrew, which had a radically different system of inflection and
> syntax. The study of Hebrew therefore forced some immediate
> revision in grammatical categories. However, it also cast com-
> mensurate doubt on how the older Latin categories could be
> held to be universal or authoritative. And since the issue of the
> meaning of the Hebrew text was still investigated largely in Latin,
> it raised a further and profoundly disturbing question of whether
> texts written in Hebrew and Latin could ever mean exactly the
> same thing.[4]

The 'older Latin categories' are, in this instance, a set of 'givens' –
those vital religious orientation points whose persistence seems
(to many) to be essential to the continuity of the tradition itself.

---

[3]We might think once more in this context of Peter's 'conversion' to the realization
that he is to share table fellowship with Cornelius the Centurion, a Gentile, in Acts 10.
The decisive factor for him is that he sees the same Holy Spirit that has been poured
out on Jewish Christians incontrovertibly at work in the Gentile centurion too.
[4]Cummings 2002, 24.

The fateful introduction of *comparison* undercuts an authority that is premised on singleness, univocity and therefore a dream of universality. There is an ahistorical tendency to this dream. Comparison is generated historically; the rise of comparative grammar is the consequence of a renewed awareness of historical difference and historical process.

Cummings outlines three core difficulties faced by the Catholic Bishop of Rochester, John Fisher, in a sermon he preached in 1521 (the year of Martin Luther's formal excommunication). All of them touch on the issue of 'Englishing' the Bible. There is something especially intriguing about this sermon, in that (although subsequently translated into Latin) it was itself delivered in English. The three core difficulties, as Cummings outlines them, are as follows. First, there was 'a lack of technical terms of established usage' in English, and this generated in an unnerving way the 'necessity for coinages'. Coinages involve judgements of appropriateness, or 'fit', as well as requiring an inventive power. This can give them a destabilizing aspect. They do not obviously deliver a secure foundation for discussion and interpretation.[5] Second, the vernacular can seem coarse or indecorous, especially in its ability to express abstract ideas. Third, it is a language ill-suited to the defence of doctrinal tradition, because in itself it has no tradition of conveying (authoritative) doctrine. That tradition had until then been 'inscribed exclusively in Latin':

> On what authority could Fisher claim tradition in English, in which that tradition was as yet unwritten?[6]

Another great Roman Catholic apologist (and theological pugilist) of the period, Sir Thomas More (1478–1535) takes up similar issues in his controversy with Tyndale. One of his principal objections is precisely Tyndale's coinages – the decision to use the word 'love' instead of 'charity' in order to translate the word *agape*, for instance; or to deploy 'congregation' rather than 'Church' to translate the Greek *ekklesia*. 'Church' and 'charity' carry with them a set of resonances that channel the power of the Latin of the *Vulgate*, and this means that they carry a particular *doctrinal* charge with them too. 'Church', for example, evokes the Latin *ecclesia*,

[5]Ibid., 189.
[6]Ibid.

which triggers associations with a particular (Roman) doctrine of the Church. Tyndale's innovative renditions of them – using the opportunities afforded to him by English – aim to dislodge these embedded associations, making the words strange again in order to release possible further meanings, which – he believes – will be equally if not more appropriate ones. This is not, of course, an entirely easy matter, in that English itself (as a whole language) is profoundly influenced by Church Latin: a millennium and a half of it. But Tyndale is resolute in making the effort – and faced with More's (and others') citing of St Jerome's historic strictures on the dangers of translating 'ye texte of scripture out of one tongue into another . . . for as moche as in translacyon it is harde alwaye to kepe the same sentence hole',[7] Tyndale can be bolstered by the fact that the translation of the Greek text in Latin was precisely the achievement of Jerome: 'the very translation which More uses as his authoritative "text"'.[8]

The explicit intent of More's *Dialogue Concerning Heresies* is to dispute a series of doctrinal claims with an imaginary Protestant interlocutor – 'pestilent heresies' like the doctrine of *sola scriptura*, or justification by faith alone – but it finds itself inevitably embroiled in the issue of how to dispute theologically in the vernacular, and how to deploy the words of the Bible *when* disputing in the vernacular. A 'new exegetical practice' seems impossible to avoid, whether it is wished for by the Catholic traditionalist or not. The basic fact is that 'the signification of English is different from the signification of Greek or Latin'.[9] As Cummings points out, it is not only Lutheran theology that divides Tyndale from his opponents, but also English grammar.

Speaking with double tongue: The fear of equivocation

Paradoxically, the opponents mirror one another in their concern to avoid 'equivocation', while seeing the path to its avoidance lying

---

[7]More, 315; cited in Cummings 2002, 193.
[8]Cummings 2002, 193.
[9]Ibid., 191.

in quite different directions. For More, and others of his persuasion, a multitude of translations of Scripture inevitably represents a multitude of variant interpretations, while a single Latin Bible represents a solid rock on which to build the necessary edifice of doctrine. For Tyndale and his ilk, the single Latin text permits a multitude of *glosses* which are undertaken (more often self-interestedly than not) by a clerical and academic elite and imposed upon the laity. As Tyndale puts it, the Latin has the effect (which More too, by all accounts, would deplore if he thought it were true) that 'mans wisdom scatereth/divideth and maketh sectes'.[10] A democratically accessible Bible in the vernacular will clarify this situation, Tyndale argues, enabling everyone to confront the plain sense of Scripture without interference.

Is a translation into English playing its part in the creation of a new Babel? Or is it one stage in a movement that – like a new Pentecost – will enable 'an infinity of possible auditors' to receive the Word of God 'as if by simultaneous translation, each in his vernacular'?[11]

One of the issues that translators like Tyndale found was held very forcibly before them was that – even if they returned to and worked solely with the words of Scripture in their original languages – the meaning of those words was far from 'given' in every instance. Or at least, their meaning was not 'given' in a mode from which all equivocation could easily be banished. Cummings points out the ambiguity of the Hebrew constructions in Gen. 2.15-17, which the NRSV translates as follows:

> The Lord God took the man and put him in the garden of Eden to till it and keep it. And the Lord God commanded the man, "You may freely eat of every tree of the garden; but of the tree of the knowledge of good and evil you shall not eat, for in the day that you eat of it you shall die".

---

[10]Cited in Cummings 2002, 199. The quotation is from *The obedience of a Christen man and how Christen rulers ought to governe*, C3ʳ. See Tyndale 1530. It is a matter for remark that Tyndale's insistence that in hearing the word of God in their own languages all will hear it alike is elsewhere contradicted by his suggestions that English is superior to other languages as a vehicle for scriptural meaning, partly because of a special affinity to Hebrew.

[11]Cummings 2002, 199.

The first 'command' need not in fact be read as a command. It could be read as permission ('you *may* eat') or as a simple prediction ('you *are going to* eat'). The verb is in the imperfect form; the Hebrew enshrines a choice between an imperative and a future tense.

Tyndale's instinct in such situations may have been to try to resolve the ambiguity. Sometimes he did, and sometimes he did not. In this particular case, he opted in both cases for an imperative meaning, rendered in the peculiar and now somewhat archaic constructions 'se thou eate' and 'se that thou eate not'. The later Authorized Version, meanwhile, would preserve the ambiguity of the Hebrew with 'thou shalt not eat': this could be imperative or future (or a mixture of both?) as the reader happened to receive it.

This 'shall' is a window onto a fundamental feature of the English language, which no interpreter of Hebrew, Greek or Latin could ignore. In grammatical terms, 'shall' here is a 'modal auxiliary'. The modal auxiliary is that interactive variable which in its relation to the main verb can open its meaning in a series of very different directions, or (as we have just seen) precisely preserve an ambiguity of meaning that will have its own proper and perhaps productive effects by being left alone. Tyndale's refusal of the option of a modal auxiliary ('shall') in his translation of Genesis 2 required him to add a new imperative verb alongside 'eat' – namely, 'see' – in order to fix a meaning that would otherwise be slippery (possibly disconcertingly serpentine . . .). But it was not as obvious a faithfulness to the open possibilities of the text as we might have expected from a self-proclaimed servant of that text (there is, after all, no actual 'see' in Gen. 2.15-17; Tyndale *added* it).

Modal auxiliaries and life in the Spirit

Modal auxiliaries are manifold in English: they include not only 'shall' but 'should', 'may', 'must', 'might', 'let', 'can', 'could', 'do', 'did' and so on. When functioning as auxiliaries (rather than acting as main verbs themselves), their existence or appearance depends upon their relation to main verbs, but the main verbs they modify cannot be themselves without the auxiliaries. At the risk of being trinitarianly glib, this might be explained as a sort of coinherence, or correlationality, in which there is mutual difference as well as the profoundest unity at the level of the morpheme, or unit of meaning – a unity made more apparent by the fact that what sometimes appears in English as an auxiliary-plus-a-main-verb may in another language appear as a single verb but in a particular conjugated form.

For the first translators of the Bible into English, the auxiliaries became the medium of a series of energetic improvisations, as they struggled to render the meanings of given texts accessible to new audiences with the help of fresh linguistic resources. Improvising with modal auxiliaries is inhabiting a fecund realm of meaning, in which discoveries may and do happen. Sometimes, there will be a recognition that a proposal which a Biblical writer struggled tortuously to express within the limits of Greek, and which required even more complex circumlocutions when translated into Latin, can find itself made more limpid by the decision to use one modal auxiliary rather than another in English. Sometimes, there will be a (re-)discovery of an underdetermined meaning in a word or phrase in Scripture that had long been regarded as clear. That word or phrase can be assisted to return to its original ambiguity (if the translator is bold enough to let it). On balance, the fecund world of improvisation required by English's relatively unregulated grammatical forms (in which modal auxiliaries are used 'interchangeably to do different jobs'[12]) tends more to complexify and multiply the possibilities of meaning than to fix them.

Tyndale's temptations in respect of Genesis 2 (as, no doubt, elsewhere) once again reveal him to have more in common with the adherents of a Latin Bible than he might have liked to admit, at least insofar as the loyalists to Latin were quintessential promoters of the fixed and clear meaning. For them, as Cummings points out, 'Latin grammar stood as a paradigm for all languages.' Indeed, 'grammar' *meant* 'Latin grammar':

[E]ven early grammarians of English such as [William] Bullokar assumed the norms of Latin applied equally in English, and advertised their works as much as aids towards the acquisition of the learned languages as primers in the better use of the vernacular. Tyndale's own terms, used indiscriminately of Hebrew, Greek, and English, bear this imprint of Latin indoctrination.[13]

---

[12]Ibid., 205.
[13]Ibid., 206; Bullokar was author of the 1586 *Bref Grammar for English*.

The early sixteenth century, when the Bible was being so contro-
versially Englished, was at the same time witnessing the first efforts
of grammarians to give a systematic account of how English worked.
Or, better, how it *should* work. Rather like a somewhat chaotic
but creative institution being visited by management consultants
or health and safety inspectors, attempts were being made to
regulate English better, and the principal form this regulation took
was to make it conform more systematically to the givens of Latin.
An instructive example of this process at work is the *Rudimenta
Grammatices* of William Lily[14] (c.1468–1522), the first High
Master of St Paul's School in London. It is precisely the modal
auxiliaries that appear to present Lily with his biggest challenge,
and to provoke his most elaborate exertions.

Lily's premise was that 'whenever English morphology differed
in function from Latin grammar' it would be possible to show
that it was nonetheless after all 'identical in fundamental semantic
structure'.[15] So, in an opening section of the *Rudimenta* enunciating
the rules 'To make latyn', he lists English morphemes which he
believes match their already-given Latin form.

Here are some of the things that happen when a very precise
equivalent is sought for in English for every Latin conjugation:

Optatiue present tens	*Amem*	God graunt I loue
Preterimperfect tens	*Amarem*	Would god I loued
Preterperfecte tens	*Amaverim*	I praie god I haue loued
Preterpluperfecttens	*Amavissem*	Would god I had loved
Future tens	*Amavero*	God graunt I loue hereafter[16]

The outlandishness of these phrases needs no labouring, and is the
product of Lily's driven determination to corral the 'uncategorized
irregularities of English' within the regimented borders of established Latin form. Elsewhere, he takes exactly the same series of
Latin verbs, declined this time as 'potencial', to produce another,
and almost equally improbable, set of English constructions (once

---

[14]*Grammatices Rudimenta* was first published with John Colet in 1509 and appeared
in various versions thereafter. See, for example, Lily 1970.
[15]Cummings 2002, 208.
[16]*A Shorte Introduction of Grammar*, B4ʳ; cited in Cummings 2002, 210.

again wholly dependent on a battery of auxiliaries): 'respectively "I maie or can loue", "I myght or coulde loue", "I myght, shoulde or ought to haue loued", "I myght, should or ought to had loued", "I maie or can loue hereafter"':[17]

> With tongue-twisting ingenuity, Lily's grammar finds twenty-eight different phrasal forms of "to love" in order to satisfy the conjugal demands of his Latin exemplar, and another twenty-eight for the passive equivalents. The result is a grammatical monstrosity, born of Lily's desire to marry two languages.

One could hold this up as a parable of how *not* to relate the found to the given, and to a considerable extent that is my intention here. One of the unintended outcomes of the process, however, is generated by the manifest friction between the two languages that still persists even after Lily has expended all that energy and ingenuity on squaring them. This can be read as the found continuing to assert itself, breaking open the givens to which it is meant to submit, opening up a new historical horizon and a new historical task that does not replace or occlude what has been given already (in this case, Latin), but enriches the field of language study more generally by taking account of the idiosyncrasies of a *new* language (in this case, English). Through his 'effort of misalliance', Lily ironically *highlights* certain resistances in English to his Latin paradigm, and because these are 'features which cry out for independent analysis', momentum begins to gather, historically, for a new analysis of vernacular linguistics on its own terms.

In this way, the modal auxiliaries of English triumph in their indeterminacy, despite Lily's wish to 'keep up linguistic appearances'.[18] Like the Holy Spirit, they keep meaning in motion. In Lily's own language, they are like 'signs' – signs of how to read the verbs to which they are auxiliary. They are co-significative with the verb they accompany, and by whose agency that verb's meaning can be directed or permitted to flower. 'Shall' and 'will' in particular hold open a space for an unknown future – or at least for a future that is as yet not fully known – in which we know we will have obligations, and hope we will have rewards. They mark the space of

---

[17]*A Shorte Introduction of Grammar*, B4ᵛ; cited in Cummings 2002, 210.
[18]Cummings 2002, 209.

a coming reality in which we are certainly implicated but for which
our givens only partly prepare us. Cummings observes that:

> The English form "shall" derives from a Teutonic root meaning
> "debt" or "guilt", and "will" is still used as a verb to mean to
> "desire" or "intend". Statements about the future usually prove
> nearly impossible to make, and languages hedge them around
> with various modalities of supposition, inference, wish, fear,
> stipulation, threat, hope, or resignation.[19]

The Holy Spirit who, as Jesus promises in the farewell discourses
in John's Gospel, will convict the world about sin and righteousness
and judgement (Jn 16.8); and who causes the creation to groan
with eager longing (according to Rom. 8.22-23); and who will
give the disciples what they need in order to cope with future trials
(Mt. 10.19-20 and parr.), is a Spirit most especially geared to the
modalities of utterance where the future is concerned, and at work
in shaping them. This is an idea that we shall be keeping in play in
the chapters that follow.

'[S]ubmitting vernacular grammar to a foreign paradigm'[20] can
at least function as an *analogy* for what goes on when the found is
forced to conform to the given, with the attendant closures or losses
of meaning, and the violence and uglification of native forms, that
that can entail. Attending to issues of translation and translatability
can generate a more self-aware theological method when these paro-
dies of style and meaning are recognized for what they are. They represent a fantasy of univocity. For it is hardly ever that an imprecision
in an original text can be translated *precisely* into a new imprecision
in a new language; it is more likely that in some cases a new language
will enable the display of an imprecision that is 'in keeping' with the
original imprecision. 'Precise' and 'in keeping' are different things.

Calvinist convolutions

We turn now to a more typically Puritan set of issues, with its own
concerns to safeguard a set of 'givens', and above all the 'given' of

---

[19]Ibid., 217.
[20]Ibid., 208.

divine election. This given (election) was read by strict Calvinist thinkers as a function of the radical 'gift' of grace, such that to compromise the givenness of election was to compromise the sovereignty of the divine initiative *per se*. But there is a conflation of givennesses here. Givenness as 'graciousness' (which asserts that human beings do not produce the wherewithal of their own salvation from within themselves, nor possess their salvation as something to which they are entitled) is elided with givenness in the sense of brutely irreversible fact. Attempts to insist on the former – grace as *donum* – have the effect of turning grace into *datum*. In Brian Cummings's analysis, for Calvinists like William Perkins (1558–1602), past, present and future circumstances all end up sharing the aspect of past ones, because when a thing is forewilled by God, it is foregone as well. There is no room for contingency here – and no room, as a consequence, for *finding* in the sense that concerns this book.

Cummings explores these issues, in part, by way of a contrast between the 'epistemic' and the 'deontic'. The 'epistemic' is a stance in knowledge which anticipates, or predicts, a state of affairs that is yet to be; a state of affairs that might in principle not happen (in other words, that is contingently possible). The 'deontic' is a fact of existence, according to which something is, or will be, *of necessity*.

Perkins, says Cummings, merges the epistemic completely with the deontic in his work (translated in 1591) *A Golden Chaine; or, The Description of Theologie, containing the order of the causes of Saluation and Damnation.*[21] Perkins writes:

> For that, which beeing hereafter to be, is foreknowne of God, that assuredly will come to passe, and shall be . . .[22]

The effect of this conflation is severe for the world of modal auxiliaries that we began to tease out in the earlier part of this chapter. Our conclusion was that modal auxiliaries give a 'space' for the engagement of the human will (in forms of obligation or responsibility as well as in forms of desire) in the utterances that the human person makes to or about God.

---

[21]Perkins 1591.
[22]Ibid., i.98; cited in Cummings 2002, 260.

The richly varied world of 'modalities of supposition, inference, wish, fear, stipulation, threat, hope, or resignation', in all of which human freedom has a part to play, can be read as the richly varied world opened up by the Holy Spirit, who distributes tasks in the Church, and educates human desire. This is one of the fundamental claims of a pneumatology that thinks history matters, and the modal auxiliaries' way of situating the human agent in history (not above it), and equipping the human agent to negotiate history in ways that are not vauntingly confident of outcomes, nor quietist and despairing of making any difference, make them a 'site' of profound pneumatological importance in relation to human activity.

This is to insist, as I do, that language use is not to be contrasted with the domain of human action (as though it constructed a world outside or parallel in some way to the world in which material processes unfold and bodies interact). On the contrary, language use *is* a form of bodily, material and historical human action, and words themselves are material things, bodily formed and bodily transmitted. There are, incidentally, wider implications here for the way that theology itself is to be understood, for it can too easily be dismissed as a 'mere' word game, self-enclosed and without reference to the 'real' world, where people's actual experiences are rooted; indeed, it can collude in this caricature. This is a failure to understand how language itself constructs experience, and how all experience is 'thick with' language.[23]

But to say that all experience is shaped and given content by language is not to collapse all difference between the meanings language carries and the way the world, or God, is – between, once again, the epistemic and the deontic. No linguistic system can hold

---

[23]Brian Cummings puts this brilliantly when disputing '[t]he presiding assumption . . . that theology is an activity separate from the personal and psychological sphere of religious experience':

> Theology is conceived as a language subsequent, and supplementary, to the spiritual life which it (merely) "describes". This mistakes the way that spiritual life is invested in theological language. Any experience, any psychology, is inseparable from the language in which it operates and by which it is identified. To ascribe to language a secondary role of description is to accord to experience an instinctual status appropriate only to a life without such capacity for description. An experience that is rationalized is thick with linguistic description. (Cummings 2002, 378)

a flawless mirror up to the workings of the divine will. Perkins, however, seems inclined to think just this. Cummings writes that in Perkins's theological system (which is also a linguistic system), '[a]ll modal meanings are constrained . . . by [the] overpowering deontic "shall" of God':

> Every epistemic prediction of what "will come" is expressible only as a deontic "shall be" attributed to the direct agency of "the will of God", so that what will be shall be his will.[24]

The auxiliaries that speak of human mood are to be chastened and disciplined if they threaten to mislead us into thinking that we have choices and contributions to make in relation to our own salvation. They must instead be recast as epiphenomena of the divine *fiat*: dispositions that God himself ordains within our minds and hearts; 'givens' of the psyche. The deployment of a theologically driven grammar in which this suspicion of the modal auxiliaries is so deeply enshrined does a strange sort of violence to ordinary speech just as it does to our natural sense of our agency in time. To reiterate an earlier point made in passing, it makes all events – past, present and future – *like* past events, inasmuch as there is nothing that is not foreknown by God (or else God would have to be responsive in some way), and inasmuch as everything foreknown by God is forewilled (or else God would be less than omnipotent), and everything forewilled is foregone (and thus has this quality of 'past-likeness').

The eradication of 'all sense of conditionality in the action of grace' is perhaps the most definitive mode in which Protestant tradition allows the given to triumph over the found.[25] Its most grotesque flaw, according to critics of the Calvinist position like Richard Hooker (1554–1600) and Lancelot Andrewes (1555–1626), is that it renders what is unsearchable (except by God) into a body of knowledge that can be marshalled by the human intellect. The anti-Calvinists' typical way of resisting this excessive confidence in speaking of election is not typically to propose an alternative doctrinal argument, but to highlight the appropriateness

---

[24]Cummings 2002, 260–1.
[25]Ibid., 290.

of humble deference in the face of God's unsearchable purposes. In Andrewes's words:

> Yet are there in the world, that make but a *shallow* of this great deepe: they have sounded it to the bottome. GOD's secret *Decrees*, they have them at their fingers ends, can tell you the number and order of them just, with 1.2.3.4.5. Men, that (sure) must have beene in GOD's *cabinet*, above the *third heaven*, where *Saint Paul* never came.[26]

It is almost a moral appeal; one that recognizes the epistemological disciplines that serve spiritual health, and the sheer unattractiveness (or laughability) of supposing you sit in God's private offices. This epistemological resistance is a mode of life in the Spirit: 'not the difference between one doctrine and another but between assertiveness and uncertainty, articulation and inarticulateness'.[27]

My claim here is that – even if it is not explicitly a difference in doctrine – this is not just a difference in style, without theological import. More than 'mere' style, this is a difference in method. And theological method is of first-order and not only second-order theological importance when it is seen as an aspect of life in the Spirit.

The subjection of foundness to givens (whether the givens of an ecclesially sanctioned language, like Latin, or of a doctrine of divine election) has the effect of breeding a confidence in theological speech, and the judgements that are made in theological speech, that a doctrine of the Spirit's home in God's unsearchable heart will want to question. It might do so in the name of a theology to which the 'found' (and the act of finding) is central.

The principal challenge here, it seems, is how to find a way of conceptualizing human agency – including human speech – that honours the Calvinists' concern to prioritize divine initiative, and makes God's action the embracing context of all human action, while not evacuating modal auxiliaries of all their natural meaning. Or, to put it another way, that makes human intendings and wishings into integral moments *within* a divine framework of gracious provision for human destinies. This will require both a

---

[26]Andrewes 1629, 548; cited in Cummings 2002, 317.
[27]Cummings 2002, 317.

language of intention and desire and a model of cause and effect (within which that language makes sense and to which it testifies) in which agency is both affirmed and relativized at the same time. One key form this might take is in the affirmation of agency in the very act of relinquishing it.

Making oneself prone: Searching and ascribing

How may theology allow for a human engagement with, and investment in, the call to follow and serve God – in desire and responsibility – in a way that neither eradicates any point to human agency (which would make a nonsense of the New Testament's language about Christian discipleship, and above all the New Testament's language about how God the Spirit works in human lives) nor overrates it? A vision is needed that will suggest how human beings may make themselves 'prone' to God without commanding his action. The suggestion I want to make is that 'finding' has something of this quality. It is both an event in which one has agency, and yet it describes at the same time something 'happening' to one.

This delicately poised orientation towards the found is theologically underwritten by the vision of God vouchsafed to Moses in the Book of Exodus. The resolutely peculiar Hebrew of God's announcement of his name – *ehyeh asher ehyeh* – is notoriously difficult to translate, partly because of the underdetermined meaning of *asher* (inadequately: 'what' or 'that'), partly because the tense of the verb *ehyeh* has a futural implication which the most common English translation 'I AM' does not capture, and partly because the verb itself suggests not so much a static state of merely subsisting as a dynamic state of coming to pass. For this reason, I have translated it in the title of this chapter as 'I will happen as I will happen';[28] which could equally though less flowingly have

---

[28]The root verb is still, of course, 'be', so I am here taking something of a liberty by introducing a different English verb to translate it. I do so in order to make my point vividly. A further alternative might be to translate the phrase 'I will come to be as I will come to be'; this would give it much the same sense as the one I am after. I am grateful to my colleague Jonathan Stökl for his advice on this matter.

been rendered: 'I will happen as what I will happen as.' This is not a God whose 'meaning' may be possessed, nor whose actions may be predicted simply on the basis of already-given states of affairs. This is a God awaiting discovery in new and radical action, to which human beings do well to be open and receptive. It is worth noting that in order to translate this incandescent verse in the heart of the Pentateuch, English has the option of resorting to auxiliaries, and in many cases does so, using (as I have) the auxiliary 'will'. The argument of this chapter is that this does not have to be seen as a falling away from the more pristine meaning of the original Hebrew, but can be seen as a possibility contained within it, hatched by the demands of a new situation in which English itself (and the embeddedness in, and commitment to, a world in which English – like any language – encodes and facilitates life) is pressed to host biblical meaning. Faith in a God who 'happens' – and, more than that, who 'will happen as what he will happen as' – should inspire confidence in the idea that the act of translation itself might be a God-given 'happening' in which meaning is added to or unlocked in its source language, rather than diminished.

The most typical sort of agency at work when there is finding is, of course, searching; searching ensures a 'proneness' to finding, but does not guarantee a find. Searching is an openness to the found that is not mere passivity, yet the finding is not wholly in one's own hands. In theological terms, this suggests some possibility of placing oneself in the way of grace. Moses in Exodus 3 can stand as a good exemplar of this 'proneness'. He searches. The searching is at the most basic level a precondition of his finding. And yet, he does not obviously know *for what* he is searching at the beginning:

> Moses looked, and the bush was blazing, yet it was not consumed. Then Moses said, "I must turn aside and look at this great sight, and see why the bush is not burned up". (Exod. 3.2-3)

First, he simply sees it, and computes it as a peculiar physical fact. This makes him turn aside, and at that moment he becomes a seeker (he becomes 'prone' to finding). But, at the same time, it might be that all he is expressing here is a 'natural' curiosity about some anomalous state of affairs. Still not aware what finding is about to happen to him, he *goes over and looks* at the bush – a further looking which deepens his investment in the search. And at this point, the terms of his search are themselves wholly transformed by the agency of the God who 'happens as he happens'.

Brian Cummings identifies a particular facility to suggest this proneness to finding in the ambiguity of the model auxiliary 'let', which can enshrine a Calvinist concern to honour the total sovereignty of God at the same time as being a vehicle for the expression of human desire. 'Let', as Cummings puts in in a specific discussion of the poetry of Robert Southwell (c.1561–95 – and not, of course, a Calvinist!), 'places the sinner in the way of grace, without congratulating itself on the achievement'.[29] This is because 'let' has an optative sense ('consignifying a wish', as Cummings puts it) and also an imperative sense ('addressed to an unnamed third party, to "let" the action occur').[30] Thus, Southwell:

Lett grace forgive, lett love forgett my fall.[31]

Southwell here is more expectant of the possibility of the 'surprise' of grace than Moses seems to be in Exodus 2. It is not clear that Moses wishes his epiphany at all. Nevertheless, we see here a pressure stemming from the Christian doctrine of God to construct a theological method which 'lets' God happen; and it is the fruits of this that I have so far been calling Found Theology.

A somewhat old-fashioned word that achieves the same poise as the optative-imperative ambiguity of 'let' is one that proved immensely rich in the context of the English translation of the Psalms which was eventually incorporated in the *Book of Common Prayer*: the word is 'ascribe'. In the context of Psalm 96, for example, the verb takes its place as the kingpin of an utterance whose whole tenor it sums up:

1 O SING unto the Lord a new song: sing unto the Lord, all the whole earth.
2 Sing unto the Lord, and praise his Name: be telling of his salvation from day to day.
3 Declare his honour unto the heathen: and his wonders unto all people.

[29]Ibid., 362.
[30]Ibid., 363.
[31]Southwell 1595, l. 785.

4 For the Lord is great, and cannot worthily be praised: he is more to be feared than all gods.

5 As for all the gods of the heathen, they are but idols: but it is the Lord that made the heavens.

6 Glory and worship are before him: power and honour are in his sanctuary.

7 Ascribe unto the Lord, O ye kindreds of the people: ascribe unto the Lord worship and power.

8 Ascribe unto the Lord the honour due unto his Name: bring presents, and come into his courts.

9 O worship the Lord in the beauty of holiness: let the whole earth stand in awe of him.

10 Tell it out among the heathen that the Lord is King: and that it is he who hath made the round world so fast that it cannot be moved; and how that he shall judge the people righteously.

11 Let the heavens rejoice, and let the earth be glad: let the sea make a noise, and all that therein is.

12 Let the field be joyful, and all that is in it: then shall all the trees of the wood rejoice before the Lord.

13 For he cometh, for he cometh to judge the earth: and with righteousness to judge the world, and the people with his truth.

Ascription is a human action, which is at the very same time an attribution of agency to another. In this sense – though it is an activity of worship – it is even more eloquent than the verb 'to worship' in suggesting how one may put oneself in a position of receptivity in relation to God's activity. This God 'cannot worthily be praised'. The activity of worship may still smuggle in the idea that it is offering a praise that is worthy. The activity of ascription, at least as we encounter it here, has no such pretensions. It encapsulates what the psalm as a whole enacts. A self-subverting intention to sing praises to one who cannot be praised is a performed ascription of total agency to God, which is nonetheless a transformative human act. The singer of this psalm becomes mobilized for generosity ('bring presents'), and for witness ('tell it out'), becomes a victor over idolatry ('as for all the gods of the heathen . . .') and enters a new fellowship with the non-human creation ('the heavens . . . the earth . . . the sea . . . the field . . . the trees'), as well as locating righteous judgement with God alone.

Ascription not only of worship but of power allows room for the possibility – as with Moses – that one's proneness to receive may yield an unexpected finding, for there is no trammelling this God's initiative. He will happen as he will happen.

The insights delivered to this chapter by a close study of the Reformation period in England, and especially by the challenges of making an English Bible, and making English as a language do theological service, have prepared the way for a more theoretical examination of what may be good for theology in a biblical text which is not, in Cummings's word, 'terminist'.[32] In other words, there may be a generativity in a biblical text that has openings, irregularities and rough edges within it. The gaps and tensions that open up between different translations of the Bible may signal a latent 'gappiness' – a capacity for tension and multiplicity of meaning – that is already the property of the 'original' text itself.

What the modal auxiliaries highlighted to the more discerning early grammarians of English (those, at least, who did not bend over backwards to make the language more compatible with Latin than it was) was an almost *precious* discrepancy between the language of the Church and the vernacular. John Wallis's *Grammatica linguae Anglicanae* of 1653 proclaims 'an *immanis discrepentia* in structure and usage between English and the classical languages'. But this is not for him a matter of regret. It highlights the positive need for a '*nova methodus* founded on vernacular principles'.[33] The theological argument being advanced in this book is that such a *discrepentia* may be read as a divine gift, a pneumatological finding; and that the newness of the approaches it provokes may be read as divine gifts too.

---

[32]Cummings 2002, 426.
[33]Ibid.

3

Maculation

Introduction

In each of three pairings of chapters (Chapters 2 and 3, Chapters 4 and 5, and Chapters 6 and 7, respectively), an extended case study will be followed by the exploration of a theoretical resource that seems to me to help make sense of the case study – not exhaustively, but usefully. The case study should give body to the theoretical material, and the theoretical material distil and clarify some key issues raised by the case study.

In this first pairing of chapters, we have begun by looking at various challenges and developments that were presented by the Englishing of the Bible: what textual ambiguities were raised by the business of translation; what ideals about the very nature of the English language needed to be sacrificed or revised in this process; and how some doctrinal commitments found help while others found resistance as it unfolded. My implicit claim was that doctrinal commitments which honour the role of locality and historicality in God's self-revelation to the Church are more likely to be helped by observation of the process of translation, and doctrinal commitments which minimize the role of locality and historicality are more likely to be discomfited by it.

The translation of the Bible, along with the theological perspectives which that untidy business showed itself capable of generating, gives us an insight into the capacity of an unstable sacred text both to make its readers anxious and to make them creative. The sixteenth- and seventeenth-century Christian desire for a text that was above ambiguity – whose 'plain sense' was self-evident and did not vary with context – embodied itself in both Catholic and

Protestant forms. A version of the Catholic desire could be seen in a continued commitment to Latin, and a version of the Protestant desire in a theology that claimed an unchanging 'Word in the words' that would successfully shine through any particular human language, provided the translation was undertaken by faithful scholars of the text. (That said, it must be acknowledged – in connection with the latter claim – that by no means all Protestants shared such theological confidence, and the evidence on the ground must certainly have made the notion seem to many like a triumph of wishful thinking over the facts.)

What I want to propose at the outset of this chapter is somewhat bold. If my proposal has plausibility for the reader, then it should help to justify the connection I intend to make between the case study in Chapter 2 (which has dwelt on the challenges of scriptural *translation*) and the theory in this chapter (which, as we shall see, is a response to the challenges of scriptural *restoration*).

My bold proposal is this: the instability manifesting itself in the gaps or tensions that open up between the Bible's instantiations in two or more different languages (i.e. when it is translated) can in turn be seen as a heightened instance of something that is discernible within the canonical biblical texts themselves, even in their original languages of Hebrew and Greek. These texts likewise are not free of inconsistency or oddity. Here too there are gaps and tensions to be noted.[1]

---

[1]David Weiss Halivni, my principal dialogue partner in this chapter, highlights just a few such gaps and tensions in relation to the Hebrew Bible/Old Testament:

> According to Exodus 13:13, on the subject of unclean animals, only the firstlings of an ass must be redeemed with the offering of a lamb. However Numbers 18:15 dictates, "The firstlings of unclean animals shall you redeem," with no limitations. According to Exodus 21:7, "When a man sells his daughter as a slave, she shall not go out as the male slaves do." Deuteronomy 15:17, however, states that a female slave must be handled just as a male. Following Numbers 18:26, one would present the agricultural tithe to the Levites, but Leviticus 27:30 states that it must go to the priests alone. The Levitical law (Lev. 12:1-13) appears to assign the Passover rite to the home, whereas Deuteronomy 16:2 consigns it to the Temple grounds alone. . . . In describing the Passover sacrifice, the Chronicles (2 Chr. 35:13) employs an awkward Hebrew construction, declaring that the flesh was "cooked" (from the root *bshl*) in the fire. *Bshl* is elsewhere understood to denote boiling, and fire is associated with roasting. The phrase is unaccountably strange. . . . (Halivni 1997, 24–5)

Unaccountable strangeness is a property of the biblical texts, which may be disguised or elaborately explained away if it is seen as a problem. Alternatively, it may be regarded as a divine provision for some generative purpose: something made to be found, and to stimulate further finding. And if this positive reading can be offered in relation to the canonical text in its original languages, then there is at least a possibility that it can be extended further, and made the basis of a welcoming engagement with the interpretative challenges that open up when the Bible is rendered in many languages. This, then, is the subject of the present chapter's enquiry.

David Weiss Halivni: A story of scriptural degradation

The theoretical resource that will be employed in this chapter is that of the distinguished Jewish scholar, David Weiss Halivni; specifically, his analysis of what he calls 'maculation' in the texts of Scripture.

Maculation in Scripture is described by Halivni early in his 1997 book *Revelation Restored* as 'the insufficiency of the Pentateuch's literal surface'.[2] He discerns even the very earliest redactors of Hebrew Scripture struggling with this issue as they canonized it, and it has remained an issue in every age afterwards.

[T]he literal surface of the canonical Pentateuch is marred by contradictions, lacunae, and various other maculations . . .[3]

One of Halivni's central proposals involves a remarkable attempt to satisfy both the critical norms of modern, Western historical scholarship and the commitments of a devoutly Orthodox Judaism, by claiming that there was indeed a perfect, or immaculate, Torah given by God to the people of Israel on Sinai at Moses's hands (thus safeguarding one of the principles of orthodoxy), but that this is not exactly the text that now constitutes the – evidently maculate – written Torah. The written text has a history, and it is the history made for it by the repeated disobedience and apostasy of

---

[2]Halivni 1997, 2.
[3]Ibid.

the people who were given it. (This continual neglect of God's Law over many centuries, incidentally, created the conditions in which prophets were necessary: calling to the people in their distance from God's Law and trying to draw them back to faithfulness.) These centuries of neglect had the effect of allowing the immaculate text to degenerate to a significant degree.

It was only at the time of the ending of the Babylonian exile – so Halivni proposes – that the people finally found themselves collectively ready to embrace and keep the Law. This is the hour in which Ezra the Scribe comes into his own (and in which prophecy ceases, for it is no longer needed).

> Whereas Moses must be seen as a passive conduit, the recipient of a perfect, divine Torah, Ezra must be seen as a prophet whose task was to rebuild that Torah. Ascribing this role to Ezra is not only a theological maneuver (that is, not merely a proposition posited in order to uphold faith) but an academic one as well (that is, a plausible historical assertion).[4]

Ezra repristinates the text, so far as he is able, so that the people may live by it at last. We see this narrated in the Book of Nehemiah – and especially in Chapter 8.

But the written Torah is now a 'troubled text'. It now has those lacunae, contradictions and maculations to which we have already referred. The people must find a way to accommodate themselves to such instability.

Halivni identifies two responses on the part of the people and their religious leaders (the 'stewards' of the text) to this 'trouble'. Both responses express the strong desire to have a firm source of divine authority to which to refer; 'an enduring record of God's will'.

Two remedial responses

Adjunct explanation

The initial strategy put in place by Ezra and his entourage to ensure that the Pentateuchal canon – though maculate – can continue to play

---

[4]Halivni 1997, 4.

the role of 'majestic and unchallenged law', and function effectively
as a rallying and orienting point for the people, is to appeal to an
oral law alongside it which will help with its interpretation. The
text itself 'requires adjunct explanation', as Halivni puts it – and it
may well be exactly this that is documented in Neh. 8.7-8[5] in which
we are told that Ezra's assistants work with the people to help them
to understand what is being read from Scripture. By giving 'explicit
instructions as to how the text was to be employed', these teachers
use oral material that ensures that '[i]n spite of textual maculations,
coherent law is introduced.'[6]

This is a strategy of extreme importance for the purposes of the
present study, because of the way that it seems quite content to celebrate an essential role for human agency in stewarding the Scriptures
(a role actually *elicited* by the scriptural maculations) alongside a
robust claim about their divine origin. The relationship between the
two is to be a continual one. The oral Torah does not work to correct
the maculate written Torah once off, and then retire. On the contrary,
the written Torah is left in its maculate state – as the best and nearest
version that can now be had of what was once immaculately delivered to Moses, never to be tampered with or neglected again.

> Ezra and his scribes were aware of problems in the text. Never-
> theless, the fact that these maculations were allowed to remain in
> place indicates that the scribes themselves had reverence for the
> scriptures they had inherited. [They were] aware that centuries
> of imperiled textual transmission, through dangerous and hostile
> times, had made them heirs to a troubled scriptural inheritance.
> Yet we can be sure that these canonizers were also convinced
> that their scriptures were the legacy of Sinai, that their Torah was
> beyond reproach.[7]

But by this very decision, the oral law that accompanies it is
given a permanent role to perform too, for the maculations in the

---

[5] Also Jeshua, Bani, Sherebiah, Jamin, Akkub, Shabbethai, Hodiah, Maaseiah,
Kelita, Azariah, Jozabad, Hanan, Pelaiah, the Levites, helped the people to
understand the law, while the people remained in their places. So they read from
the book, from the law of God, with interpretation. They gave the sense, so that
the people understood the reading. (Neh. 8.7-8)
[6] Halivni 1997, 27.
[7] Ibid., 37.

written text will (if not suppressed) continue grittily to stimulate and to provoke its readers, thereby galvanizing questions that need resolution. Suppression, however, remains a real temptation.

Suppression of memory

Halivni, as I have said, outlines *two* responses to the troubled nature of the text and its maculations. The second is somewhat less healthy, involving as it does a degree of self-deception by the tradition about just how fissured the sacred text is. In this second response – broadly – 'the memory of canonization itself became less palatable'.[8] The reasons for this, speculates Halivni, have to do with the instincts of piety. '[W]hatever its purveyors, the scribes, may have known about the book, to the people at large its absolute perfection was self-evident,' he says – and this because a holy writ that was also a maculate writ seemed like an oxymoron.[9]

> A holy text ought to be smooth, free of blemish; its indispensable instructions should emanate from within.[10]

This fuelled a suppression of memory – the memory of canonization itself – until, eventually, 'the actual history of the text seemed impossible, or even absurd, when suggested to the religious mind'.[11] Along with a forgetfulness about canonization, there was a concomitant forgetfulness of what the initial relation of the oral law to the written text might have been. No longer a body of adjunct material that was appealed to in order to deal correctively with maculations in the written text, the oral law had to be made to cast no aspersions on scriptural wholeness at all.

Halivni sees two successive historical stages in rabbinic thought that seek to smooth over the problem in two different ways. (a) The first is the way of exegesis, which says that everything in the oral law can in fact be read out of the written Torah; it is, thus, not so much an adjunct to as it is derivative of, and dependent on, the written Torah. (b) The second is to say that Moses had two bodies of material revealed to him on Sinai that are both immaculate, and that are

---

[8]Ibid., 52.
[9]Ibid., 48.
[10]Ibid., 50.
[11]Ibid., 52.

complementary when taken together. The written Torah and the oral
Torah have both been handed down without blemish. Halivni writes:

> The trend of Tannaitic times[12] was to impute all authoritative law
> to scriptural sources in an effective move away from external oral
> law, toward exegesis. As the written Torah had been canonized
> and was venerated as the book presented to Moses on Sinai, the
> desire of the age was to demonstrate that all valid laws were
> deducible from the text itself. Toward the end of the Talmudic
> period[13] and thereafter, the rabbinic viewpoint came full circle,
> with existing law – even rules attached to well-known exegetical
> arguments – being imputed to a separate body of nonscriptural
> information, revealed explicitly and transmitted faithfully along
> with the scriptures – *Halakah le-Moshe mi-Sinai*.[14]

Let us look briefly at these two stages in turn, before bringing
some comments to bear on the strategies that were used in each of the
stages, drawing upon the theological resources that the present book
has begun to develop. It is here that some of the key issues that emerged
in the previous chapter's 'case study' will demonstrate their use.

The first stage (a), which Halivni calls 'the trend of Tannaitic
times', knows that 'the very existence of oral law militates against
the notion of scriptural self-sufficiency', and it feels uncomfortable
with this. Thus – in service of defending Scripture's adequacy – it
makes oral law appear so dependent on Scripture that any tension
will 'dissipate'.[15]

> Once the written word was canonized – that is to say, once the
> scriptures were fixed in form and sacred in popular opinion – the
> religious leadership, the scribes and their successors, began to
> believe in earnest that all laws to be observed had their origins in
> the written text itself. Generations of exegetes maintained that the
> scriptural word was capable on its own of giving rise to a body of

---

[12]The classical Tannaitic period begins after Rabbi Hillel (first century BCE) and
Rabbi Shammai (c.50 BCE–c.30 CE) and ends in the early third-century CE after
Rabbi Yehuda ha-Nasi. See the entry on 'Tanna' in Berlin 2011, 720–1. For entries
on Hillel and Shammai, see 347, 670.
[13]The Talmudic period runs from c.200–500 CE. See the entry on 'talmud' in Berlin
2011, 714.
[14]Halivni 1997, 64.
[15]Ibid., 50.

law that once had been viewed as strictly oral tradition (and that, as we shall see, was later to be regarded in just that way again). Correspondingly, if the composite nature of the scriptures had ever been acknowledged, its history of compilation evaporated in the heat of exegesis.[16]

By contrast, the approach (b) that will govern rabbinic interpretation throughout the Middle Ages, and which (says Halivni) originates at the end of the Talmudic period, works instead from the premise that Moses received a good deal more on Sinai than the written text of the Torah alone, and that he initiated a chain of transmission of this other (oral) material in a way that foresaw virtually every later issue or application of the Torah that would ever arise. In this view, 'the entire oral law was given to Moses on Sinai . . . not only the written text, but also the interpretations offered by the rabbis (the scribes), were revealed to Moses by God'.[17] Halivni identifies what he calls a 'maximalist' version of this position whereby 'not only sacred literature and interpretations of the scribes, but also what any scholar at any time will innovate (i.e. whatever passes as halakha), was already provided to Moses on Sinai'.[18] This could include, for some, even the melodies that would later be used when chanting different parts of the Scriptures, and even the decisions that would later be made about how to calculate the Jewish calendar. The claim that something had been revealed to Moses on Sinai, *Halakah le-Moshe mi-Sinai* – whether it was in the written Torah or not – became an untrumpable card, against which no amount of exegetical argument could prevail.

The allure of the pure

In this statement by a medieval rabbi – R. Y. Abarbanel (1437–1508) – we see the passion deployed in defence of a scriptural text that simply must be without flaws:

> How can I believe and bring to my lips that Ezra the Scribe found God's Torah, and the books of the prophets and others

---

[16]Ibid., 51.
[17]Ibid., 58.
[18]Ibid., 59.

who spoke while possessed by the holy spirit, to be faulty and confused? . . . The cardinal belief which the great Rabbi [Maimonides] bequeathed to us in his commentary to the Mishnah [is] to believe that the Torah which we possess is the one that was given to Moses on Sinai without change or variation at all.[19]

The motivation for a new emphasis – alongside this supposed perfection of the written Torah – on the perfection of the *oral* Torah might well be explained (as Halivni explains it) as a new fearfulness about imperfection. It is one that goes well beyond a distaste for admitting maculation only in the scriptural texts. The imperfection of *exegesis itself* was now the additional concern; an immaculate oral Torah was the solution to it. The criterion of the divine perfection that Abarbanel particularly associates with the teaching of Maimonides, means that nothing given by God as a means of knowing God can easily be treated as less than perfect. Exegesis certainly did not seem to meet this criterion:

> It was assumed that a perfect God could create only perfect things, and if the Torah had been given to Moses by God, a belief shared also by Christianity and Islam, it could not be changed or abrogated. The weakness of exegesis – its subjective nature and its vulnerability to error – made it intolerable as a basis of law for philosophers of Maimonides' time.[20]

Assuming Halivni's account of developments in rabbinic interpretation to be a defensible one, how might we evaluate the two attempts, outlined earlier, to 'smooth the problem' of the grittily maculate written Torah? In particular, how might we evaluate them in terms that are informed by the 'case study' in Chapter 2, and the theological reflections that have begun to be developed in the book so far?

Keeping time

The first thing to note is that the move from an emphasis on exegesis to an appeal to an immaculate oral Torah signals a contraction

---

[19]R. Y. Abarbanel's introduction to the Book of Jeremiah; cited in Halivni 1997, 72.
[20]Halivni 1997, 71.

of the sphere of human creative activity in the interpretation of Scripture – or, at the very least, an occlusion of the actual creative activity that does inevitably go on in the interpretation of Scripture. Halivni points out the change by comparing the *Mekhilta* tractate *Bahodesh* (Chapter 9) and Sifrei on Deuteronomy (on the one hand) with the later Song of Songs Rabbah (on the other).[21] The former texts emphasize the excellence of the interpretative involvement of the Israelites themselves as they received the Torah at Sinai, and identify hermeneutical activities that helped them draw out and apply its wisdom – like inference and analogy. But, in the latter text, we find a very different outlook:

> Let him kiss me with the kisses of his mouth; (Song 1:2) – R. Yochanan said: An angel carried the utterances at Mount Sinai from before the Holy One, blessed be He, each one in turn, and brought it to each of the Israelites and said to him, Do you take upon yourself this commandment? So and so many rules are attached to it, so and so many penalties are attached to it, so and so many precautionary measures are attached to it, so and so many precepts and so and so many rulings from minor to major. The Israelite would answer him, Yes. Thereupon, he kissed him on the mouth. The Rabbis, however, say: The commandment itself went to each of the Israelites and said to him, So and so many rules are attached to it [etc.] and he would reply, Yes, yes. And, straightaway, the *commandment* kissed him on the mouth.[22]

This is a model of the revelation of the Torah which Halivni rightly describes as a 'spoon-feeding' model – for whether it is an angel or the commandment itself that comes down and delivers not only the bare commandment but all the interpretations and applications of the commandment, all that the human recipient has to do is say 'yes' (and be kissed). If the only role of the human being is to say 'yes' then all sense of searching and finding, and of arriving at implications that are initially only latent in a text, is lost. No agency is awoken and fostered in the interpreter. As Halivni says, '[m]an

---

[21]The *Mekhilta* tractate *Bahodesh* and Sifrei on Deuteronomy are dated to the period of the Tannaitic Midrash in the first and second centuries CE; the Song of Songs Rabbah is sixth century CE. See entries in Berlin 2011, 482, 687, 697.
[22]Cited in Halivni 1997, 67.

contributes no intellectual input, divinely gifted with wisdom or otherwise'.

Ascribing man's interpretive powers to commandments themselves is, in essence, attributing each derived detail to *Halakha le-Moshe mi-Sinai*. Exegesis is short-changed and a reliance on divine supernatural powers is substituted.[23]

This, to use the working vocabulary of the present book, is to make everything given and to leave nothing to be found. The contraction it represents may look like the closing of a worrying space that threatens to weaken the Law's authority, and thus be a welcome underpinning of some vital foundations for a religious life. But the space being closed is the space of human ratiocination and constructive enterprise; and (in the terms proposed by this book) it is a wrong turn to rule out this space as a space of divine agency just because it is self-evidently also a space of human agency. The Song of Songs Rabbah presents a relation between divine giving and human finding that has elements of the zero sum game about it, premised as it is on what seems a competitive model of the relation of divine to human agency: a model which says that where one increases the other must necessarily decrease. As angels or personified commandments take the stage, the human contribution is reduced to a deferential monosyllable.

However, identifying the problems that attend the rejection of exegesis in favour of a set of meanings that is comprehensively given – in every detail – in oral fashion still leaves us with the problem that (as we have seen) exegesis itself was used at an earlier point by the rabbis as a way of 'smoothing' the maculate text. What might be the problem here, as measured by the criteria we have been developing?

In fact, the issue here is not with exegesis as such, but with its use to change the interactions of the oral Torah with the written Torah from being creative and/or corrective ones into being derived ones. Exegesis becomes a form of 'explaining away' any tensions between the written Torah and the oral tradition rather than generating new readings within new horizons from out of those tensions. So, actually it might be better to say that the loss here is not so much

---

[23]Halivni 1997, 67.

human agency (for all sorts of ingenuity can and are brought to bear on the exegetical task) but history itself: the text's history (which shows its maculate state), and the history of reparative engagement with its maculations, which is a continuous process of reading and rereading, to new ends. In this process, we who read will have to reckon with our own historical specificity and finitude as well as the fissures in the text. Peter Ochs summarizes the implications of this:

> God beckons the reader by way of apparent errors in the text . . . [E]ach reading [must then] fulfill its reparative task within the finitude of this world, provided we recognize that the maculation is not merely "in the text" but also "in the reader" or, otherwise put, in the specific relation that binds this text to this reader (within his or her community of reading at this particular time). In these terms, the text's maculations are also signs of context-specific problems within the reader's community. A reading completes its task when it identifies these problems and contributes to their repair.[24]

In Christian terms, the 'explaining away' achieved by certain sorts of exegesis can be recognized as a common tendency in the development and transmission of doctrine. Exegesis that is made to serve predetermined doctrinal goals, or to reinforce established positions, will almost always seek to minimize the oddities and challenges of the text: to smooth it, and remove its grit.[25] Exegesis, whether Jewish or Christian, that is undertaken in the vein of 'explaining away' is not predisposed to find anything really new in its readings of the scriptural texts – or, indeed, anything really problematic. The doctrine served by such exegesis will take on the aspect of a body of material that is ahistorically true (rather than the product of context-specific and reparative judgements, arising out of human needs and urgencies, of the sort that Ochs describes). Brian Cummings makes a similar point in his study of the literary culture of the Reformation. It is only in 'the artificial world of

---

[24]Ochs 2011, 237.
[25]For a very helpful discussion of this tendency with specific reference to Augustine's treatment of the parable of the Good Samaritan, see Higton 2003, 447–56. I owe my language of smoothness and grit to Higton.

intellectual history', he observes, that '[d]octrine exists as a single stratum of dogmatic propositions':

[W]ithin its historical formation it is a complex series of intersecting speech acts.[26]

Here, perhaps, is our first explicit point of contact with the issues raised in Chapter 2. The attraction of a Latin Bible, as well as a Latinate system of doctrine that correlates neatly with it, is that its language has developed settled meanings that over time have smoothed both the surface of the canonical text itself *and* the borderline between the Bible's surface and the surface of a great body of Christian doctrine. The business of (as far as possible) circumventing Latin's hegemony in order to turn Hebrew and Greek into English exposed the Bible's rough power to provoke and interrogate once again – and its need to *be* interrogated in order to be understood.

We may now turn again to the second of the two rabbinic 'solutions' to the maculate text that Halivni explores: that of a perfect oral Torah, fully and finally communicated to Moses on Mount Sinai. The issue here is not unlike the issue that arose in relation to certain Calvinist doctrines of predestination whose lineaments we traced in Chapter 2. These doctrines found themselves struggling hard to overcome or subdue the biblical text, and particularly to evacuate that world of meaning and action, which English portrays in its modal auxiliaries, of any sense of real moment. As we observed, the doctrine of predestination risks making both the present and the future effectively indistinguishable from the past. All is already decided; history is only a platform for the illustration of the given. The idea that Moses was given not only the written text of the Pentateuch by God on Sinai, but also the interpretations that would later be offered by the rabbis – in short, the entire oral law – is tantamount to a claim that the history of the people with its Law is already a *fait accompli*, in which there is no room for any free or improvisatory contribution to be made.

If the problematic alternatives that Halivni diagnoses in rabbinic tradition seem to have analogues in Christian history, there is reason

---

[26]Cummings 2002, 285.

to hope that some of the positive aspects of his alternative to them (which is a sort of recovery of the spirit of Ezra for today) will find an answering echo in Christian theology as well. I believe this is so, and that the particularly resonant echoes will be found in the meeting point between Christian pneumatology and a theology of Scripture.[27]

A Christian account of scriptural maculation

In what follows, I shall be referring to Stephen Fowl's typology of determinate, anti-determinate and underdeterminate accounts of scriptural meaning in his book *Engaging Scripture, A Model for Theological Interpretation*.[28] Our main dialogue partner, however, will be Rowan Williams in his essay 'Historical Criticism and Sacred Text'.[29]

Williams points out how overly determinate accounts of scriptural meaning have trouble giving an adequate description of how God's relationship with his people throughout history unfolds by way of the new meanings that arise from that people's continual reading of Scripture. Accounts of Scripture that seek to identify the original meaning of a text through a knowledge of the historical context of its production – and to make this probable original meaning its single meaning – are examples of such determinacy at work. Williams argues that scriptural texts have far more of a quality of 'excess' of meaning than this determinate account allows. What gives his account interesting affinities with Halivni's is that he ties this power of excess to 'contradictions', 'stresses' and '*aporiai*' in the text (elements of disturbance or irresolution which we may now gloss as 'maculations').[30] When reading, Williams proposes, one should be 'alert to the fresh contradictions or strains set up by the text, inviting further textual elaboration – the unfinished business of any and every text'.[31] So the contradictions – or maculations – of

---

[27]I am grateful to my former graduate student Rachel Greene for many points in the discussion which follows.
[28]The categories of determinate, anti-determinate and underdeterminate are themselves drawn from Fowl 2000. See, for example, 10–11.
[29]Williams 2004, 217–28.
[30]Ibid., 222.
[31]Ibid., 221.

the scriptural text, which show as marks of 'intra-textual strain' – are also signposts of Scripture's readiness to give more than has so far been yielded. In resisting our desire for determinate readings, they also free us from a naïvely unified picture of what we have in Scripture, and an entrapment in our own preconceptions about what it ought to say. This makes the underdeterminate character of Scripture a generative force.[32]

In a set of key respects, Williams, Fowl and Halivni are very close to one another, and can be read compatibly. Determinate accounts of Scripture (Fowl's term) are undermined by Scripture's maculations (Halivni's term). Moreover, these maculations (which render the body of Scripture underdeterminate, rather than determinate) demand an ongoing, diachronic relationship with the text through time (Williams's point).

Williams does, however, make a further suggestion that is bolder than anything we find in Halivni. Williams insists that a doctrine of Scripture (for which we may read 'maculate Scripture') cannot be separated off from a doctrine of God, and he proposes that the generativity of underdeterminate scriptural texts derives from the generosity of God – a God characterized by (or even *as*) excess. 'A theological exegesis', writes Williams, '. . . looks for . . . marks of

---

[32]We should note that Williams is cautious in his essay about the use of spatial language to describe the way in which Scripture generates communities of interpretation (language of the sort I have been reproducing in this chapter whenever I have talked in terms of lacunae or fissures, for example). With good reason, he warns that talking about some putative spatial expanse in a text can suggest that engagement with that text will be an ahistorical affair – not a gradual and diachronic process. The only time that matters will be the interpreter's present moment, as she or he (so to speak) *enters a space* in the text. It should be apparent from the whole thrust of this chapter (and indeed of this book) that this is a picture of the interpretative process that I in no way want to commend. I can partially meet such concerns by pointing to the fact that Halivni's language of maculation has been my principal language of choice, and that this language does not have to be conceived spatially. Indeed, Halivni, as we have seen, is very clear that scriptural maculations are themselves the product of time, and not features of a supposedly timeless architecture of Scripture. But having said that, I want to go further and say that the image of lacunae or fissures in Scripture can be quite compatible with a diachronic attitude to interpretation; in other words, one does not need to choose between spatial and temporal models. What are conceived of as spaces in Scripture can be revisited in time. A theological interpretation that occurs in such a space, or opening, is a temporal occupation of that space but not a closure of it. The space is not sealed shut; the process of engaging with (and in) it is always capable of continuation.

excess and of intra-textual strain that might have to do not only with immediate ideological context but with God.'[33] Halivni, meanwhile, always remains reserved in his discussions of God's purposes and nature, and does not wish to say that it was God who put the grit in the text. For Halivni, the maculations in the canon of Scripture are 'more human than divine' in their provenance.[34] God, in a final flourish of prophetic commissioning, gives through Ezra the means of *dealing* with the grit – but that is something rather different from saying that God had any role in originating that grit.

One very important consequence of Halivni's standpoint is that the innovative actions of Ezra in restoring revelation are not offered as, and cannot be, a paradigm for later interpreters. Ezra can claim to be a prophet and not just a scribe; subsequent interpreters may not claim the same thing:

> This [i.e. Ezra's time] was the age in which idolatry ceased in Israel; it was also the end of prophecy. Once the nation had embraced a book, no need remained for the admonitions and the visions of the prophets.[35]

Ezra's position is unique; as unique as Moses's was. He stood at what Halivni calls a 'crossroads of Jewish history',[36] an unrepeatable point at which a set of historical and religious forces came into alignment 'to bring about a constellation where God encountered human beings and revealed himself to them'.[37] He lived and acted 'at a time in which the people of Israel wrought their greatest revolution, reversing almost seven hundred years of rebellion with their enthusiastic reception of the Torah'. *This* is what makes 'Ezra so pivotal and his mission so climactic'.[38]

Moses passed down the perfect Torah to a people not yet ready; Ezra redelivered the maculate Torah to a people now – at

---

[33]Williams 2004, 225. I use the language of generosity here because of Williams's argument that theological exegesis 'assumes that reader and text are responding to a gift, an address or a summons not derived from the totality of the empirical environment' (Williams 2004, 224).

[34]Halivni 1997, 2.

[35]Ibid., 83.

[36]Ibid., 78.

[37]Ibid., 88.

[38]Ibid., 78.

last – prepared. The maculations of the Torah are the price paid for the history that allowed the people to overcome their own shortcomings.

On this basis, Halivni concludes *Revelation Restored* with a rejection of two sorts of appeal to the idea of 'continuous revelation'. I summarize them as follows:

1   One is the claim that the indeterminacy of meaning generated by certain texts can occasionally – at a certain moment in history – give way to a final and binding decision. This may be because of an overwhelming consensus on the part of the community, or it may be because an incontrovertible authority (and paradigmatically a voice from heaven) pronounces on and decides the issue once and for all.

2   The other sort of appeal to the idea of continuous revelation says that even what has in the past been held to be true and binding can in new historical circumstances be revised. Laws can be changed by their new interpreters, who set themselves up as the equals of ancient sages: 'each generation determines the content of revelation, which may at times require the canceling of some old laws'.[39]

Halivni does not find either option palatable, rejecting the idea of continuous revelation altogether, and making a firm distinction between *revelation* and *interpretation*. His problem with each can be summarized like this:

1   The first appeal to continuous revelation claims a certainty that is inappropriate. It claims that the revelation delivered on Sinai and renovated by Ezra needs additional supplementation by way of direct divine interventions, and such interventions disenfranchise many of the divergent interpretations of difficult passages from earlier times by ruling them out retrospectively. This theory of continuous revelation is therefore disrespectful on two fronts: to the Torah, which (though maculate) is to be revered even in its less than perfect state; and to the community in its legitimate and proper variety of viewpoints on certain issues of interpretation. In short,

---

[39]Ibid., 88.

it is impatient with interpretation (which we have been calling 'finding') and wants to substitute for it something more decisive: extra revelation (which we might call more 'givenness').

2 Halivni's problem with the second appeal to continuous revelation is that it is hubristic, claiming a level of insight into and authority over the tradition that will too easily pass judgement on it simply on the basis of whether it satisfies some perceived present-day need or not. 'Givens' are always under question, but – perhaps paradoxically – there is not a great deal of actual openness to finding (or being found) by the complex and resistant text either, because it is rendered subject to suppression or manipulation.

These rejections of ideas of continuous revelation enable Halivni to make some Christianly valuable points about the importance of the found in its relation to the given. There is immense richness and suggestiveness in his theorization of scriptural maculation as a legacy that awakens one to one's creative historicity. He is able to commend a continual relationship between the human stewardship of the Scriptures and their divine origin, and to resist proposals that diminish or bypass that human stewardship. However, he will not dignify this ongoing relationship with the title 'revelation'. This is one key respect in which he does not go as far as I (and, I think, Rowan Williams) wish to. As I have said, he wants a hard and fast line to be drawn between revelation and interpretation. Yes, there are many things to be 'found' in working out the details of the religious community's life, but these findings are interpretative and not revelatory in character. Revelation is already and finally given. God gave it – through Moses, through Ezra and through the prophets who appeared in the time between them. Interpretation is human activity, and must be kept formally distinct from revelation which (even when it comes through human conduits) is *divine* activity.

One might want to register a theological worry here over the implication that as the influence of human action increases, the influence of divine action decreases; or at least that human interpretative activity risks compromising the divinely given status that revelation ought to have. This can too readily reinforce the construction of divine agency as like creaturely agency in its making of particular finite differences in the world (rather than all the difference in the world), and of human agency as being somehow in competition with divine agency. What I want to suggest – as I have suggested before[40] – is that there need be no 'either–or' here. In other words, any human origin to the maculations in Scripture (and the interpretative task they engender) need not preclude the claim that they are also attributable to a divine providence that can use even human sin and put it to good ends.

The claim that an ongoing, fallible human interpretation of Scripture (generated by the grit of Scripture's maculations[41]) is capable of being read as part of the divine generosity is a claim that may draw special justification in Christian tradition from a trinitarian understanding of God. Here, we turn back to Rowan Williams, who in the two different essays we have looked at so far in this book formulates two ways of thinking in trinitarian fashion about maculation. It is in the 2000 essay 'Trinity and Revelation' that he most clearly suggests a christological valorization of maculate Scripture; and it is in that same essay and also in the 2004 essay 'Historical Criticism and Sacred Text' that he suggests a pneumatological complement to that valorization. In both cases, he suggests that the maculate text can indicate divine plenitude, and thus, paradoxically indeed, be part of the text's 'perfection'.

We begin with his christological remarks in 'Trinity and Revelation'.

Christological maculation

One of the ways that Williams works out the idea that (some sorts of) maculation and (some sorts of) perfection may not be mutually contradictory is by exploring what is the common, and well-justified, analogy drawn by Christians between the Torah and Christ. Both are perceived as revelatory, and both as constituting 'a distinctive social organism'. Indeed, the constitution of a new and distinctive social organism is, as Williams highlights, part of

---

[40]See the discussion in Chapter 2, especially on p. 48ff.
[41]A gritty Scripture that is to be protected and safeguarded not because we are never again going to have access to any better version (which is Halivni's point) but because the grit is precious in itself.

what justifies the claim that they 'reveal'. To be revelatory is to be generative in a manner that 'breaks open and extends possible ways of being human':

> Torah is experienced as a new and distinctive definition of a human community; and if the pattern proposed is right, the same must be true of Jesus of Nazareth. His revelatory significance is apprehended by way of what it means to belong to the community whose character and limits he defines – not simply as "founder" but as present head and partner in dialogue and relation.[42]

If we were to seek to reintroduce Halivni's theory of maculation in the Torah at this point, it might be interjected that the analogy between the Torah and Christ breaks down immediately. Christ, for Christians, is, after all, the definitive revelation of God; the image of the Father. Even if Christians are prepared to concede fissures and lacunae in their scriptural texts, they may well be loath to accord anything like them to the incarnate one to whom Scripture witnesses.

This deserves a second thought, however. Williams speaks of Christ in a way that makes the analogy harder to write off, for Christ's teaching and his actions seem, among other things, to have the effect of bequeathing a lot of uncertainty in relation to certain issues:

> If the early communities exhibit a profound puzzlement about their boundaries, about issues of purity and separation (virginity, abstinence from idol-meats, circumcision), this assuredly reflects the memory of the Church's Lord as a man who, in his own words and actions, generated immense confusion on this subject, sharply challenging the available models of distinctiveness and "cleanliness".[43]

Now, of course, this confusion cannot straightforwardly be equated with Halivni's account of the occasional confusingness of the text of the Torah, and his putative history of how it became so confusing. According to Halivni, the text of the Torah underwent

---

[42]Williams 2000, 136.
[43]Ibid., 136–7.

decay; Christ's confusing teachings, according to Williams, are *generatively*, perhaps even *deliberately*, underdetermined. They are not the product of a decline, but a refusal of tidiness, which may, in turn, offer liberation from enslaving certainties. Nevertheless, Williams invites an interesting question here. If the faithfulness (the adequacy, aptness, even perfection) of the New Testament witness to God's revelation in Christ consists in part precisely in its faithful registration of the generative uncertainty that was central to that primary revelation in Christ, then it is a 'troubled' text not by accident or omission, but by design. And if this is accepted in relation to the New Testament, then Christians may find themselves with resources to wonder whether something comparable may be true of the maculate Old Testament; something which may lead to a parting of the ways with Halivni's insistence on the immaculate nature of the (partially lost) Torah given to Moses. Might the maculate Torah be readable – just as the New Testament is readable – as *properly* maculate; *properly* a troubled, and creatively troubling, text? At the risk of putting it too crudely, might the Mosiac text have been designed for a process of accompaniment in which the people's interactions with it (even their disobedience to it) would be part of how that text would achieve its full purposes – become itself more completely, both at the time of Ezra, and even beyond?

This is already the beginning of a move from a claim about how (a) the maculate nature of the text may have been a product of the text's faithfulness to its (divine) source (i.e. to the 'giver of the grit'), to a claim about how (b) the ongoing history of the text's interpretation may *also* be a form of faithfulness to the divine intention. Indeed, a legacy of ongoing interpretation – as in claim (b) – may be precisely what was envisaged in the divine origination that ensured maculation-at-source – as in claim (a). To put this in Christian doctrinal terms, this move – from source to ongoing history – is a move from a christological claim to a pneumatological claim (these being, of course, claims that mutually inform one another). Christ may have lived and taught as he did in order to engender a witness that would make not just a people but also that people's history of interpretation. (And God may have given Moses the Torah in the way that he did for analogous reasons.)

Rowan Williams is of help once again in formulating the issue in its pneumatological dimensions.

Pneumatological maculation

As we have seen, in his 'Historical Criticism' essay, Williams
deploys the language of 'excess' to account for passages in Scripture
that are resistant to easy appropriation. This is pneumatological
language, because for Christian tradition it is the Holy Spirit who
opens up the 'moreness' of meaning in the unfolding of history:
the Spirit who, in new historical sets of circumstances, discloses
the abundance of God's loving purposes;[44] the Spirit who guides
Christians from glory to glory[45] in their assimilation to the perfect
form of Christ; the Spirit who unfolds the riches that are in Christ.
In opening what has been received in the past to its transformed
possibilities in the future, the Spirit is therefore also the key to
the way Christians read Scripture; the Spirit unlocks and sets in
motion the power of Scripture to speak in each new historical
moment, and thus to reconfigure each new 'present' such that it
is never simply a reproduction of the past. My suggestion here is
that the grit of Scripture may be read as an intrinsic part of how
this unlocking and reconfiguring is initiated; if so, it can be read
as divine gift.

Halivni does not have any account of how maculations might
become generative in their own right: generative of new findings
despite being the products of a sort of falling away. Without such
an account, the maculations present themselves principally in his
thought as a problem to be coped with. Williams, by contrast,
allows an account in which even fallings away – even the effects of
sin – may be the occasion for revelatory discovery. This is part of
a larger pneumatological account of a historical process that does
not keep interpretation sealed off from revelation. God the Spirit
can use even the effects of sin to generate new benefits and new
blessings, thereby increasing the 'gladness'[46] which God's activity in
history (as Spirit) delivers back to the Godhead.

That these new benefits and new blessings can be called revelatory
is a key point made, once again, in 'Trinity and Revelation'. Having

---

[44]   When the Spirit of truth comes, he will guide you into all the truth. (Jn 16.13)
[45]   And all of us, with unveiled faces, seeing the glory of the Lord as though reflected
       in a mirror, are being transformed into the same image from one degree of glory
       to another; for this comes from the Lord, the Spirit. (2 Cor. 3.18)
[46]Eugene Rogers's concept, following Barth, proves valuable here. Rogers Jr. 2005.

claimed, as we noted earlier, that to be revelatory is to be generative in a way that 'extends possible ways of being human', Williams claims that the forward-moving hermeneutical labours of the Church in the Spirit (a sort of interpretative spiralling forward which combines return with advance[47]) are as worthy of being called generative as the new pattern of life that was instantiated by Christ, and are even – in their own way – as generative as the creation-from-nothing which brought the world into being at the beginning of days. In other words, he breaks down Halivni's divide between revelation and interpretation, and as a consequence gives interpretation the highest dignity imaginable. This is because he holds the history in which interpretative work goes on to be capable of being shaped by the Spirit into an offering acceptable to the Father through Christ. Temporal process is made an 'internal' moment of the trinitarian life, so to speak – though this requires all the caveats about the risks of spatializing language (time as 'inside' something else) that Rowan Williams highlights, and that in another context I have also attempted to head off.[48]

Halivni, as I have shown, does not have a direct correlate in his thought to this pneumatological valorization of maculation as a stimulus to interpretation. But despite the centrality of a narrative of decline in his narration of the period from Moses to Ezra, and his determined resistance to the idea of continuous revelation, there is nonetheless something quasi-pneumatological to be unearthed in some of his closing remarks in *Revelation Restored*. He makes a distinction between 'the giving and the receiving of Torah', which is a distinction 'according to the Bible itself': the giving being the event over which Moses presided, and the receiving the event over which Ezra presided. They were, as he says, 'not one and the same event'. And yet, they were intrinsically related:

> Divine revelation unfolded and completed itself in the time of Ezra, and the written Torah is the result of this unfolding.[49]

Effectively, what Halivni is saying is that the 700-year history of the people's errors was simultaneously a period in which the

---

[47]See Chapter 1, p. 26.
[48]Quash 2005.
[49]Halivni 1997, 84.

written Torah was abraded *and* a period in which the people came progressively to themselves, 'improving themselves sufficiently to embrace monotheism':

> The people might not have allowed revelation to dissipate; they might not have stood idly by as the Torah slipped away through their uncareful fingers. Yet Israel would never then have embarked upon the improving journey of the Torah's restoration. In the end, true repentance and self-improvement are more valuable than an artificially instilled resolve. God does not change the nature of man, with whom he was pleased at the time of creation. Israel is forced to find its own way. Though the wounds and scars of the journey remain, the holiness endures as well.[50]

This time period of seven centuries, and the experiences that the people had during this time, thereby become inseparable from the consummation of the covenant. They become internal to the covenant's completeness. The language that Halivni uses to describe this consummation is that of Ezekiel,[51] but it is language that Christian tradition has used pneumatologically:

> The very essence of the Mosaic covenant is the belief in a unique God, whose will is reflected in the Torah. This belief was absent in the wilderness, but it was present in Ezra's day, and thus the Sinaitic covenant was finally complete. The covenant of Sinai was realized by means of Ezra's canonical Torah; thus Ezra's canon received retroactively a Sinaitic imprimatur. The destiny of the nation began in earnest, and our canonical Torah was born, etched in inviolable holiness – not by fire on tablets of stone, but by faith upon human hearts.[52]

This almost Pentecostal description has the curious effect of celebrating temporal process as a means of holy and revelatory 'finding', but then of framing the results of that process as fixed and subject to no further additions. 'With Ezra, revelation was completed', as Halivni puts it firmly. This is not an arbitrary cut-off point: reasons are given for it. And indeed, Christians would not generally demur

---

[50]Ibid.
[51]Ezek. 11.19 and 36.26. See also 2 Cor. 3.1-4.
[52]Halivni 1997, 85.

from the canonical implications of such a move: they too claim that at a certain point the shutters came down and there was no further admittance to be had to the scriptural party. But it invites the question: why might not the ongoing relationship that Christians have *with* this body of Scripture also deserve the dignity of being called revelation?[53]

And this returns us to the issue with which we began: the issue of translation as itself – potentially – a medium of ongoing revelation. The canon may be fixed, but interpretation never ceases. Translation is interpretation in a concentrated and unusually exhaustive form. A fully pneumatological affirmation of ongoing history (not just a 700-year period, or some equivalent of that, but history in its open-ended continuation towards a future horizon we cannot yet see) may want to endorse translation as a pneumatological imperative.

There is a positive ground for such an endorsement in the New Testament witness to the way that the Spirit works with many languages on the Day of Pentecost. This can be seen as an imprimatur for translation. The Spirit who comes in tongues of fire at Pentecost does not eliminate the many languages of the known world, making them all one, but enables the Gospel to be proclaimed and heard in all of them, and across (and maybe also by way of) the

---

[53]Peter Ochs is with Halivni in treating this idea with caution. He does seem more ready than Halivni to speak in terms of post-Ezra moments when a radical reappropriation and reconstrual of the inheritance of the Jewish faith is required – including its Scriptures – but he does so while deploying what we might gloss as a 'pull only in an emergency' principle. In other words, he does not think such moments of finding (and consequent reconstrual of the given) are so much a day-to-day affair as they are a response to exceptional disruptions in experience. Like the Book of Job, such moments will be 'about epoch-changing trauma rather than everyday protestations against tradition' (Ochs 2011, 213). By analogy, the sort of 'new Reformation' he sees in some post-liberal Christian theology is not for him an everyday event, but is likewise 'to be enacted only periodically, in epochs of inordinate stress when, in the judgment of potential reformers, the dominant practices of theology obstruct rather than enable efforts to unify the body of Christ' (Ochs 2011, 264). Furthermore, as far as I can see, Ochs is like Halivni in not using the language of revelation even of such epochal changes. My own account in this book does also address the particular status of experiences of 'emergency' (see the discussion of the 'founding trauma' of the English Commonwealth in Chapter 6, p. 168), but it is less cautious about identifying as revelatory a more low-level and (quite legitimately) *constant* creative interaction between given and found. What I am proposing might be more akin to the Protestant principle of the Church as *semper reformanda*. It is assisted by other parts of Ochs's account which, even though they do not talk about revelation, do

complex boundaries and overlaps that all of them have with each other.[54]

But another, and perhaps equally important, ground for endorsing the ongoing (never-complete) translation of Scripture is that the God to whom Scripture witnesses is better gestured to in this never-completeness than in the presumed fixity of a particular linguistic matrix. This is to return to Rowan Williams's point about excess. It is not only the work of reading that is never complete. The 'unfinished business' of these texts – which is the effect of the divine excess on them – may mean that the work of transmitting them in human language is never complete either. Languages are systems that carry conceptualities within them, and reinforce such conceptualities by their repeated use. But, writes Williams, 'if God is as the narrative presents God, it will not be possible to present God without remainder into either narrative or conceptuality':

> The only "translation", for the Christian reader, is the action of Jesus . . . God names God in Scripture as the unconditioned and

---

talk about 'reparative reading' (a concept also developed by the Christian theologian Nicholas Adams: see, Adams 2008, 447–56), a process which denies that the givens of revelation are ever merely static but sees them in perpetual motion as they are called to make context-specific contributions to new needs. Ochs writes: '[T]he reading I perform speaks only now, and the next moment may call for new reparative readings. From this rabbinic perspective, we would label such renewed readings a "futile series" only if we took our lives and efforts in this world to be futile. But we don't, since we do not imagine a wholly alternative world. From this perspective, to pray for the fulfillment of history is not to seek another world, nor to understand the work of this world as tragic. It is, instead, to take deep satisfaction in the fulfillment offered in each and every moment of reparative reading and worldly repair, while awaiting a time in this world when no human would lack such fulfillment' (Ochs 2011, 238).

[54]I do not think one should too rapidly dismiss the idea that this Pentecost experience forms at least part of the reason for Christianity's progressive embrace of multiple translations of the Bible, by contrast with rabbinic Judaism's pedalling back from even the one great translation that had achieved such currency by the first century CE: the Septuagint. At the time of Jesus, the Greek text of the Septuagint was the shared possession of Jews and Christians. Judaism would eventually return to a privileged focus on the original Hebrew, whereas for Christianity translations of the Old Testament's Hebrew and – in due course – the New Testament's Greek would not generally be regarded as less sacred by virtue of their translation. I said earlier that there were aspects of the very content of the Christian Bible that seemed to press for its translation, and Pentecost is perhaps the best instance of such a pressure at work.

uncaptured, apprehended as such only in the upheavals and new beginnings of the history of those God encounters in grace and freedom.[55]

Translation is a fundamental means by which we are reminded that the God witnessed to in the language of the text is not 'captured' by it. In translation (as in all interpretation) the text 'spirals' – returning to itself and moving forward at the same time. The apparent destabilizations of the text that accompany this movement are ways in which the text is permitted to continue to display its true and gritty nature perpetually and productively, until the Last Day.

A covenant in pieces

After these things the word of the Lord came to Abram in a vision, "Do not be afraid, Abram, I am your shield; your reward shall be very great." But Abram said, "O Lord God, what will you give me, for I continue childless, and the heir of my house is Eliezer of Damascus?" And Abram said, "You have given me no offspring, and so a slave born in my house is to be my heir." But the word of the Lord came to him, "This man shall not be your heir; no one but your very own issue shall be your heir." He brought him outside and said, "Look towards heaven and count the stars, if you are able to count them." Then he said to him, "So shall your descendants be." And he believed the Lord; and the Lord reckoned it to him as righteousness.

Then he said to him, "I am the Lord who brought you from Ur of the Chaldeans, to give you this land to possess." But he said, "O Lord God, how am I to know that I shall possess it?" He said to him, "Bring me a heifer three years old, a female goat three years old, a ram three years old, a turtle-dove, and a young pigeon." He brought him all these and cut them in two, laying each half over against the other; but he did not cut the birds in two. And when birds of prey came down on the carcasses, Abram drove them away.

---

[55]Williams 2004, 227.

As the sun was going down, a deep sleep fell upon Abram, and a deep and terrifying darkness descended upon him.

When the sun had gone down and it was dark, a smoking fire-pot and a flaming torch passed between these pieces. On that day the Lord made a covenant with Abram, saying, "To your descendants I give this land, from the river of Egypt to the great river, the river Euphrates, the land of the Kenites, the Kenizzites, the Kadmonites, the Hittites, the Perizzites, the Rephaim, the Amorites, the Canaanites, the Girgashites, and the Jebusites." (Gen. 15.1-12, 17-21)

In this momentous encounter with God in Genesis 15, Abram undergoes a dramatic change – a profound reorientation of his entire self and his sense of destiny. Even his name changes, never to revert. In this respect, he is himself being 'translated'. He will, once and for all, be Abraham – the father of many nations and a blessing to all of them. Like Moses, and (as we shall see) like Job and Jacob, he is a paradigm of what it is to 'find' and to have his 'givens' radically reconfigured as a result of such finding.

But, in concluding this chapter, it is more the strangeness of the covenant on which I want to focus, rather than Abraham himself. In particular, what I want to focus on is how the peculiar and disturbing material features (we might say, the maculations) of this covenant work to open it to a future where it can be further interpreted by future covenantal moments, while being quite compatible with a sort of absoluteness (we might say, perfection) residing in the terms of the covenant itself. The most remarkable material features of this covenant in Genesis 15 are the role that darkness and dismemberment play in it. Frightening confusion and the deliberate disintegration of things are key aspects of its *mise en scène*.

Abram falls into a trance and, we are told, a *great dark terror* descends on him; and in the midst of this terror and this darkness, he looks at the pieces of dead animal he has – at God's instigation – lined up on the ground before him, and he sees strange shapes moving down this sacrificial corridor – a smoking oven and a flaming torch. Then the Word of God comes once again to Abram to confirm the promise that the host of descendants which is to issue from his loins will have, eventually, a land. The promise was made before the vision. Now it is sealed in the form of a covenant; and with this, the episode is concluded.

Reading or hearing this passage can be a bit like entering a darkness oneself, with its attendant terrors – or, at the least, feelings of real disturbance. Some things we can guess at, *maybe*. Some things seem irreducibly odd. What, for instance, is the terrible darkness? Perhaps, we may conjecture, it is the cloak God must wear if Abram is not to be destroyed by the sight of him. That Abram experiences this darkness means God is drawing very near to him indeed – nearer than could possibly be safe were protective measures not in place.

How, then, shall we interpret the things Abraham *is* allowed to see: the apparition of a smoking oven and a flaming torch?

Here, what we have been calling the material maculations of this covenant event offer their own particular stimulus to interpretation – and echo, though non-identically, Halivni's arguments that maculation has at least some good sides when it comes to making room for creative human agency.[56] Recorded as they are in scriptural form, they make something possible for the reader (that may, of course, not have been possible or appropriate for Abram), and that is the crisscross reading between different scriptural texts that begins to build up a mesh of interpretation. Scripture makes its maculations into 'perfections' by stimulating and licensing a process of reading some texts in light of other texts (and thus too, as it happens, creating a community of readers who dedicate themselves to this activity).[57]

In this case, the broken (maculate) pieces laid out on the ground before Abram (and, by extension, before us as later readers of the text) may be a stimulus to put on Exodus lenses, and to read one 'event-series' in the light of another. The 'event-series' that

---

[56]Halivni's discussion of the relation between God's covenant with Moses and the people's renewed embrace of it at the time of Ezra – which has been such a focus for this chapter – suggested (as we have said) that maculation was a human intrusion upon the Mosaic covenant, which the dispensations of Ezra remedied but did not eradicate. In Genesis 15, however, the covenant with Abraham is in some more unavoidable way 'maculate-at-source' – though admittedly we are stretching Halivni's idea of maculation somewhat by putting it like this. The point is: God is *in* the pieces. Even were we to concede to Halivni that there is a radical difference in the origination of the maculations in Abraham's and Moses's respective covenantal encounters, there are, nonetheless, important analogies in the effects of these maculations: they make the reader (or hearer) active as interpreter.

[57]Tractate *Bahodesh* 8 from the *Mekhilta* tells us that 'where something is imperfect Scripture seeks to make it complete' (Lauterbach 2004, 333).

incorporates Abram's hearing of God's voice, God's promise, the creation of a passageway of dismembered bodies, the darkness, the terror, the moving fire and smoke, may reach out to the 'event-series' that is the account of the Israelites' redemption from Egypt. Indeed, the language God speaks in Genesis 15 makes this connection seem even more legitimate if one allows oneself to hear 'Egypt' when the passage says 'Ur of the Chaldeans': 'I am the Lord who brought you out from Ur of the Chaldeans to give you this land as your possession' (v. 7). This is a text about a promised land, and about deliverance. So, in that perspective, what we have opening out between the broken pieces of animal carcass is a *covenant corridor* like the pathway from Egypt through the waters of the Red Sea, and on through the desert with all its hardships, to the land made ready by God for his people. And the oven and the torch may tell interpreters of this passage that God is present on this pathway in the form of smoke and fire – the two pillars that assure the people that he is with them. They are his saving holiness rendered visible for them in a material form, to guide them and keep them strong. So the covenant made with Abram in this dark vision is the covenant that will ensure the Exodus of a whole people in a generation yet unborn.

The pathway of the broken pieces may foreshadow the pathway of liberation from Egypt, but it is also a pathway from Genesis to Exodus, from Abraham to Moses. It is therefore not only a pathway signifying physical release from bondage at some point in the people's future, but also a pathway to a fuller interpretation of Scripture for those who will one day read both of these 'event-series' together. And for this reason, the covenant of the pieces described in Genesis 15 seems particularly apt in the context of this chapter, for this discussion of maculation has, in at least one way, been a celebration of a disintegrated corpus which is, by the same token, a pathway. The disintegration may (as this chapter has suggested) or may not (as Halivni has argued) be perceived as a good in itself. However, there is no doubt that it has creative and re-creative effects. Something of the outline of salvation history is brought into view as a consequence of the gritty provocation of this difficult text, and the labour that it evokes.

Devout readers of maculate Scripture are to enter the covenant, as Abram did. This may mean being 'eclipsed', as Abram was. It may mean a radical transformation of self, and a new mission.

It may mean being plunged into terrifying darkness. It may mean being faced with all sorts of confusing images or signs, and having to wrestle hard to interpret them. But this is precisely what the covenant invites – *requires*, even. One of the gifts of the covenant that Jews and Christians have is our Scriptures, and (as in Genesis 15) much of what the Scriptures offer us needs long contemplation and imaginative work if we are to possess it properly. This process is not necessarily a bad thing, or a problem – wrestling with Scripture can itself be a mode of relationship with God. It can be covenantal. When Scripture seems to lie before us in pieces on the ground, then it may be that God is waiting for us in the midst of them, and the best thing we can do is 'enter the pieces'. The apparent gaps and tensions and oddities in our texts may be signalling places where *we* should be, as energetic interpreters. As we have seen, this is what many Jews celebrate as Midrashic indeterminacy, and it promotes a level of engagement with the text that is hard to achieve by any other means. In this perspective, what seem to be the numerous gaps and inconsistencies in Genesis 15 may not be a sign of inferior redaction, but a deliberate device to engage the reader – to make the reader participate more fully in the text.[58] If we are bold enough to go into the gaps, we may find God's fire burning there.

A Christian pneumatological reading of the covenant of the pieces may be tempted to see the burning presence in the midst of the maculations as a sign of the Spirit, the living and guiding divine agency who does not erase the brokenness of the pieces but works within them.

And – again in Christian terms – it is quite hard to avoid making a further connection with eucharistic practice and the theology of the atonement here, for here too the pieces of a disintegrated body are pulled apart to make a pathway for a pilgrim people. Jesus's torn body is also maculate, and perfect, at the same time: perfect in its maculation for the purpose of making a people. But that is a discussion that must wait for a later chapter.[59]

---

[58]Lipton 1999, 215–16.
[59]See Chapter 5.

PART TWO

4

'In my flesh I shall see God'

(JOB 19.26)

Introduction

Analogical thinking is imaginative thinking. You need an able and an agile imagination to draw good analogies, and inasmuch as the task of translation is a form of analogical reasoning – feeling for the aptness of one verbal form to render another in the context of a new language (which is also to say, a new set of particularities) – then it is a highly creative activity. Of the three 'case study' chapters that occur in this book, the one on the translation of the Bible into English (Chapter 2) may seem to be the odd one out, in that it seems to have least to do with art. But my claim is that translations *are* forms of artistic making in their own way.

The subject of the second case study, which will be the focus of this present chapter, needs no argument to be made for its character as art. It is a painting, created in Venice in the first years of the sixteenth century. It shows us a landscape both beautiful and dreadful (Figure 4.1).

A gentle, even light bathes the sandy foreground. This recedes to a middle distance where steep hillsides and rocky outcrops protrude, and past these, a more verdant expanse of countryside opens up, disclosing the distant outline of mountains on the horizon. The gradual recessions of this illuminated world create fields of colour that interrelate with immense delicacy: browns and greys in the foreground, unfolding to brownish yellows behind them. Flashes of brighter colour are hosted by the figures and objects that are located here – red, blue, dark green and hints

FIGURE 4.1 *'Die Grabbereitung Christi'.* The Entombment of Christ *(or* The Dead Christ*). Painting, oil on canvas, c.1505. Vittore Carpaccio (c.1465– 1525/1526). Dimensions: 145 × 180.5 cm. Inventory number: 23 A. Copyright: bpk/Gemäldegalerie, SMB/Jörg P. Anders.*

FIGURE 4.2 *The Meditation on the Passion, Vittore Carpaccio (c.1465–1525/1526). New York, Metropolitan Museum of Art. Oil and tempera on wood, 27¾ × 34⅛ in. (70.5 × 86.7 cm). John Stewart Kennedy Fund, 1911. Acc.n.: 11.118 © 2013. Image copyright: The Metropolitan Museum of Art/Art Resource/Scala, Florence.*

of violet. Meanwhile, the most far-off reaches of the scene are a backdrop of lighter green and azure. These are all aspects of the landscape's beauty.

The greatest concentration of light is in the white body of a man that – almost preternaturally long and elegant – stretches horizontally across the painting, laid out on an altar-like embalming slab. The waxy pallor of his flesh is made all the more vivid by contrast with the deep green of the cloak spread out on the ground behind him, against which the contours of his body are highlighted. It is not only the landscape that is beautiful. There is also great beauty in this body; and from one perspective it seems perfectly of a piece with the prevailing atmosphere of stillness and repose. It could almost be sleeping.

But, at the same time, the dreadfulness of the scene finds its focus here too. For the unnatural length and luminosity of this body awaken us to other weirdnesses in the scene: the turbulent sky, which is so much more energetic than almost anything else in the picture; the outlandishness of some of the rock formations; the fact that a single tree has a branch dense with foliage alongside a blasted and barren branch; the disturbing darkness of the open mouths of caves; the ruined and shattered stonework; the fact that upon the ground human pieces in various stages of decomposition are sprinkled with a sort of profligate abandon; and the odd, semi-clothed figure of an old man who sits at the foot of the tree staring at (or past?) the dead Christ on the slab.

That it *is* the dead Christ whose body we are presented with is beyond doubt. The gash made in his side by the lance is bloody, and one of the wounds in his feet is clearly visible. High in the top left-hand corner of the painting – tiny, but crazily tall in proportion to the human figures at their feet – are the three crosses of Golgotha. And to the right of the main tree, the two Marys (the mother of Jesus and the Magdalene) are shown seated and weeping, with St John (standing with his back to us) cradling the side of his head in a gesture of mourning.

These are just some of the ways that the painting manages to be both beautiful and dreadful; or, in the words of another commentator, both 'horrifying and lyrical'.[1]

---

[1]Klessmann 1971, 166.

Why start here? The remainder of this chapter will be needed in order to answer that question properly, but – in short – it is because of the way that this painting highlights the core concerns of this book. Above all, it provokes thought about how particular historical circumstances create opportunities for new theological insight, and about what role the human imagination can play in responding to such opportunities and expressing such insight.

The painting is by Vittore Carpaccio (c.1465–1525/1526), one of the most distinctive artistic hands at work in the Venetian Renaissance – a period with an unusually heightened sense of historical movement, and a location with an unusually intense exposure to cultural difference and exchange. Carpaccio, even by the standards of his day, developed a capacity for idiosyncratic self-expression that gave his imagination all sorts of opportunity to take flight. My claim is that in key respects – and certainly in paintings like the one I have begun this chapter by describing – it was genuinely a theological imagination, to the extent that I believe it quite proper to consider his paintings works of theology.

His painting of the dead Christ is both a window onto the historical flux and excitement that marked the time of its production, and also in its afterlife (in its own subsequent role in 'art history') an exemplary reminder of the energetic and, in its own way, creative reappropriation that is necessary if *any* work is to continue to have life and meaning in subsequent eras. The *Dead Christ*, and other works like it, may all too easily become 'dead letters' unless not only the *factual knowledge* but also the *imaginative sympathy* is marshalled that will make them 'speak' again. And if, as I believe, the *Dead Christ* and other works like it are indeed *theology* of a kind, then there is a lesson here about how theology itself needs to understand its task, its place in and relation to history, and its reliance on the imaginative sympathy of its audiences as well as its authors.

We must return to the painting at greater length to see just how it gives this object lesson. This will require us to do two different things in combination. First, we will look at what the content of the picture tells us about the influence on it of a unique historical period. This will be a meditation on its special context of production – so far as we can reconstruct that context and its fields of experience and expectation. There will, of course, be a good deal of speculation involved in this enterprise, given that no documentation survives about the identity or concerns of the patron who commissioned it, and almost none about the intentions and character of the artist himself.

Second, we will look at the theological ideas that appear to have been made thinkable by that context when an imagination like Carpaccio's set to work in its midst. This too will involve a close examination of the painting's content, but it will handle it as a work of theological as well as of painterly art, capable of rendering new theological insight conceivable. A subsequent chapter on reception theory (Chapter 5) will return to these same issues in a more sustained way.

Carpaccio's dead Christ: The subject of the painting

So, what is this painting, now hanging in the *Gemäldegalerie* in Berlin, plausibly *about*? In terms of the New Testament narrative, the answer could be relatively simple: this is a scene in which we see preparations going on for Christ's entombment, in a burial ground near Jerusalem, while some of those people closest to him grieve. We do not know whether the painting originally even had a title, let alone what that title might have been, but it has variously been referred to as the *Lamentation over the Dead Christ* and as an *Entombment*: the former title takes it cue more from the group of figures to the right of the painting; the latter more from the group of figures to the left. The basin-carrying figure standing at the mouth of one of the open tombs, and attended by two men in oriental headdresses, could be Nicodemus or Joseph of Arimathea. Perhaps he is here to wash the body, but the association of the basin with the sacrament of baptism parallels the association of the embalming slab with the sacrament of the Eucharist.[2]

---

[2]This might reinforce the idea that it is more likely Nicodemus than Joseph, given the former's nocturnal conversation with Jesus in the Gospel of John, in which he is told that he must be born again of the Spirit (Jn 3.4-8). Nicodemus is the subject of a certain amount of later Christian narrative material, which recounts his conversion to Christianity, and subsequent missionary activities. According to a story of St Athanasius, Nicodemus made a crucifix that was brought to Beirut and gushed blood and water, causing the conversion of many Jews. See Sgarbi 1994, 188.

Most of the painting's details are (loosely) drawn from the Gospel narratives, or at the very least they are plausible extrapolations from them. Even the bodies that 'seem to have been recently exhumed or to have been arrested in the act of emerging from the ground'[3] might be explained as the dead who rose and walked about after the earthquake which (Mt. 27.52 tells us) was triggered by Christ's death.

There is also, of course, a great deal of symbolism here (the narrative quality notwithstanding). Carpaccio sets things up so that that most mechanical of art-historical approaches – iconographic analysis – has plenty to get its teeth into. The supports of the altar-like slab can be read as representing the five wounds of Christ. The column lying on its side in the centre of the picture (reddish in colour) might echo the column of flagellation. The tree is an ash tree (a symbol of holiness, according to some accounts) and the leafy branch (*arbor bona*) contrasts as a symbol of the Church with the bare branch (*arbor mala*), a symbol of the synagogue (this is a codification made well-known by the *Liber Floridus* of Lambert of St Omer [c.1120]).[4] Together, these images represent an *iter salvationis* – a 'way of salvation' – between the pre-Christian and the Christian aeons: the transition of one world to another, turning on the sacrifice of Christ. The wounds by which sinners are healed, the sacraments by which they are united with Christ's life through his death, the overtaking of barrenness by fruitfulness, all these are markers on the way of salvation, and all are – arguably – visually encoded in this work.[5]

But the real interest of this painting lies not in the fact that it can be deciphered like some sort of crossword puzzle; the various items of meaning contained in it being ticked off one by one. There is a far greater density and interlacing of signification at work in the way that its subject matter is arranged, and in its complex reciprocal relation to certain other key paintings (and, indeed, texts and traditions) to which it seems related.

Lamentation or *Entombment* might, respectively, capture various aspects of this peculiar painting, but it might also justify the title *Contemplation of the Dead Christ*. It would be at least as apt a title

---

[3]Hartt 1940, 31.
[4]See O'Reilly 1992, 188.
[5]Gioia Mori is the source of much of this iconological reading. Mori 1990, 188–92.

as any other. Indeed, as we have noted, the old man leaning against
a tree in meditative pose rather mysteriously models precisely this
contemplation. He is, we might say, setting a tone for the painting.
But who is *he*? And why, in a painting full of narrative references to
the New Testament texts that deal with the Passion of Christ, has
he been allowed to intrude himself so centrally here? What justifies
this interloping?

Who is the old man?

To answer this question it is necessary to transfer our attention from
the content of the painting, taken on its own, to its relationship with
other works – and to take a detour through a later art-historical
detective story which unlocked a key part of the painting's meaning
that had for a long time been lost.

As if to compound uncertainties about its title, the circumstances
of its commission, its original home and ownership, and even the date
of its manufacture, the painting acquired a fake signature as early
as the seventeenth century.[6] This, along with a number of stylistic
affinities and similarities in subject matter and mood, linked it to
another painting which – by the early twentieth century – had found
its way to the Metropolitan Museum in New York (Figure 4.2).
The New York painting, too, had the signature (overpainted, as it
would turn out) 'Andreas Mantinea' – for Mantegna. And, indeed,
both of the paintings have their first documented mention in association with one another: they were listed together as being in the
Canonici Collection in Ferrara in 1632. In other words, they have a
shared provenance for at least as long as that provenance is trace-
able at all.[7] It was not until 1911, however, that the New York
painting was correctly attributed to Carpaccio by Claude Phillips[8]
and this only finally confirmed as late as 1945 when Carpaccio's
original signature was discovered under the fake one. And to confirm that one of the paintings was actually by Carpaccio, and not
by Mantegna, was effectively to confirm it of both.

---

[6]Lauts 1962, 246.
[7]Sgarbi 1994, 50.
[8]Phillips attributes it to Carpaccio and calls it 'Meditation on the Passion'. Phillips
1911, 144–52.

That is a considerable detective story in itself, but it is equalled if not surpassed in its interest by the subplot of how the old man in the Berlin painting came to be identified correctly. This too only occurred in the mid-twentieth-century and, in this subplot, the New York painting emerged as the repository of the crucial clue to the meaning of the Berlin painting (that is, the one that has been our principal focus until now).

There are notable differences between the New York picture and the Berlin one, but there are profound similarities as well. The New York one has more of the quality of a static set piece. It is not even so much a *tableau vivant* as a quasi-heraldic construction. The detail of the New Testament drama is eliminated, and the symbolism is laid on even more thickly. In the centre, as if to confirm this greater degree of stylization, the dead Christ is not lying down but *sitting*, supported on a crumbling throne of red and cream marble. His eyes are closed. The composition has elements of a *pietà*, the images that depict the Virgin Mary mourning over the dead body of Christ; even more directly, it echoes a genre of paintings of the dead Christ supported by angels, of which many were painted in this period. The throne divides the background, and all the paraphernalia symbolizing the *iter salvationis* are ordered rather more systematically than in the Berlin painting so that those on the left are marks of a world in need of transformation and those on the right are the fruits of a world transformed (here, *two* trees, and not just two branches from *one* tree, are employed to suggest the 'old' and the 'new' orders). His crown of thorns propped up rather tidily against the base of the throne, Christ slumps sideways, revealing stylized Hebrew letters inscribed on the marble behind his head. On the left, like one of the heraldic supporters of a coat of arms, sits Jerome (c.347–420), the great biblical scholar of the ancient Church, identified by the iconography of the books, rosary and the figure of a small lion peeping out from behind him. Across from him, in the direction in which Christ slumps, sits another ascetic-looking figure.

The great continuities with the Berlin painting – despite all these differences – are of course (i) the fact that this is a depiction of the dead Christ, and (ii) that in this context the painting prompts thoughts about the epochal shift marked by Christ's passage through death. But the other, most visually arresting, continuity is precisely (iii) the other ascetic figure, the other heraldic supporter, sitting as he does on the right-hand (the 'redeemed') side of the composition. For in his posture and in his clothing, he is unquestionably the same old man whom we see in the Berlin painting, sitting at the foot of the tree.

His seat in the New York painting is a marble block, which has its own set of Hebrew and perhaps, in some cases, pseudo-Hebrew characters carved upon it. It seems extraordinary that no one thought to pay attention to these before 1940, until then proposing that Jerome's companion was probably an obscure desert saint called Onuphrius.[9] But it is the Hebrew which unlocks not only the identity but also the sheer (substantial) significance of this man, and arguably of both of the paintings in which he appears. For the inscription on the side facing us (echoing part of the inscription on the throne itself) can be deciphered as: 'My redeemer [lives] 19'.[10]

We are being pointed to the Book of Job, and – more specifically – to Job 19.25. Even the location of the inscription could be meaningful, for as Frederick Hartt reminds us, the preceding verse is: 'Who will grant me that my words may be written? Who will grant me that they be marked down in a book? With an iron pen and in a plate of lead, or else be graven with an instrument on a flint stone?' (Job 19.23-24).[11]

The link with Jerome thus becomes a little clearer too. Jerome was one of the first theologians, through his translations, commentaries and letters, to give a Christian symbolic interpretation of Job. He strongly influenced later Christian tradition in its interpretation of Job not only as a paradigm of patience, and not only as one who suffered to a degree that was comparable to Christ's own suffering, but also as a *prophet*, and more particularly and uniquely the prophet who foretold Christ's resurrection. In an often-quoted passage in a letter to Paulinus, Jerome sums up his interpretation:

> Then, as for Job, that pattern of patience, what mysteries are there not contained in his discourses? . . . To say nothing of other topics, [he] prophesies the resurrection of men's bodies at once with more clearness and with more caution than any one has

---

[9]Lauts 1962, 246.
[10]Once again, I am grateful to Jonathan Stökl for his help with the Hebrew here.
[11]Hartt 1940, 28.

yet shewn. "I know," Job says, "that my redeemer liveth, and that at the last day I shall rise again from the earth; and I shall be clothed again with my skin, and in my flesh shall I see God. Whom I shall see for myself, and mine eyes shall behold, and not another. This my hope is stored up in my own bosom." (Job 19.25-26)[12]

The emergence of this crucial piece of information makes a huge difference to the overall force of the Berlin painting (as it does, in its own way, to the New York one). That is not to claim that the painting is somehow 'solved' by knowing that the old man is Job. Far from it, the sheer innovatory oddity of the way that the figure of Job is deployed here expands rather than reduces the field of possible interpretations. For our purposes, there are questions to be asked in two key areas as a consequence.

The first is: what historical conditions (or, in terms of this book, what 'findings' in Carpaccio's own context) might have made this use of Job thinkable in the first place? What was it that was unpredictably thrown up in the path of early sixteenth-century Venetians that made them capable of such Joban innovation; that led them also thereby to 'find' Job again? Although elsewhere in this book (and especially in Chapter 5 on reception theory) I will raise questions about the presumptions and priorities of the historical-critical method – and its occasional naïvety in supposing that there can be objective pursuit of a probable original meaning – I do not thereby mean to dismiss absolutely the value or the possibility of enquiring into the historical conditions for the production of a particular work. Art historians use similar tools to historical-critical text scholars – I will show debts to them in what follows – and both often use them to good effect. I think that Rowan Williams' insight is a good one here. Texts (like paintings) represent in two obvious ways. They represent some aspect of the world (which might include a train of thought or a feeling), and they also and at the same time (though less consciously) represent 'the conditions of [their] own production'. The task of interpretation, says Williams, is 'to make plain the contradictions between what the text says it represents and what it represents of its own conditionedness', and this is only possible with the help of some capacity to look into

---

[12]Jerome 1989, Letter 53 (to Paulinus), section 8.

those conditions.[13] Like Williams, I think one *can* look into those conditions to a valuable extent, though without stepping outside one's own historical locatedness.

The second question that needs to be asked of Carpaccio's painting is consequent upon the first: what theological insights does this Joban innovation help to bring to light; what does it help later viewers of the painting, in turn, to *find*?

These are risky questions, without watertight answers. We might say: this is an enterprise that, in theological terms, has elements of dread as well as of beauty.

Nevertheless, conscious of the dangers but reluctant to be disabled by them, I turn first to the first question: what circumstances in Venice in around 1505–20 (which is when the scholarly consensus assumes that these two paintings were created) made Job findable again in the particular way that Carpaccio found him?

What made Job findable by Carpaccio?

Artistic traditions

In strictly art-historical terms, the paintings in New York and in Berlin seem to have precedents not only in the 'Dead Christ Supported by Angels' and the *pietà* genres that we have already noted, but also in at least two other significant traditions. The first is most often encountered in the North of Europe, and the second is from the Orthodox East.

The North, as Gert von den Osten has argued,[14] had in medieval times a fascination with the figure of Job as a type of patient suffering, and it developed a typical way of representing him as a proto-'Man-of-Sorrows'. He is illustrated in books and carved in sculpture, seated alone and covered in sores or else being addressed by his wife, by his inept comforters or by the Devil, but he is always in misery. He is less often depicted in paintings, but as a visual type he is established and recognizable. Both in texts (sermons and commentaries) and in visual schemes, a clear link is

---

[13]Williams 2004, 220.
[14]Osten 1952, 193–6.

established between his misery (and the patience with which he is alleged to have faced it) and the misery and patience of Christ. He becomes a figural representative of this patience – notwithstanding the scriptural material in which he is so unabashedly belligerent in his arguments with God.

The rise of the image of Christ seated 'on the cold stone' – alone, dejected, awaiting his final execution – displays a whole set of visual echoes of this seated Job. It is squarely the product of the *devotio moderna*, the tradition of emotional appeals made by texts and images in the later medieval period to the devout viewer's sympathy and conscience.

In a moment, I want to argue that if he is indebted to this visual tradition, Carpaccio's adaptation of it nonetheless takes it in a significantly different direction. But the likelihood remains that the tradition was a part of his inherited artistic vocabulary, and therefore acts as one of the factors that makes conceivable his linkage of Job with the dead Christ.

From a quite different direction comes the influence of Byzantium. Venetian artists were unusually exposed to such styles on account of Venice's uniquely extensive trading relations with the Eastern powers – both Orthodox and Islamic. Venice was still a maritime trading hub of unparalleled reach in Carpaccio's day. In retrospect, its slow decline can be said to have been underway already while Carpaccio was at work – in motion ever since the fall of Constantinople in 1453. But even if the tectonic plates of power were shifting in a barely perceptible way in this period, the Republic remained the major player in the economic life of the Mediterranean, and there would be no impact on the city's patronage of the arts until well into the 1500s:

> Indeed, between the 1460s and the first years of the sixteenth century the policy of withdrawal westward only increased the extraordinary interest that the local ruling class showed for all the forms of decoration that might contribute to clothing the "state on the sea" in adequate finery.[15]

For a powerful piece of evidence of Venice's special openness to the East, one need look no further than the Byzantine predilection

---

[15]Sgarbi 1994, 12.

for mosaic, which lasted longer in Venice, and had a more defining impact there than anywhere else in the West (as the glittering walls and domes of San Marco testify).[16]

Carpaccio's borrowings from the East are evident not only in the headdresses he so evidently enjoyed painting (for example, on the men preparing the tomb for Christ's burial) but also in many of his architectural fantasies, which are frequently oriental in style. The very theme of the dead Christ laid out in preparation for burial is itself the product of Eastern influence. It stands in continuity with the *epitaphios* icon of the Eastern churches – most frequently embroidered on cloth and used in the liturgies of Good Friday and Holy Saturday, but painted on walls and panels as well.[17] Indeed, the earliest surviving embroidered *epitaphios* icon was preserved precisely in Venice, and dates from around 1200.

A part of Carpaccio's genius, however, is to be not only a debtor but also an innovator, combining the tradition of the Byzantine dead Christ with the motif of the contemplative Job to do something new with both. We will return in due course to ask just what his achievement is in this regard.

Religious influences

Job himself may not have figured in *epitaphios* icons proper, but there is a particular way in which not only the dead Christ motif but Job too is put in Venice's way by the practices of the Byzantine world; the world that haunted and often crossed its eastern boundaries. That is to say, Job does not only approach from the North, and it may be that the North cannot claim sole credit for his appearance in Carpaccio's paintings. The key influence to note here is the typically Eastern practice of treating the patriarchs,

---

[16]On Venice and the East see Demus 1970 and Howard 2000.

[17]The name means winding sheet/shroud and the icon often appears in the medium of an embroidered cloth although painted versions also exist. It shows Christ after the deposition, ready or being prepared for burial. For a discussion of the role of the *epitaphios* composition and its liturgical use, and for further references, see Belting 1980/81, 1–16. On the *epitaphios* and the Edessa Icon, see Scavone 1999, 1–31. My thanks to Chloë Reddaway for her research into this.

and other great figures of the Old Testament, as though they are Christian saints.

So far as I can discover, it is only in Venice that Job is patron saint of a church: San Giobbe in the Cannaregio area, one of the earliest Renaissance churches ever built (it was completed in 1493). He is not the sole Old Testament figure to hold this distinction – 'St Moses' is a dedicatee elsewhere in the city. But he was a very rare beneficiary of the honour. In all of Western Europe, it seems to have been the Venetians alone who undertook the transgressive 'local canonization' of Old Testament saints, and this may have gained not only a sense of permissibility but also an aura of attraction as a consequence of exposure to Eastern practices. Venice's broad horizons made Job's adoption into sainthood an enriching possibility, which the Venetians seized upon and made distinctively their own.

In Giovanni Bellini's famous altarpiece, made for the church of San Giobbe, Job stands in an intercessory posture, among a group of other saints gathered in a classic *sacra conversazione* formation around the enthroned Virgin and Child.[18] The other saints are all figures from Christian history; in this sense, Job is the odd one out. Yet, of all of them, he stands in the closest proximity to the Christ child (as he will again in relation to the body of the dead Christ in Carpaccio's Berlin painting). It cannot be denied that this was viewed by patrons and artists alike as a special relationship.

If the unique historical and geographical circumstances of Venice make it peculiarly open to 'findings' from outside the Roman Catholic world, in the form of Orthodox ideas and images, it may be important not to forget, either, some of the distinctive aspects of its relationship to another religious group – one which stood outside Christianity altogether: the Jews. Suggestions about the role of the actual relationship with the Jewish community in Carpaccio's (or his patron's) choices of subject matter must be extremely tentative – far more so even than suggestions about the role of Eastern Orthodoxy. It is also undeniable that whatever openness

---

[18]Giovanni Bellini, *San Giobbe Altarpiece*, 1487. Gallerie dell'Accademia, Venice. The painting can be viewed online via the Web Gallery of Art (accessed 15 August 2013) at http://www.wga.hu/

Carpaccio (or his patron) may have had to Jewish ideas and people, he does not eschew the highly supersessionist pattern of contrasts between the old and the new orders that are represented by the *iter salvationis*, as we have already observed. But with this caveat, one may at least note the fascination with the Hebrew language that the New York painting displays. Does Carpaccio (who also made work for the church of San Giobbe) work in an atmosphere of permeability to the Jewish community that that church's dedication may also have signalled? Dedicating a church to San Giobbe may of course have been a forceful statement of Christian rights to Job, or even a thoughtless assumption of such rights. But it might also have been a bridging gesture, at least implicitly acknowledging a shared ownership of Job (just as – for all the brutality of the contrast between bare and leafy branches in the Berlin painting – the tree at least has a single root).

Venice always maintained a clear distinction between citizens and foreigners: foreigners could hope for concessions but never full integration in the life of the Republic. But it did grant them a degree of relative autonomy and a power of self-regulation that was far from typical of other parts of Europe. Protestants and Orthodox were tolerated partly because Venice's relations with the Roman Curia were perpetually antagonistic – but there were also good commercial reasons for admitting minorities who brought mercantile and artisanal skills with them, and that meant Jews had an important place too.[19] Venice was, after all, a city that lived by trade. Furthermore, the 'consolidation of these nuclei' of various minorities certainly did not lead to their isolation, partly because they were limited in number, and partly because the very fabric of the city (bounded by water and densely criss-crossed by thoroughfares) ensured such minorities' active presence to, and participation in, the commercial and social life of the city.[20]

We must leave it as the most open-ended of suggestions, but there seems a slight possibility that Venice's particular settlement with the Jews – generally more civil than elsewhere in Europe despite

---

[19]Jews in Venice were ceded the right to exercise the ragman's trade in 1264 and in 1305 in competition with the recognized ragmen. The right was reconfirmed in 1515, at about the time Carpaccio was painting his dead Christs and Jobs. See Sgarbi 1994, 27, citing Sandri and Alazraki 1971, 101.

[20]Sandri and Alazraki 1971, 105; cited in Sgarbi 1994, 27.

the predictable tensions and prejudices[21] – may have played some part in making Job, both Semite and saint, so unforeign to Venetian Christians.

Other social influences

Why did the Venetians take so much to Job in particular, given all the contenders for their attention that the Old Testament had to offer? Again, there is necessarily a high degree of speculation involved here, but the posture of Job in the Bellini altarpiece is a major clue that Job was regarded by the Venetians as a well-qualified intercessor. Savonarola, preaching in Florence, promoted the idea of Job as a mediator through his virtues and sufferings,[22] but it is much more particularly in Venice that this idea gets taken up and developed – especially in art.

This is an epoch in which, in both immediate historical experience as well as in the reflections of those with time to entertain larger philosophical and existential questions, death was a major preoccupation. Horrific plagues and famines visited Venice frequently.[23] It is perhaps in keeping with this atmosphere that Carpaccio's somewhat gruesome preoccupation with human body parts displays itself – and not only on the sun-baked earth of the

---

[21]It is possible to claim, as certain recent historians have done, that the gradual establishment of a *ghetto* during the sixteenth century actually solidified the Jewish position in Venice, and in some ways enabled relations. There is evidence of boundary crossing, Christian Hebraism, Christians attending Jewish sermons out of interest, etc., in the autobiography of Rabbi Leon Modena (1571–1648) and the writings of Azariah dei Rossi (c.1513–1578). See, for example, Cohen 1988. See also Katz 2011, 233–62. My thanks to my colleague Aaron Rosen for his guidance on this issue.

[22]Most notably in his series of Lenten sermons of 1496, the first of which he preached on 1 March. Savonarola's text is available in Ridolfi 1957, I, 188–9. See also Weinstein 2011, 145.

[23] Outbreaks of bubonic plague were the most merciless killers and the greatest inspirers of terror encountered by the inhabitants of early modern cities. . . . One of Venice's most powerful administrative organs was designed to fend off plague and to control it when, despite all precautions, it invaded the city. The Health Office, ruled by the Provveditori all Sanità, had a continuous existence from 1490 onwards, and its powers were subsequently, in the late 1520s and late 1530, extended to include the co-ordination of poor relief, the suppression of vagrancy, and the control of prostitution. . . . There were fourteen outbreaks of plague in Venice between 1456 and 1528. . . . (Chambers et al. 1992, 113)

Berlin painting. On closer inspection of the New York image, Jerome's famous rosary seems to have been constructed from human vertebrae, and the top of his cane is made from a bone. Nor is Carpaccio's morbidity restricted to the two paintings with Job and Christ in them. His celebrated image of St George defeating the dragon, completed for the Scuola di San Giorgio degli Schiavoni in around 1504–07, has the same proliferation of ghastly remains scattered about the ground as the Berlin painting of Christ and Job – indeed some are identical.[24] This is the debris of the dragon's deadly appetite. Lizards, vipers, toads and vultures lurk among these fragments. The superficial differences in subject matter between the paintings should not deceive us – both paintings are about death and the defeat of death. But while in one, death is metaphorized as a murdering monster and its conquest personified as a knight on horseback, in the other, death is concentrated in a holy corpse and if we are to see signs of its conquest anywhere, we have to work a good deal harder. That it is worth such hard work is a case I will argue in the following section.

The key point to make at this stage is that one of the ways in which Job offers himself to the Venetian religious imagination is as a 'saint' acquainted with grief: himself plagued, himself brushed by death. For the same reason that they developed an especial attachment to St Roch (or San Rocco), the plague saint whose very attributes included the sores on his skin, the Venetians *found Job meaningful* in their special circumstances, and, as a consequence, *used him meaningfully*. A suffering servant, he was necessarily also a well-qualified and sympathetic intercessor – one who in Bellini's imagination 'has the ear' of Christ, and will use it to pray for those who are threatened by plague and death.

So then, a preoccupation with plague and death is one additional feature of the Venetian context that may have helped to place Job in Carpaccio's path. There is, however, a final feature of Carpaccio's context about which we may speculate. This final feature is less specifically an explanation of the choice of Job *per se*, and more a suggestion about what might have resourced the sheer boldness with which Carpaccio was prepared to use him in the unusual way that he did, that is, in the context of a painting of the dead Christ.

---

[24]Vittore Carpaccio, *St George and the Dragon*, 1502. Scuola di San Giorgio degli Schiavoni, Venice. The painting can be viewed online via the Web Gallery of Art (accessed 15 August 2013) at http://www.wga.hu/

Carpaccio is a genre bender. He has a fantastical imagination. The secondary literature which discusses his *oeuvre* returns again and again to his inventive powers. He is a maker of 'dream-like' realities which at the same time bear the marks of almost scientific precision.[25]

> Science and fantasy seem to be the principal ingredients in Carpaccio's poetry, and this formula distances him from the masters who preceded him.[26]

Yet, in the wake of what may well be a certain Byzantine influence, he likes static rather than dynamic compositions, with lustrous surfaces in which colour glows while human figures are poised motionlessly. But what is energetically at work throughout is a visionary power to summon new worlds into being and make us believe in them even though they are impossible:

> When one thinks of Carpaccio's paintings, an enchanted world entirely alien to the [Florentine one] rises before one's eyes; stillness pervades the wide piazzas, the wealthy towns on the seashore with their marble palaces and oriental towers, the fantastic landscapes and secluded interiors, flooded with sunlight which seems to live a life of its own. . . . A secret shadow seems to lie even over the festive splendour of [the] courtly ceremonies. True, the people wear Venetian or oriental dress of the artist's period, and their existence belongs to a definite historical epoch. This can be seen in a thousand details but in details only: as a whole this world is lifted out of its time; it is a Venice of dreams, an Orient of a thousand and one nights. Like a fairy story, like a consummate creation of the imagination, it convinces us and compels us to believe in its own special reality.[27]

Carpaccio's imaginative ability to blur the line between truth and fiction – to construct 'real' spaces out of landscapes and architecture that are invented, and to play confidently with 'probable Orients' in order to envision 'possible Venices'[28] – is perhaps itself not so much a communing with infinity as the very particular product of

---

[25]Lauts 1962, 33.
[26]Sgarbi 1994, 20.
[27]Lauts 1962, 7–8.
[28]Mason 2000, 26.

a place and a time. His Venetian context licensed and fuelled genre bending; all that was needed was a sufficiently supple imagination to respond creatively to circumstance.

A visitor to Venice, on diplomatic business in Carpaccio's heyday as a painter,[29] remarked on its own fantastical qualities:

And I marvelled greatly to see the placement of this city and to see so many church towers and monasteries and such large buildings, and all in the water; and the people have no other form of locomotion except by these barges, of which I believe thirty thousand might be found; but they are very small. In the neighbourhood of the city within a radius of less than half a French league there are some seventy monasteries (and all of them are on islands; they are for men as well as women and they are extremely beautiful and rich in buildings as well as in what decorates them, and they have beautiful gardens), not including those which are within the town, which comprise the four mendicant orders, some seventy-two parishes and many confraternities; and it is a very strange thing to see such beautiful and large churches constructed in the sea.[30]

Carpaccio lived in a city-state that was ready to experiment in the most extraordinary ways. Its artists took completely new steps in their use of light and perspective; its churches, as we have seen, canonized Old Testament figures; its buildings seemed to float on water. He would have seen it changing before his very eyes as he grew up there.[31] Might this have instilled in him the confidence to

---

[29]Philippe de Comines (sometimes spelt Commines or Commynes) was an ambassador from France in the service of Louis XI, and stayed eight months in Venice from October 1494 to May 1495.

[30]Philippe de Comines, *Mémoires*, 1489–98. Various manuscripts survive: see Kinser 1973, 81–3. The quoted passage is cited in a different translation in Sgarbi 1994, 10–12. See also Kinser 1973, 489.

[31] Vittore Carpaccio grew up in a Venice that evolved with him. . . . This is the Venice in which work began on the Scuola Grande di San Giovanni Evangelista (1478), Santa Maria dei Miracoli (1480), the Scuola Grande di San Marco (1485), the Palazzo Dario (1487), the Palazzo Corner-Spinelli (1490), the Torre dell'Orologio and the Procuratie Vecchie (1496), and the church of San Giovanni Crisostomo (1497): real architecture in a continuous dialogue with Vittore's painted architecture, to the point of suggesting mutual substitution, a simple inversion whereby Carpaccio's paintings become solid architecture and the Venice of stone becomes a large painted backdrop. (Sgarbi 1994, 19)

put Job into a scene from the Gospel of Matthew, or a motif popular in Northern Europe into his own version of a Byzantine *epitaphios*? Might this explain the 'absolute iconographic originality of [his] themes'?[32] Like the place of which he is a visual spokesperson, he moves easily to confer 'verisimilitude' on 'unreality', and 'precision' on 'fantasy':

> In doing so, he was doubtless helped by the fact of working in a unique city, a creation at the boundary of the impossible, that physically reconciles the irreconcilable; a city where the line between reality and imagination is not easily drawn.[33]

What theological findings are made possible by Carpaccio's Job?

The twentieth-century British art critic Roger Fry had little time for Vittore Carpaccio. Here is just a sampling of his comments, written in 1908: 'Carpaccio was, at least so far as he reveals himself in his art, singularly devoid of religious, or indeed of any rarefied or spiritual imagination';[34] he was 'the most thoughtless, gay, irresponsible painter of the Renaissance';[35] he was 'never real enough to hurt'; and '[t]here is no dramatic suspense, no real issue at stake' in his paintings.[36] Finally (the killer blow): 'His taste, in the matter of form, is constantly at fault; he inclines in all his accessories to a futile repetition of meagre units.'[37]

One wonders whether any of this invective would have been modified if Fry had been able to take account of the painting of the dead Christ which has been the main subject of this chapter. As it was, he was working with the erroneous attribution (noted earlier) of this and the New York *Meditation on the Dead Christ* to Mantegna, thereby leaving Carpaccio's corpus more slender and,

---

[32]Sgarbi 1994, 50.
[33]Ibid., 19.
[34]R. Fry 1908, 491; the article is a review of Ludwig and Molmenti 1907.
[35]R. Fry 1908, 493.
[36]Ibid., 495.
[37]Ibid., 503.

conceivably, more trivial.[38] But if these paintings are approached as the product of Carpaccio's hand and imagination, then it seems to me impossible to judge him today exactly as Fry did then. As unusual and thoughtful forms of religious meditation, they are fascinating paintings. The later of the two may not be anything like as immediate and impressive in its use of form as the earlier picture (or, moreover, as the great Mantegna *Dead Christ*[39] whose existence may well have influenced the false attribution of both these Carpaccios to him), but it is *serious painting*.[40]

The previous section of the chapter was principally concerned to pursue an extensive case study whose main aim was to show that the 'foundness' of particular historical circumstances can play a profoundly important role in facilitating new experimentation, both artistic and theological. The section was about context and its often surprising effects on the creative imagination. It traced the many idiosyncracies – the historical uniquenesses – of Carpaccio's Venice, with the aim of suggesting how, taken together, these might have generated auspicious conditions for an art like his, and (even more particularly) for a painterly experiment like his image of Job contemplating the dead Christ.

This final section of the chapter is about the insights – or, to stick with our chosen vocabulary, the 'findings' – that such context-fuelled experimentation may, in turn, permit. Its assumption is that, in such encounters with the particulars thrown up by historical process, theology does not necessarily stand still and reiterate the self-evident truths it has at its disposal already, but makes new steps and learns new things.

---

[38]It is also unquestionably the case that Fry was partly driven by a desire to reverse some of the effects of John Ruskin's adulatory promotion of Carpaccio (Ruskin having been mainly responsible for the revival of Carpaccio's reputation in the nineteenth century).

[39]Andrea Mantegna, *The Lamentation over the Dead Christ*, 1490. Pinacoteca di Brera, Milan. The painting can be viewed online via the Web Gallery of Art (accessed 15 August 2013) at http://www.wga.hu/

[40] The quality of Carpaccio's use of colour and his power of expression and invention decrease even further in his last religious paintings, for the most part executed by his assistants But in at least two of his late works, where the subject matter stimulated his imagination, Carpaccio returned to the creative levels of his earlier periods. (Valcanover 1989, 68)

Carpaccio's painting, I therefore propose, is working out a delicate theology of prophecy, time, death and hope.

As we have seen, in the New York picture, Job was made sense of more artistically than anything else; this is what helps us to see him as an 'indissociable factor in the whole'. But in the Berlin picture, 'Job appears as an intruder from another time and place, a sort of commentator on the scene, who has just wandered in.'[41] The question is, what sort of 'commentary' might he be offering? My suggestion is that Carpaccio (and his patron, to a degree we cannot now determine) is prompting a range of theological insights, one of which is at the same time a recovery of a more ancient patristic habit of mind (thus demonstrating that some of the most fruitful findings are actually *re*findings).

Job keeps the company of the saints. That is one of the messages of this picture. It is also, as we have noted, one of the messages of the Bellini altarpiece for the church of San Giobbe, and of the Venetian 'transgressive canonisation' of Job. But here, the suggestion is made more concretely and vividly than a *sacra conversazione* could ever make it, because the normal rules of the contemporaneity of persons are *always* suspended in a *sacra conversazione*, which is why St Francis can rub shoulders with John the Baptist (for example) without anyone raising an eyebrow. But this is not a painting of some timeless gathering in the mansions of eternity. It is too laden with narrative.

The assumption we have been working with so far is that what we have here is Job being admitted to a New Testament 'space'. The Gospel scene is the 'literal' context, and Job is the product of a figural flight of fancy – an embellishment of a New Testament moment. But maybe there is greater ambiguity at work here than that. Might it be that this is a painting first and foremost of Job, in his 'literal' context, but with the vision vouchsafed to him in that context made visible to us too – unfolding all around him? Might it be that the contents of his inward sight are being rendered external and shareable (as a prophet's visions should be)? Is it, in other words, first a painting of Job and then of Christ, rather than first a painting of Christ and then of Job?

---

[41]Hartt 1940, 32.

By this ambiguity, the painting invites us to ask the question 'who is in whose landscape?'. Is Job admitted into the dead Christ's landscape because he was a 'seer' of Christ?[42] Or are we witnessing the entry of Christ (and his history) into Job's landscape, because God came to meet him in just this mode, as a God in the strange form of human flesh? In this case, the painting would become a creative meditation on the act of prophetic seeing itself, in which the painter aligns himself with a person who anticipates Christ (rather than someone who simply recalls him), and – perhaps – feels thereby a special affinity with an Old Testament perspective. The work of the artistic imagination, which in turn shapes and inspires the imaginations of the viewers of its work, would thus find itself compared with that of the prophetic imagination.

There is implicit in this an attitude to time, for what permits Job and Christ to occupy the same visual 'space' – legitimating this artistic connection between them in what I have called a 'narrative-laden', or history-like, context[43] – is an assumption that God assures their meaningful relation to one another. This is a stronger bond than the merely fortuitous usefulness of Job's example to illustrate something about Christ's suffering. It is perhaps better described as a belief that all times are present to one another in God, and that there is a divinely ordained patterning of history such that one moment can carry a connection to another within itself. This is what I referred to earlier as one of those 'findings' of Carpaccio's painting that is at the same time a refinding, inasmuch as he can be said to have achieved the visual analogue of a patristic 'figural reading'.

John David Dawson traces with unusual subtlety the concerns and the reasoning behind the figural readings of the patristic period – and, above all, those of Origen, that master of the practice.

---

[42]We might ask whether Job in this painting is taking the place of John, the Beloved Disciple (and also, of course, a 'seer' in Christian tradition). Here, Job is the person in closest proximity to Christ (as John was at the Last Supper), while John himself is placed at some distance away. Yet, it could be argued, they echo one another pictorially, not least by the colouring of their clothing. Perhaps one prophetic vision (from the Old Covenant looking towards the New) adumbrates and invites a further one (John's yet-to-come visions on Patmos, in which a thoroughly risen and glorified Christ will reveal the 'Last Things').
[43]'History-like' is the phrase that Hans Frei used to describe the character of the Gospels in his book *The Eclipse of Biblical Narrative, A Study in Eighteenth and Nineteenth Century Hermeneutics*. Frei 1974, 10.

In Origen's view, it may be that an Old Testament prophet like Isaiah, by seeking 'to render *intelligible* a certain divine performance', is able to refer 'in some oblique fashion to the person of Jesus'.[44] The 'intelligibility' of any event in history – when construed as divine performance – is a mark of the divine Logos at work, and the Logos (generatively fertile in all times and places, though only coming into full visibility at a certain point) is, for Christians, a christological reality made knowable in the Spirit. Thus, Gregory of Nazianzus (330–89/90) writes in Oration 41:

> [The prophets] foreknew the future, having their master part [i.e., their ruling faculties] moulded by the Spirit, and [were] associated with events that were yet future as if present, for such is the power of the Spirit.[45]

It is a point that could be confirmed by appeal to the New Testament itself, which says of another Old Testament figure, King David, that it was by the working of the Holy Spirit in him that he was able proleptically to call Jesus 'Lord' (see Mk 12.36 and Mt. 22.43). Gregory makes the point in relation to Jonah, who (he claims) 'foresaw the fall of Israel, and sensed the transfer of the grace of prophecy to the Gentiles'.[46] This is a very particular sort of 'seeing' – and there may be a crucial clue here to how Carpaccio decided to make his Job 'see' – and, more particularly, *contemplate* – the dead Christ.

For these patristic writers, the words and the actions of prophetic figures from the Old Testament can refer forward to the incarnation. Indeed, at times, the very power of their actions is seen as deriving from this proleptic connection (this 'referring forward'), because it is an ontological, God-given bond between the times, and not just an imposed one. Thus, the outstretched arms of Moses in the battle of Israel against Amalek in Exodus 17 channel the redemptive power of the Cross whose cruciformity they figure. Such a view does not require any claim about authorial intention: in some cases, the pointing forward is unwitting but nonetheless effective for that.

---

[44]Dawson 2002, 6.
[45]Or. 41.11. See Gregory Nazianzen 1995, 383.
[46]Or. 2.109. The translation here is Ben Fulford's own. See Fulford 2013, 141.

As Ben Fulford has argued, the incarnation is central to these figural relations and their interpretation.[47] Gregory of Nazianzus is once again one of the most articulate exponents of the theory. The incarnate Christ – 'that great . . . Victim' – was 'a purification, not for a part of the world, nor for a short time, but for the whole world, and for all time'.[48] This way of conceiving the effects of Christ's sacrifice is a way in which Christ – even dead – can be seen as visiting Job in his affliction, or making Job capable of 'access' to the Paschal Victim.

It may not be far-fetched to suppose that Carpaccio had some feeling for this patristic way of thinking about time and figural relations in time, which was less rigidly codified than the typological readings that remained prominent in the art and preaching of the Middle Ages. The passage from Jerome quoted earlier in this chapter is also quoted (in full) in the Cîteaux manuscript of Gregory the Great's (c.540–604) famous *Moralia in Job*, which builds on and elaborates Jerome's interpretation of chapter 19,[49] and we know that in 1480, and again in 1494, Venice saw reprints of this work.[50] Perhaps Carpaccio had access to it. In any event, it is likely that it was a subject of discussion among the theologically minded in late-fifteenth-century Venice, and Carpaccio's pairing of Job with Jerome in the earlier (New York) altarpiece does, as I have suggested, seem more than fortuitous.

So then, the 'findings' made possible by Carpaccio's imagination at work in its distinctive historical circumstances have so far been shown to include a fresh iteration of a theology of time, and a (related) meditation on the power of prophetic sight. We now turn to the theme of death, which is a natural correlate to these themes of time and prophecy. The prophetic-artistic imagination, turned to the future, will be hard-pressed not to contemplate mortality. Carpaccio foregrounds it unapologetically in these works.

> [A]s one looks at [this] dead body . . . one cannot help asking
> oneself the peculiar, arresting question: if such a corpse . . . was

---

[47]See Fulford 2013, 139–40.

[48]Or. 45.13. See Gregory Nazianzen 1995, 427.

[49]A full translation can be found at http://www.lectionarycentral.com/Gregory MoraliaIndex.html (accessed 13 August 2013).

[50]By Reynaldus de Novimagio Teoteutonicus. See Hartt 1940, 29.

seen by all His disciples, by His future chief apostles, by the
women who followed Him and stood by the cross, by all who
believed in Him and worshipped Him, then how could they
possibly have believed, confronted with such a sight, that this
martyr would rise again?[51]

Though it might have been written about either or both of
Carpaccio's images, this passage about looking for an answer from
Christ's body – perhaps looking for an answer from death itself – is
in fact about Hans Holbein's *Dead Christ* of only a few years later
(1521–22), and now in the Basel Museum of Art.[52] The passage
is written by the philosopher and psychoanalytical theorist Julia
Kristeva. But its preoccupation with a subject so close in content
to the Carpaccio images is interesting here, for Kristeva makes a
powerful argument that the rise of such images is precisely a mark
of an emergent early modern consciousness, even as it draws on so
many older artistic traditions of the kind we have already traced.

In the Carpaccio paintings of the dead Christ, as in the Holbein
image, death is made the subject of our contemplation. Carpaccio,
as we have seen, also makes it the subject of *Job*'s contemplation.
The intentness of his contemplation is perhaps intended to educate
ours. If death is, as one famously sentimental Victorian meditation
has it, 'only a horizon',[53] then the Berlin painting in particular
(which is, in Hartt's words, 'a mysterious and profoundly moving
dialogue between life and death') both reinforces and also queries
that horizon.

To be clear, there is nothing new about showing Christ dead;
dead Christs are a staple of Western art throughout the medieval
period. Nevertheless, it can be suggested (as Kristeva suggests)
that in the particular period of Western history in which Carpaccio
and Holbein find themselves, a newly interrogative attitude to
death is awakening. New artistic responses mirror this new relationship to death; this more unsettling sense of human finitude

[51]Kristeva 1989, 108.
[52]Hans Holbein the Younger, *The Body of the Dead Christ in the Tomb*, 1521.
Kunstmuseum, Öffentliche Kunstsammlung, Basel. The painting can be viewed
online via the Web Gallery of Art (accessed 15 August 2013) at http://www.wga.hu/
[53]This phrase appears to have originated with the author, Rossiter W. Raymond
(1840–1918).

and – possibly – of human ephemerality. When once a painting of
the dead Christ might have invited a penitential self-examination
by the viewer of the manifold sins and wickedness by which this
death was made necessary, now an additional option presents itself:
a contemplation of *oneself* in Christ's dead body. A contemplation
not of the vicarious death of the Saviour but of the ubiquitous
death of everyman.

In this newly arrived early modern moment, what 'findings' might
these paintings of the dead Christ make possible? For Hartt, the
Carpaccio paintings, and especially that in Berlin, offer a 'haunting
suggestion' that with sufficient attention, 'an answer may be elicited
from death' – one that relates to our own deaths too.[54] For Kristeva,
the Holbein painting, at least, faces the hard truth that no answer
will come, and that human beings are henceforth to live in a manner
unencumbered by false consolations.

My own view is that Carpaccio's picture – though very much
a part of its early modern world – does still retain a marked sense
of hope in the resurrection, and in this respect I wish to endorse
but go further than Hartt. Meanwhile, I wonder whether it is right
to deny *any* such hope in *Holbein*'s image, and in this respect I
think Kristeva's conclusions are at risk of being too hasty, or too
ideologically driven.

Admittedly, the Holbein image is starker in its intense focus on
the body alone; and in its omission of all other figures or narrative
references. It can thus be read as a profoundly lonely image, in a way
that Carpaccio's images cannot. Kristeva takes this solitariness –
combined with a 'realism, harrowing on account of its very parsi-
mony' – to be a sign that 'transcendence' has been lost to this early
modern vision:

> With no intermediary, suggestion, or indoctrination, whether
> pictorial or theological, other than our ability to imagine death,
> we are led to collapse in the horror of the caesura constituted by
> death or to dream of an invisible beyond.[55]

Kristeva finds there to be both continuities and (more importantly) discontinuities between Holbein's image and two earlier

---

[54]Hartt 1940, 32.
[55]Kristeva 1989, 113.

ways of painting Christ's corpse: (i) the sweetness of the Italian
tradition, which acted as a sort of theodicy, and (ii) the brutalism of
the Northern tradition, which was nonetheless not so much God-
doubting as designed to elicit a heightened sense of the divine presence and summons in the guise of Christ's consummate sacrifice. He
uses elements of each to correct the other, and in so doing makes a
new statement of his own. It is as if:

> Holbein had picked up the anatomical and pacifying lesson taught
> by Mantegna and Italian Catholicism, less sensitive to man's
> sin than to forgiving him and influenced more by the bucolic,
> embellishing ecstasy of the Franciscans than by Dominican
> dolorousness. And yet, always heedful of the Gothic spirit,
> Holbein maintains grief while humanizing it, without following
> the Italian path of negating pain and glorifying the arrogance of
> the flesh or the beauty of the beyond.[56]

In other words, crudely to paraphrase Kristeva, Holbein is not hung
up on sin, but is honest about suffering. This, she says, makes him
more humane.

Kristeva is perhaps too prejudiced against the idea that this image
could ever be the basis of (admittedly crepuscular) hope. She will
not entertain the possibility for more than an instant. The edging of
the painting, which (she is forced to concede) 'seems . . . always to
have been part of Holbein's painting':

> includes, between the words of the inscription [*Jesus Nazarenus
> Rex Judaeorum*], five angels bearing the instruments of the
> martyrdom: the shaft, the crown of thorns, the scourge, the
> flogging column, the cross. Integrated afterwards in that symbolic
> framework, Holbein's painting recovers the evangelical meaning
> that it did not insistently contain in itself . . .[57]

But Kristeva is determined to credit this 'evangelical meaning' to
some other source than Holbein's creative genius and truthfulness.
She says that the edging 'probably legitimized it in the eyes of its

---

[56]Ibid., 117.
[57]Ibid., 114–15.

purchasers'[58]: she reads it, in other words, as a piece of marketeering that merely adopted the guise of piety.

What Carpaccio does, meanwhile, is more deliberately hospitable to such 'evangelical meaning'. There are subtle signs of it to be picked up in the two figures making music on a ridge in the middle distance. While some critics have seen these as fluting shepherds – the denizens of some soothing pastoral idyll – it seems clear that one of them (the standing figure) is playing a brass instrument. This is 'no bucolic melody, but a fanfare . . .'.[59] We may be reminded of the triumphant blasts that are so much more prominent in Carpaccio's painting of St George baptizing the Selenites.[60] Although more discreet, might it be that some similar sense of Christian victory over death is being signalled here? Moreover, in the distance on the right-hand side of the Berlin *Dead Christ*, three figures can be discerned making their way along the road towards the place where Christ is. They are a clear visual echo of the three figures approaching the scene of Christ's re-emergence into life in Giovanni Bellini's *Resurrection*, now also in Berlin.[61] They, like the resurrection itself, are further away in Carpaccio's painting than in Bellini's, but might their steady advance act as an assurance that the resurrection of which they are a visual mnemonic draws nearer too?

But it seems to me that if it is also a painting about hope (as well as a painting that treats of prophecy, time and death), the real success of Carpaccio's picture lies not in the way these little visual signposts hint at something better to come. It lies in its refusal to dodge the challenge in the face of which Christian hope has to sustain itself. It lies in the fact that it can be read as a painting about the resurrection not *despite* but *because of* the fact that it shows a dead Christ, and that it shows him alongside the most afflicted of all Old Testament figures: Job. That the resurrection can be anticipated even in the midst of so much death and mourning means that we are not being hoodwinked with false consolation;

[58]Ibid., 115.
[59]Mason 2000, 28.
[60]Vittore Carpaccio, *The Baptism of the Selenites*, 1507. Scuola di San Giorgio degli Schiavoni, Venice. The painting can be viewed online via the Web Gallery of Art (accessed 15 August 2013) at http://www.wga.hu/
[61]Giovanni Bellini, *The Resurrection of Christ*, 1475–79. Staatliche Museen, Berlin. The painting can be viewed online via the Web Gallery of Art (accessed 15 August 2013) at http://www.wga.hu/

resurrection hope is offered as strong enough to hold up in the face
of a tangible mortality. To borrow Job's own words, it is only 'in
our flesh' (which includes our mortality), and not by some escape
from it, that we can hope to 'see God'; moreover, it is only in God's
sharing of that flesh, which is also our flesh.

The brilliance of Carpaccio's artistic invention in this regard is
to make Job the 'presence' of Christ's resurrection in a painting that
holds off from showing the resurrection explicitly (and wisely so,
because visualizations of the resurrection usually fail – for good
theological reasons as well as for artistic ones). Job, the resurrection-
seer, keeps the flame of resurrection promise alive while Christ
himself is dead.

If this is a plausible reading of Carpaccio's painting, then it
is at least worth entertaining the possibility (*pace* Kristeva) that
Holbein's painting – though raising the stakes somewhat – is inviting
our hope to test itself in a comparable way. In this case, however, *we*
must play the Joban role:

> Holbein's Christ is alone. Who sees him? There are no saints.
> There is of course the painter. And ourselves.[62]

This is a heavy task, and for Holbein's first viewers it was no doubt
fraught with the newly emerging anxieties and doubts that were
the product of the unique social and intellectual revolutions of
their new century. But their sense of how and in whose company
to meditate on the dead Christ may have been a more devotionally
shaped (and artistically informed) one than Kristeva allows – and
no less authentic for that.

A Kristevan question

This chapter's case study has aimed to show two key things. First,
particular emerging historical circumstances (i.e. certain 'found
things') inform particular possibilities for theological thought in
a profound way; and second, some of the theological thoughts
that emerge in new historical circumstances can be genuinely

---

[62]Kristeva 1989, 137.

innovatory (i.e. they can properly be called 'findings'). Historical and local particularity are themselves correlates and conditions of 'enfleshment', such that to say – with Job – 'in my flesh I shall see God' is to say that this God will be vouchsafed in particularity to particular persons and communities, persons and communities who must learn to look with their own eyes and not those of another.

Carpaccio has been explored as an exemplar of this process at work, through a combination of an active historical sensibility and a lively creative imagination. In this light, Carpaccio can be evaluated in a far more positive light than the one in which Roger Fry cast him – not on merely technical grounds, but on genuinely *theological* grounds, for he is arguably a theologian of some originality and brilliance. Carpaccio's 'visual theology', as we have seen, is imbued with a remarkable power of association, and in his paintings of the dead Christ being contemplated by Job, he is a midwife of extraordinary theological discovery.

Julia Kristeva says that the genius of the Christian narrative of Christ's death and resurrection was its ability to represent and provide catharsis for the splittings and rejoinings that 'necessarily structure our individuation'.[63] The Christian narrative recognized the reality of 'hiatus and depression' – indeed, she says, it *started from* these things – but it also offered an 'antidote' to them.[64] And if, as she suggests, the hiatus opened up by Christ's death somehow discloses an aspect of the trinitarian relation between Father and Son, then the cathartic restoration that is the 'antidote' to this hiatus somehow discloses an aspect of the rejoining work of the Holy Spirit. The Spirit's restoration of all things issues in what Kristeva calls the 'forgiveness inherent in Redemption'; this is, she says, 'one of the most interesting and innovative instances of trinitary [sic] logic'. She describes that thirdness in the Christian doctrine of the Trinity which Christians call the Holy Spirit as Christianity's 'antidepressive carrier wave'.[65]

The trouble is that she does not believe in this thirdness; she does not think it is a defensible modern object of faith. Moreover, she does not think it is a feature of the painting by Holbein that she

---

[63]Ibid., 132.
[64]Ibid., 134.
[65]Ibid., 135.

discusses at such length. The painting is, as she puts it, '*stripped*' of its antidepressive carrier wave (my emphasis).

And yet, Kristeva has confidence in the power of art to communicate meaningfully across the divide of centuries; she has confidence, in other words, in a rejoining that can be accomplished across historical divides that many see as mere hiatuses. How is *this* antidote to the depressive effects of splitting to be accounted for?

Although I have allowed Kristeva to help formulate the question, I want to turn to other theorists to help articulate the answer, which will, as the next chapter unfolds, take on a pneumatological shape as it discerns the Holy Spirit as the 'carrier wave' of historical insight, by way of a theological appropriation of the theory of reception.

5

Reception

Introduction

We turn in this chapter to the idea of reception. More particularly, for the purposes of this book, we turn to the reception theory developed in the 1960s and 1970s by Hans Robert Jauss (along with Wolfgang Iser and other members of the Konstanz group of literary historians), and his account of what happens when literary works continue to live and speak through time in new receptions by new communities of readers. Our especial focus here will be Jauss's inaugural lecture at the University of Konstanz in 1967. While this theory of reception – and more particularly of the sorts of aesthetic judgement that characterize reception – has been fairly widely put to work by biblical scholars, it is still relatively neglected by theologians.[1] This deserves to be remedied, for Jauss's theory has much to offer.

The case study of Carpaccio's painting of Job contemplating the dead Christ very effectively foregrounds many of the issues that are of greatest concern to reception theorists. As we have seen, the specific historical conditions in which Carpaccio was painting unlocked particular avenues into the subject matter for him. The painting was a creative reception of a whole range of earlier works (both artistic and theological works, and sometimes both in one), in a way that had been facilitated by the passage of time.

In line with that insight, this chapter will ask what is happening when people in new contexts find themselves able to do new things

---

[1] One notable exception is Ormond Rush. See Rush 1997.

with old things – whether they are biblical narratives or texts, or doctrinal formulae, or works of art and literature. (Following Jauss, and to avoid verbosity, I will generally use the shorthand 'works' to describe all these productions.) It will assess the processes of estrangement and rediscovery that mark some works' later destiny; and how these processes (inasmuch as they show themselves capable of generating further theological thought as well as literary-critical or art-historical insight) may be instructive about the very practice of theology itself.

This will open again – as so many of the examples and themes of this book do – onto a reflection on how theology can think in its own proper terms about history and historical process, and how it might go about describing such process.

Why be receptive to reception aesthetics?

'[T]he quality and rank of a literary work', wrote Jauss, 'result neither from the biographical or historical conditions of its origin [*Entstehung*], nor from its place in the sequence of the development of a genre alone, but rather from the criteria of influence, reception, and posthumous fame, criteria that are more difficult to grasp.'[2]

It helps to be clear about the problems that Jauss was attempting to solve. They were (i) whether you can have literary history at all, rather than only the discrete study of individual texts; and (ii) whether this literary history has any relation to general human history.

He wanted to say yes to both, and contrasted his new proposals with those of a series of paradigms in literary criticism that had dominated the field in the preceding decades. These included positivism (causal explanations for all literary phenomena which reduce the innovative creativity of the literary artist herself or himself to a set of outside influences), and *Geistesgeschichte* (the idealist notion that there are quasi-mystical archetypes in great literature, and that literary history is about spotting the recurrence of atemporal ideas and motifs).

---

[2]Jauss 1982, 5.

These problematic paradigms had more recent relatives in Marxism and Formalism. The Marxists reductively sought to limit the meaning of a text to being a record or deposit of the historical and economic relations that pertained at the time of its production. To read the text 'truly', on this account, required a reconstruction of that milieu. They reduced the text to a single, fixed place in a larger historical process. Meanwhile, Formalist approaches (and principally that of the New Critics) saw the text as a free-standing entity, whose only interest to the reader should be the internal relations of its constituent literary parts. Once it had been created, authorial intention (so far as that could ever be reconstructed) was of no relevance to the text, nor were other prevailing circumstances at the time of its birth. They cut the text free from historical process.

The new school of Reception Theory wanted to get the text back in touch with history – history as an unfolding medium of interpretation, which could interact unpredictably and generatively with the text. Each new encounter would allow both the text and the new historical circumstances to *mean more* than they did in previous encounters, and sometimes to *have different meanings* from the meanings they had in previous encounters.

A succinct account of this view is offered by Karl Kosík, whom Jauss quotes approvingly:

> The work lives to the extent that it has an influence. Included within the influence of a work is that which is accomplished in the consumption of the work as well as in the work itself. That which happens with the work is an expression of what the work is. . . . The work is a work and lives as a work for the reason that it *demands* an interpretation and "*works*" [influences, *wirkt*] in many meanings.[3]

One key objective of Jauss and his colleagues in the service of returning the work to ongoing history was to overcome the

---

[3]Cited in Jauss 1982, 15. The quotation comes from *Die Dialektik des Konkreten*. See Kosík 1967, 138–9. For an English translation see Kosík 1976. Incidentally, art is not just a copying of or commenting on 'actual' historical process. It is *formative* of it, by being formative of readers and communities – this is the link between literary and 'general' history.

tendency of previous schools of literary criticism to focus only, or principally, on author and text. To correct the balance, Jauss wanted more focus on readers; those who represent, interpret and transmit the text in the historical process; those in whom the text lives and by whom it is mediated historically. To put it rather more bluntly than he did, Jauss intended to shift the enquiry after meaning from its fixation on two poles of a relation to an investigation of three. The way in which a work 'means' would be better understood as involving a three-way interaction between author, text and recipient-reader.

This was not in any way to imply a total relativism – some sort of infinite fluidity to a text's meaning, which is wholly reader-generated and can change completely from one reading to the next. Jauss wanted to safeguard the place of the author and of authorial intention (in this we can contrast him with, for example, Stanley Fish[4]). Reading is traditioned, and Jauss's theory also required an acceptance that texts set parameters for – or contain the seeds of – the traditions they generate. Texts have effective possibilities, some of which a prescient author may to some degree apprehend, ahead of her time, as she imagines future worlds, and some of which she may be unaware of, but which nonetheless lie dormant, perhaps as covert implications of a text, or yet-to-be-answered questions raised by it. A later interpreter ought not to disregard the text, for these possibilities are, in some way, *properties of the text*. They are not impositions on it. We should seek the horizons of the text, and then find how they interact with our own. As Jauss wrote in relation to his Thesis 4: '[t]he reconstruction of the horizon of expectations, in the face of which a work was created and received in the past, enables one . . . to pose questions that the text gave an answer to', and by that token to discover how the contemporary reader may view and understand the work.[5]

By establishing the questions a work itself was asking, and to which it was essaying an answer, we may be helped with the discovery, formulation or refinement of our own questions in our own contexts. This is not, of course, a simple business, and we can initially identify at least two forms that it might take:

---

[4]Fish 1980.
[5]Jauss 1982, 28.

1 we may adopt the work's questions again, or at least find that our questions prove very similar to the questions the work was once asking (and trying to answer) when it was made; or

2 instead of identifying with, and appropriating, the questions the work was once asking (a predominantly imitative model), we may ask quite different questions that are nevertheless provoked by the original ones; we may want to outdo or refute whatever it is we think a work was originally doing, but this will also be an 'effect' of the work in reception theory's terms, because it still involves the appropriation of that (past) work.

Jauss recognizes a third option too, namely, that:

3 we may bring wholly new questions to the work that have not been asked before – though such an approach will be governed by a sense that the work somehow has the resources to answer such questions.

All these are ways of honouring (but not idolizing) authorial intention, and of respecting a literary text's important relation to the context and circumstances of its production, while maintaining that it may have opennesses, and powers of suggestion, that exceed conscious authorial intention.[6] 'The work of art can . . . mediate knowledge . . . if it anticipates paths of future experience, imagines as-yet-untested models of perception and behavior, or contains an

---

[6] I will reiterate here a point I made in the preceding chapter. There is a place for enquiry into the historical conditions of a work's production, in relation to texts (including sacred texts) as well as in relation to works of visual art or literature. It is true that with the help of reception theory I intend to claim the unavoidability of 'looking along' tradition rather than supposing one can bypass it and go straight to an original source. But I do not intend to suggest that investigations into earlier historical contexts are bound to be utterly fruitless, so long as it is recognized that such investigations are themselves, of course, traditioned and temporally located. As Rowan Williams writes: 'the tools of the historical critical method are in fact essential – so long as they are clearly separated from an interpretative method mortgaged to genealogy, an assumption that the earlier is the authentic, or to evolutionism, an assumption that the later is the finished, the definitive' (Williams 2004, 222).

answer to newly-posed questions.'[7] These capacities of the text are
only made manifest in interaction with readers in history. Once
again, we see here Jauss's emphasis on the three-way relation
between author, text and reader.[8]

Jauss was clear, therefore, that readers do not read in a vacuum.
They come with particular assumptions and expectations, and these
are, in turn, historically informed. Readers may *make history*, in the
sense that they will inevitably generate new readings of earlier works
by the unprecedented perspectives they bring to their reception of
them, thereby bequeathing these readings to later interpreters. But
they are also *made by history*. Their new readings cannot but be
coloured by readings that have gone before.

In this respect, Jauss's thought displays clear debts to the
hermeneutical studies of his former teacher, Hans-Georg Gadamer.
It will be worth taking a little time to examine the nature and
extent of these debts before going any further. It will be especially
worthwhile insofar as it will afford us an opportunity to correct
a widespread misapprehension (not least in biblical studies) about
just what Gadamer's notion of *Wirkungsgeschichte* means, and how
far it overlaps with the field of 'reception studies', which is now a
burgeoning field in the study of biblical texts.[9] Jauss's 'reception
aesthetics' – while doing something more and/or different from
Gadamer's theory of *Wirkungsgeschichte* – is nonetheless a good
deal more hermeneutically sophisticated than much of what passes
under the name of 'reception history'.

---

[7]Jauss 1982, 31.

[8]It should be noted that a specific part of what Jauss is concerned with is how a
later work in an identifiable tradition (e.g. the tradition of French novel-writing) is
a reception of (and an innovation on) earlier works in that same tradition. In other
words, he is interested as much if not more in how works generate new works as he
is in how works generate readings, or interpretations. A work and an interpretation
are not quite the same thing. Having said that, the boundaries between the two are
blurred, and every author of a work in a tradition has first also been a reader in that
tradition. Moreover, interpretations – even when they are in different genres – are in
some way also 'works'.

[9]In the critique that follows, I share the reservations of Richard Kueh in his work
'Reception History and the Hermeneutics of *Wirkungsgeschichte*', an unpublished
PhD thesis (University of Cambridge, 2012), and I am indebted to him at a number
of points in what follows.

A Gadamerian excursus

Gadamer's notion of *Wirkungsgeschichte* has been notoriously difficult to translate into English, and this has perhaps been the cause of some of the peculiar ways it has been used to underwrite academic approaches that it ought not to underwrite.

As Richard Kueh has pointed out, it is used interchangeably with a range of terms and phrases, including: 'effective history', 'effected history', 'history of effects', 'history of influence', 'history of interpretation' (*Auslegungsgeschichte*), 'post-history' (*Nachgeschichte*), 'reception history' (*Rezeptionsgeschichte*) and 'use and influence'.[10] The discipline of biblical studies is a case in point, inasmuch as it has integrated the term *Wirkungsgeschichte* into its vocabulary to describe the practice of identifying and gathering the cumulative interpretations of a biblical passage or text through time (whether in other texts, like commentaries or sermons, or in sculptures, paintings, novels, films or comparable art forms).

This may indeed be a valuable and instructive exercise in its own right (though, as Richard Kueh says, it can often look more like the diverting pastime of collecting curios and *objets d'art* rather than a form of serious hermeneutical engagement). But it is a long way from what Gadamer's account of *Wirkungsgeschichte* aimed to achieve; indeed, in some key ways it is a contradiction of the spirit of Gadamer's proposals. This is because Gadamer was arguing, not so much for a practice of historical tourism, as for a revision in how we recognize and relate to the intrinsic historicality of all of our interpretative processes *per se*.

A dominant paradigm in modern biblical studies has had a major preoccupation with questions about the source, date, authorship and, above all, the original intention of texts (sometimes this is more modestly qualified as 'the probable original meaning'). It typically holds to a belief in the primary meaning of a text upon which other forms of interpretation may then be built, and the in-principle accessibility of that meaning to later scholarship. Reception history – at least as it is practised by many biblical scholars today – does not fundamentally question this 'objectification' of history; this

---

[10]See Kueh 2012, 3.

belief that historical events and artefacts can always, in principle, be subjected to the even scrutiny of an impartial scholarly observer. On the contrary, it continues to sustain this objectification – and indeed to extend it – by *also* objectifying *tradition*; by applying just the same methods it uses to study 'originals' to the way it studies the products of later responses to those originals. But this is quite at odds with Gadamer's intention.

'Gadamer's hermeneutics', as Kueh points out, 'were never intended for methodological application; they are, above all, designed to act as a summative narration of what happens in understanding.' In other words, Gadamer's task was 'a descriptive account of understanding, not a prescriptive model to be applied to texts'.[11] To put it another way, Gadamer's theory of *Wirkungsgeschichte* aimed to describe the *conditions* of knowledge rather than a way of constituting a set of possible *objects* of knowledge. Reception history is not, in this sense, a good translation of *Wirkungsgeschichte*, and the fruits of reception history, in practice, have proven themselves all too capable of leaving every narrow prior assumption about what we can know – and *how* we know it – firmly in place. '[F]ar from following Gadamer's radical departure from classic models of understanding, [reception history] actually capitulates to standard historical-critical practices.'[12] It simply transfers the same set of historical-critical procedures from their application to the original text to later interpretations of that text.

For Gadamer, the reclamation of tradition as a dialogue partner demanded the relinquishment of a foundationalist dream that the meaning of biblical (or indeed any) texts can be settled once and for all. This is because he did not think we are ever capable of standing outside the river of history – as though on its bank, able to walk up and down its edge and examine at will the various features of its course. We are within it, and our historical insights, such as they are, will always be formed in a historically constituted consciousness which is the inheritor of whatever the 'flow' of the river of history brings to it. This will include intermediate understandings, attitudes and interpretations which mediate between us and that towards which we look. These mediations are not obstacles or distractions to our perception of the principal 'target' of our gaze; they are

---

[11]Kueh 2012, 53; see also Parris 2009, 113–15.
[12]Kueh 2012, 105.

necessary conditions for our having any sense of what we are gazing at in the first place.

We might change the metaphor for a moment, and borrow shamelessly a now-famous image developed by C. S. Lewis: that of the beam of sunlight shining into his toolshed.[13] Lewis was principally using the image to illustrate how one knows in faith, but it can have other applications. Some kinds of knowledge presume an ability to look *at* things. A stance can be adopted which claims it has seen all it needs to see by standing outside the beam of light that shines into the toolshed and by looking *at* it. But – even in cases where it is plausible in the first place that one can ever stand fully apart from an object of one's enquiry – there are a great many things that are not seen when such a stance is adopted. An entirely different vision, and a greater wealth of knowledge, is vouchsafed to the viewer who looks not *at* the beam but *along* it.

The 'river of history' may very appropriately be described as a beam of light in just these terms, entering the darkness of one's shed through a crack in the wall. And an historical consciousness of the sort that Gadamer insists we can never escape has no real option but to look *along* this beam.

'In my *flesh* I shall see . . .'. To know under these conditions (and there are no other conditions for human knowing than those of enfleshment) is to know in a way that is also of its nature historical. Being in the flesh *is* – by its very nature – a form of *looking along the beam.*

When history is conceived, as Gadamer conceived it, as a medium of consciousness, and not an object of conscious study, then it asks to be looked *along*. This is an inescapable mode of being in the flesh.

> Gadamer's main proposal is that "understanding" always and without exception involves a bearing down of historical effects on the interpreter's being, despite whatever attempts he makes to manipulate or control understanding.[14]

Gadamer's celebrated discussion of the 'fusion of horizons' was precisely a discussion of this mediatory power of history. He was not saying that past and present are discrete entities, one of which must

---

[13]Lewis 1970, 212–15.
[14]Kueh 2012, 117.

be forced to conform to the norms of the other by suppressing its own norms before a successful event of knowledge can take place. He was, on the contrary, optimistic that we have a great deal that already relates us to the past we seek to understand. We do not need to suppose, despairingly, that a Herculean task of reconstruction is the only remedy against meaninglessness. On the contrary:

> [Gadamer's] argument is rooted in the observation that human beings are historical beings. Such historicality is, Gadamer claims, fundamentally connectedness with history and therefore the past.[15]

In the specific case of texts from the past, history does not only mark out 'the remoteness, "otherness" or "alterity" of the text to the interpreter' (though it may also do this at times, and this can be a very important reminder that traditions cannot always be trusted[16]), but also bestows the framework necessary to interpret such texts. In Gadamer's own words:

> To think historically always involves mediating between those [past] ideas and one's own thinking. To try to escape from one's own concepts in interpretation is not only impossible but manifestly absurd. To interpret means precisely to bring one's own preconceptions into play so that the text's meaning can really be made to speak for us.[17]

---

[15]Ibid., 91.

[16]Habermas is perhaps the most famous of Gadamer's interlocutors to express concerns here. The sorts of critical reflection that are, he objects, absent in Gadamer's account of hermeneutics and consciousness include the ability to ask questions about whether a text is a reliable or an unreliable source of authority; whether its writers and earlier readers had malign motives; and whether the text has lent itself to oppressive uses. Karl-Otto Apel, meanwhile, asks whether one can ever 'naively or even straightforwardly *place one's trust* in history' simply because 'history is complex and encompasses many layers, several of which simply do not command one's trust' (Kueh 2012, 128). Gadamer is not without responses to these challenges. Part of the reason why I do not think they finally vitiate his affirmation of history as a medium of connectedness are addressed elsewhere in this book (see, for example, my appropriation of Rowan Williams on the generative process of historical reading [pneumatologically construed] on p. 76ff., and of C. S. Peirce on the idea of the 'eventual' and the value of gradual community discernment on pp. 221–6).

[17]Gadamer 1989, 397.

We can draw this excursus to a close by concluding that, in Gadamer's hands, *Wirkungsgeschichte* was used to describe the productive mediating power of historical process itself. *Wirkungsgeschichte* – 'effective historical consciousness' – is thus better translated in a way that suggests not so much how our consciousness is effective when we think about history, but how history is effective in and in relation to our consciousness. The hyphen is better placed between 'effective' and 'historical' ('effective-historical consciousness') than between 'historical' and 'consciousness' ('effective historical-consciousness').

This represents a profound affirmation of the connectedness and coherence of the world, particularly in respect of its historical aspects.[18] A trust in such connectedness – a trust that the world is a world one can genuinely inhabit in the expectation of an experience of 'at-homeness' – is a fundamental aspect of the theological argument being advanced here. History, on this account, is not principally to be conceived of as a problem to be surmounted (a ditch to be crossed, in Lessing's still-famous image), but as itself a sort of effective power. We will return to this affirmation later in the chapter, and develop it further with the help of R. G. Collingwood's thought. But, for now, it makes sense to return to Jauss.

Jaussian reception aesthetics

We have identified a number of the central assumptions that Jauss adopted from, and shared with, Gadamer in relation to this optimistic account of the historical medium as a condition of productive knowing (despite the many things that can go wrong in any tradition).

If Jauss had one main gripe with Gadamer's hermeneutics overall, it seems to be that in his evocations of history's effective power, Gadamer did not place sufficient emphasis on the role of readers, and communities of readers, *in* history. Jauss did not see

---

[18]At other points in this book, different aspects of this connectedness will be given greater emphasis: they include the connectedness between the human and the non-human world, and between what are often set up over against one another as the 'subjects' and 'objects' of knowing.

enough of an account of what might be called *receptive agency* in Gadamer.[19]

Jauss, clearly, *did* wish to make the language and the analysis of reception the central concern of his work, and indeed to study what seemed to him to be going on in particular receptions within a literary tradition. Moreover, his was not first and foremost a description of historical consciousness as such; it was primarily interested in concrete examples of transmission and development in specific relation to literature. In other words, he had specific aims that distinguished his project from Gadamer's, giving it a particular focus and application. It is these, as we shall see later on in this chapter, that make his theory especially useful in analysing what Carpaccio's painting achieved as a piece of traditioned-but-innovatory theological art. And that case study can, in turn, stand as an illustration of the value of Jauss's theory for suggesting how theological interpretation in other genres (not only in the medium of painting) may develop over time as theology brings its 'givens' into dialogue with the things it finds.

Jauss's focus on the concept of reception took him beyond Gadamer, but in choosing to focus on reception, Jauss at the same time successfully avoided most of the pitfalls that we have observed in a certain sort of flat-footed 'reception *history*' – the kind we have noted, for example, within some strands of recent biblical studies. He preserved the sense that you can take account of a history of receptions while yet 'looking along the beam': seeing yourself as part of that history, and – as we noted earlier – seeing that history as one of the essential conditions for your seeing anything at all.

Jauss's decision to describe what he was doing as 'reception aesthetics', and not reception history, may be a significant marker of

---

[19]It would be wrong to conclude on this basis that Gadamer denies any agency at all to human consciousness. Human thought operates in history and has historical effects. The interpretation of a text (a law, for example) can have very direct and immediate effects indeed. However, at a more comprehensive level, Gadamer's point is that consciousness is being shaped and changed – being constituted, even, and in that sense 'effected' – in its very act of interpretation, as it looks along the beam of history and '*reads*' in each new and unique moment. To keep the legal example in play for a moment longer: the act of conscious appropriation and application of the law is not merely a decision *about* what historical effects will or will not now take place. It *is itself* an historical effect; something that history has effected, *as* an event of (and in) consciousness.

the difference. He is undoubtedly aware of that Kantian tradition of aesthetics which sees aesthetic judgement as the product of the free play of the imagination – assuming as a condition of its rationality the likelihood that others will share one's judgements, although (by contrast with what goes on in pure and in practical reason) not being able to give *a priori* conceptual reasons for why this must be so. He was therefore also aware that reception aesthetics can have the optimism but not the certainty of the historical-critical method in relation to the study of texts from the past. Jaussian reception aesthetics believes that there can be shared insight in valuing and celebrating some texts and not others, but denies any pretence of absolute methodological objectivity. (Moreover, as an aesthetics of reception rather than an exercise in reception history, it must take account at every stage of elements at work in the successive transmission of texts through time that are not narrowly fact based, or merely analytically rational, but involve affective responses too.)

How might the idea of 'looking along the beam' actually work in the particular context of Jaussian reception aesthetics? The notion of 'canon' is very important for Jauss here. As Kueh puts it:

> [F]or "classic" texts, which have a wide sphere of influence and recognition, later interpretations do not simply differ because the interpreters come from a different geographical or historical place. They differ because succeeding interpretations are themselves situated in the thought-world of preceding interpretations.[20]

Readers come with a sort of internal 'canon' of texts (or, importantly, of established interpretations) that they expect to be able to relate any new text of a similar type. They expect this text to keep a certain sort of company.[21] The text will variously confirm or confound such expectations. To the extent that it modifies them, it plays its own part in reshaping the horizon of expectations that will attend the reception of texts encountered in the future. If it proves itself a

---

[20]Kueh 2012, 50.

[21]The idea of texts – or indeed words – 'keeping company' is one initiated by Nicholas Lash in *Believing Three Ways in One God, A Reading of the Apostles' Creed* (Lash 1992, 12) and developed further by Mike Higton in Higton and Muers 2012, 71–92.

classic text by having a rich and effective influence,[22] it will itself
become part of a relevant literary canon – a text to which people
will normally expect to relate their readings of new texts of any
comparable kind. It will become a text to which you cannot but
make some mental reference whenever you read. *Madame Bovary*,
Jauss claims, achieved this in the history of novels.

A text that has once been part of a literary canon can, of course,
drop out of it if it has no obvious value or ceases to relate in any
helpful way to other texts that are now being encountered. Correspondingly, I take it, an ancient text as well as a newly written one
might enter a canon if it seems to a new epoch to be the sort of text
you cannot read without; to which it would be a mistake not to be
relating to the texts you are reading; which has crucial horizon-
forming expectations for you as a reader.

In relation to such cases – in which an ancient text 'comes back'
into circulation, and is accorded classic status when for a time it
had no such status – Jauss writes:

> [T]he past work can answer and "say something" to us only
> when the present observer has posed the question that draws it
> back out of its seclusion.[23]

To which he adds the statement that 'a literary past can return
only when a new reception draws it back into the present . . .'.[24]
And he speaks appreciatively of R. G. Collingwood's postulate –
'posed in his critique of the prevailing ideology of objectivity in
history' – that '[h]istory is nothing but the re-enactment of past
thought in the historian's mind'. This, he insists, 'is even more valid
for literary history'.[25] (As I have indicated, we will have cause to
return to Collingwood's thought later, in a concluding section that
reverses Jauss's focusing move – from history to literary history –
and that begins to open up a consideration of historical process
more generally.)

---

[22]   [T]hose historical texts which are continually read in the present are ones which
have endured through history and, as such, have passed the test of time. . . . [T]heir
quality of survival throughout history then, in turn, becomes an authoritative
attribute as they address the present. (Kueh 2012, 100)

[23]Jauss 1982, 32.

[24]Ibid., 35.

Such claims were at the heart of Jauss's 'Thesis 1' in his inaugural lecture. Unlike a political event:

> [a] literary event can continue to have an effect only if those who come after it still or once again respond to it – if there are readers who again appropriate the past work or authors who want to imitate, outdo, or refute it.[26]

And again:

> The "verdict of the ages" on a literary work is . . . the successive unfolding of the potential for meaning that is embedded in a work and actualized in the stages of its historical reception as it discloses itself to understanding judgment, so long as this faculty achieves in a controlled fashion the "fusion of horizons" in the encounter with the tradition.[27]

Aside from conscious authorial intention, particular literary works may embody a *Zeitgeist*; expressing the mores and outlook of a particular epoch. In Jauss's words: 'works are variously permeable of events in historical reality, according to their genre or to the form pertaining to their period'.[28] As we have indicated, the question this then prompts is: what happens to such works when the *Zeitgeist* changes, and history moves on? Do they cease to have anything to say, or are they doomed simply to keep on reiterating what they said when they were first made, in exactly the same form, with exactly the same meaning-content, but with a more restricted audience, whose members have a more partial ability to comprehend them? To put the question as Jauss did:

> How can the art of a distant past survive the annihilation of its socioeconomic basis, if one denies . . . any independence to the artistic form and thus also cannot explain the ongoing influence of the work of art as a process formative of history?[29]

---

[25]Ibid., 21.
[26]Ibid., 22.
[27]Ibid., 30.
[28]Ibid., 12.
[29]Ibid., 13.

His answer, as we have adumbrated already, is that the common historicality, which incorporates the common, embodied experiences of human beings, represents a medium in which there can be understanding across epochs. To adopt Rowan Williams's words – used, we may note, of the assumptions that inform the Christian reading of Scripture, but applicable to Jauss's ideas – the 'context' (of a sacred text, for Williams, or of a 'classic' text, in Jauss's terms) 'is always more than [its] social or ideological matrix'. Such readings '[assume] a continuity between the world of the text and the world of the reader'.[30] New circumstances do not necessarily therefore require our jettisoning of older texts, but rather a new configuration of them in the working canon we generate by our actual practices of reading: which texts we read most often; which we read in close proximity to which, and so on. These texts come to license one another in interesting ways, to be read together as part of an always-provisional configuration of texts (a body which, it is important to stress, I am calling a canon in the *literary* rather than the more strict *scriptural* sense).

Rather than rendering past writings alien, historical distance itself, Jauss maintained, enables a text to 'open up new ways of seeing things and preform new experiences'.[31] And while receptions by historical readers are the leading agent involved in thus determining the *variety* of responses to texts, the 'stable core of the work' nevertheless, in Jauss's words, 'limits the arbitrariness of interpretation, guaranteeing the continuity of its experience beyond the present act of reception'.[32]

One world, one history, but never one perspective

In all this there is implied a certain ontology of the historical process, and it is at this point that claims about the work of the Holy Spirit in history can perhaps suggest themselves to the theological interpreter – even acknowledging all of Jauss's proper

[30]Williams 2004, 224.
[31]Jauss 1982, 31.
[32]Jauss 1990, 60; see Kueh 2012, 134.

and conscientious concerns that the appeal to God as sustainer of a trans-historical reading context might represent a lazy short-circuit of the human processes involved in such reading, and an excuse for not paying due attention to its challenges.

The first indications of this possibility will have been evident in the similarity between Jauss's view of how classic texts are unlimited by their original context and Rowan Williams's view of how sacred texts open up '[other territories] for interpretation, potentially limitless'.[33] More specifically, there is, of course, a serious ontological claim being made whenever the idea of there being *one world* is advanced. But it is just such an idea that underwrites Jauss's belief in the communicability of texts across time. Borrowing Williams's words again, Jauss 'assumes a continuity between the world of the text and the world of the reader'. *One world*: this is, we may note in passing, just the principle deployed by the Anglican bishops at the 1958 Lambeth Conference in their statement (drafted by Michael Ramsey, then the Archbishop of York) addressing the question of scriptural authority in the face of the new historical science of biblical criticism (whose value they did not deny):

> [I]f there is faith and imagination, the Bible and the modern world are not so far apart – for the modern world is restless, torn by calamity, and seemingly near to catastrophe. It was in such an environment that the Bible was first written, and to such an environment it has the power to speak yet again.[34]

This is glossed somewhat less satisfactorily as we shall see, but in service of the same basic point, by Geoffrey Fisher, Archbishop of Canterbury, in his accompanying Encyclical Letter:

> Though our understanding of the Bible has been greatly assisted by those scholars who have taught us to see more clearly the varied ways in which the human factor has contributed to the books we call the Bible, and to the history which they record, the great realities – life and death, sin and righteousness, war

---

[33]Williams 2004, 220.
[34]Lambeth Conference 1958, 2.3.

and peace, famine and plenty, good and evil – remain always the
same, and the Bible speaks to these situations as it did when its
various books were written.[35]

It is on such grounds that some of the more explicitly theological
appropriations of reception theory for biblical studies have justified
themselves. John Collins in *The Bible After Babel*, for instance,
grounds his principle of analogy in the fact that there must be a
resemblance between the text in the past and the interpreter in the
present:

> To understand the ancient context of a text requires some
> sympathetic analogy between ancient and modern situations.[36]

And in the hands of Ulrich Luz, this point of coherence is divinely
assured, an unabashedly theological claim that, as Richard Kueh
puts it, 'the productive capability of the Bible is of the same order
as that which Paul attributes distinctively to the message of the
crucified Christ as the power of God'.[37]

But the subtlest approaches (which need be no less theological
for their subtlety) will be careful of suggesting, as Archbishop Fisher
could be read as suggesting, and as Archbishop Ramsey stopped
short of suggesting, that *all* 'the great realities', as Fisher calls them,
are equally present to *all* times. This would be (ironically) to forget
the extraordinary capacity of human beings, and human societies, to
forget. It would also be to suppose that there are no 'great realities'
yet to be unveiled. Part of the value of Jauss's account of reception
is that it admits the reality of forgetting, as well as allowing for the
possibility of later (re)discovery when circumstances facilitate such
discovery.

If literary canons change shape, then presumably the canon of
theological reference and association can do the same. The task
of theological interpretation, educated by reception theory, will
foster a sort of vigilance about what might be lying forgotten at
any particular time, and will build in a reflexivity, so far as possible,
about what may be on the brink of being lost, or what could now

---

[35]Ibid., 1.19.
[36]Collins 2005, 5–6.
[37]Kueh 2012, 156.

be re-found – or even found for the first time as an inherited text or a thought-form that finds itself in new company and utters new truths under that stimulus.

There is a question about just how much willed intention there can be in the reshaping of a canon (and the analogy here, to reiterate, is with a literary canon not a scriptural one). A few individuals may *wish* to reshape a canon, but Jauss's points relate to larger forces of influence and change. Nonetheless, we may entertain the idea that unfolding traditions of theological reflection in dialogue with historical experience have the power to re-form as well as transmit canons of thought, often though not always embodied in texts.

Moreover, the constant evolution of such canons is a signal that we are rarely, if ever, in a position to read our customary sources with exactly the horizon of expectations of an earlier generation, even if we and they do have a common worldedness. The body of material to which we habitually and instinctively relate all that we read (*including* our Scriptures) is never static.

The case study set out in the preceding chapter serves to confirm the broad lines of Jaussian reception theory in its display of how *forgetting*, and *recovery*, and *discovery* are all illustrated by the story of Carpaccio's remarkable painting. A knowledge of tradition (both theological and artistic) may – after the fact – make some sense of the work. An assertion of the 'one world' that envelops Carpaccio, Jerome and the unknown author of the biblical Book of Job may justify the work's boldness of association. But, when all that has been admitted, its innovation remains highly particular to its time and place. It was a new interpretation catalysed by circumstance: a finding. It is proof of the fact that the product of an exchange between author and context in one epoch (say, the Book of Job) can in a later time 'offer itself or invite in ways that do not wholly depend upon either factor' (the words are Rowan Williams's, though they could be Jauss's).[38] It also highlights something about the wider canon of scriptural texts, all of which have found themselves 'preserved because they speak of more than the circumstances which produced them'.[39]

The fact that the Book of Job is such a fruitful example to consider in this regard is also handy in light of its centrality to our

---

[38]Williams 2004, 220.
[39]Ibid., 223.

case study in the previous chapter. It gives licence to a final visit to Carpaccio's work before concluding the present chapter with a return to some wider considerations about historical consciousness which have been opened up by our examination of reception-in-particular.

The return and return of Job

This final visit to our case study provides an occasion to extend the field of our interest both backwards and forwards from Carpaccio's time; seeing his interest in the figure of Job as just one moment in a longer history of appropriation and reappropriation of Job; a history of which the painting (as part of a Western visual 'canon') in turn becomes a part, capable of contributing to the context for later interpretations. *Job Contemplating the Dead Christ*, if we may take the liberty of calling the painting that, elicits responses from us that would not have been capable of prediction by Carpaccio or his contemporaries as it speaks in vivid and developing ways to the modern imagination. The longer series of interpretations and the wider range of associations to which it can now be related burst the bounds of Carpaccio's own field of reference. Or, to put it another way, the painting, like any influential work of art, escapes its author in certain ways.[40] It goes beyond his or her intentions, and says more than he or she might have been able to anticipate, by virtue of its interactions with the frames of reference and the questions that later viewers bring to it. Giving some sort of theoretical account of that process has been the main concern of this chapter.

The fact that such 'escape' happens with a painting like Carpaccio's ought to be less surprising given that (*in* that painting) we are seeing just the same sort of thing happen with the 'literary' – or, more precisely, scriptural – figure of Job himself. What Carpaccio achieves in his interpretation of the scriptural Job, in other words, is echoed in what a twentieth-century interpreter might achieve in her or his interpretation of Carpaccio's painting (and thereby also, to some extent, in her or his interpretation of the scriptural Job as well). The Job of the Bible 'escapes' the conscious intentions of

---

[40]A point very elegantly expressed by Rowan Williams in his *Grace and Necessity, Reflections on Art and Love*. Williams 2005. See, for example, 37, 147.

whoever the original author, or authors, of the biblical Book of Job may have been.

Let us dwell for a brief moment once again on Carpaccio's early sixteenth-century achievement before we move outwards from it, recalling one of Jauss's most suggestive statements:

> [T]he past work can answer and "say something" to us only when the present observer has posed the question that draws it back out of its seclusion.[41]

Sixteenth-century Venice, we may say, was a good place from which to 'draw Job from his seclusion' (and at the same time cast new light on Christ). To recapitulate, the conditions that 'drew Job out' for Carpaccio included the fact that, at the cultural crossroads which Venice represented, he inherited a Byzantine tradition of depicting the body of Christ in preparation for burial, a European tradition of showing the body of the dead Christ being supported by mourners or angels, and a specifically Northern tradition of using Job as an antitype of the suffering Christ. He found himself in the European centre most receptive to Orthodox practice and ideas (including its attitude to the patriarchs and prophets of the Old Testament). He found himself in a place where an interest in the Hebrew language and thought could be indulged. He found himself in a place and time where mortality was an acute concern, and plague and death a daily threat. And, perhaps most important of all, for without this the other influences would have meant a good deal less, he found himself in a place and time which invited one to think the impossible. 'Carpaccio', so one commentator puts it, 'had to give shape and image to ideas that he had never had before . . .; he had to let his imagination bloom . . .'.[42] His historical circumstances, as I have been arguing, gave impetus to that process.

But to do this was to do something that had analogies with what the early Christian exegetes themselves did with Job. We have met some of the most significant of them already: Gregory of Nazianzus, Jerome and Gregory the Great. They too found themselves in circumstances that drew Job from his seclusion – even though in very different circumstances from Carpaccio's. Job seems to have

---

[41]Jauss 1982, 32.
[42]Sgarbi 1994, 50–2.

been of more than average interest to commentators in these early
centuries of the Church's life. So what were the questions *they*
brought to the text that the text seemed to promise an answer to?
And to what extent did their bringing of these questions unlock
the book's potential in their own situation (and make it available
for, and influential on, their Christian successors), opening up its
implicit 'horizons' even more fully than the book's anonymous
human author(s) may ever have imagined possible?

Perhaps they came to it because it appeared to have a horizon
open to the idea of redemption, but redemption in very peculiarly
progressive or unsettling terms. The Book of Job's ideas of
redemption are explored in relation to the idea of an alien God who
causes Job to suffer, while preserving his integrity: a God beyond the
Law. It is a book about the face-to-face (or as Barth would put it, the
'mouth-to-ear'[43]) encounter of Job and God when the framework
of the Law has fallen away. With the Law having dropped away,
Job's integrity comes to mean the radically contracted but non-
relativizable status he has merely by virtue of being a creature, and
God's 'godness' in the book stands as a radically non-negotiable
reminder that human beings are to act not because the Law says
so but simply *for God's sake*. These two 'integrities' – God's and
Job's – emerge into sharp view in relation to each other.[44] And
this makes the book readable as a book about grace, in Christian
terms; a book that speaks of 'being beyond the Law' in a way that
resonates with Jesus's fate as he hangs on the tree; a book that may
equip one to accept God in other 'alien forms' again than the alien
form in which Job met him (in the form of a dead human being, for
example); and a book that speaks of the indissolubility of a man's
integrity as witnessed in the resurrection. In these ways, an early
Christian context of reading may have supplied very specific points
of entry into the Book of Job.

That is to look back from Carpaccio's day. But what about our
own day and our own context? Are we in a place where Job can be
well-appropriated anew? And will Carpaccio as well as his sources
be our useful companions in doing this?

---

[43]Barth 1961, 458.
[44]These ways of characterizing the Book of Job are worked out at length in Susannah
Ticciati, *Job and the Disruption of Identity: Reading Beyond Barth*. Ticciati 2005.

In my experience, Carpaccio's Berlin image readily finds new audiences today (when I speak about it to students, for example, it awakens sharp interest and often strong identification). One definite aspect of the picture's appeal for modern viewers can be its apparent surreality. It intrigues rather as the paintings of Hieronymous Bosch seem to do. There is in the work an apparent freedom of association, a certain experimentation with strange and surprising and thought-provoking conjunctions, which is also the mark of a great many twentieth- and twenty-first-century works of art (not only painted ones). In a closely related set of responses, the painting engages interest because it feels a bit like a puzzle, and this bequeaths to us viewers a substantially constructive interpretative role – one which we are accustomed to being given in a modern context. Today, artists do not generally want to predetermine the responses of their audiences, or be thought to be telling them what to think or feel. So, the non-didacticism of the painting works for us.

This may have parallels in the way that we presently tend to appropriate the Book of Job itself. We are able to feel its landscape as our landscape, its interrogative mode as suited to us. It may be found to reveal to us *a God open to question*. It can seem to show us an agnostic moment, in some way. We can identify with a Job who is faced with suffering and death; a Job who asks questions of them, and of the universe in which they are met. We can identify with the Book's depiction of death in the midst of life, and with Job's radical uncertainty about how he stands in relation to God.

In such respects, we may be able to return appreciatively to some of Julia Kristeva's proposals, as discussed in the last chapter. For although she may have been too quick to deny that Holbein's dead Christ had an evangelical message for his contemporaries (pious patrons aside), she may be entirely right that a modern reception of it will relate to it differently – and if to that picture, then potentially to Carpaccio's image too. Indeed, Kristeva's very essay may be taken as evidence of just what a claim such images of the dead Christ seem to have on a modern Western imagination. We can relate to the death and grief Carpaccio shows us. The painting does not offer trite comforts. It shows the nobility that may be conferred upon all those who honestly, and without evasion, 'look

death in the face': an unprecedentedly modern challenge in a world
unprecedentedly without God (or 'a beyond'):

> [P]erhaps . . . because he faces his mental risks, the risks of
> psychic death – man achieves a new dimension. Not necessarily
> that of atheism but definitely that of a disillusioned, serene, and
> dignified stance.[45]

'Not necessarily that of atheism'. The special insights that a
modern set of conditions may bring to the Book of Job (as to
its tradition of interpretation in Carpaccio and others) may be
'additive' to it in the key respect that they allow the book to speak
religiously to disillusion, and affirm the dignity and value (and
not necessarily irreligiosity) of what lies beyond such stripping
away of illusions. This is not, of course, to deny that an attentive
recovery, and a sympathetic reinhabiting, of some of the Christian
concerns that may have made Carpaccio's painting eloquent in
its own day would be a waste of effort on the part of modern
viewers of it.

Our explorations backwards and forwards from Carpaccio's
painting have been necessarily, and perhaps irresponsibly, brief, and
they do not have time to tackle how the differences between these
very different retrievals of Job in very different epochs may also
merit the status of a *tradition*. What they do illustrate is the Book of
Job's fecundity across many centuries. It would be risky to say that
the questions with which early Christian commentators unlocked
it and the preoccupations with which twenty-first-century seekers
approach it are in either case straightforwardly wrong. Instead,
these forays suggest the text's repeated capacity – echoing Williams
again – to 'speak of more than the circumstances which produced it',
and this seems amply to justify its preservation by Jews, Christians
and Western cultural critics alike.

If we are to see such receptions as more than eisegesis, and to
take a further step beyond Jauss by affirming (though with critical
vigilance) that the Holy Spirit sustains traditions of reading that
foster such receptions, then we may suggest that Christian receptions
of biblical texts and received doctrines can be a sort of 'revelation in

---

process'. This would be to concur with Dale Allison in his *Studies in Matthew*:[46]

> If texts cannot be divorced from the traditions that birthed them or from the traditions they in turn begat, and if new readers inevitably make for new readings, and if multiple meanings need not always be contradictory meanings, then it makes little sense to confine revelation to the words on a biblical page. Exegetical history in its entirety rather confronts us with an ongoing, evolving divine disclosure.[47]

It is a point that is countenanced, even if a little more cautiously, by Robert Morgan in a recent paper:

> Both literary classics and authoritative legal texts, to say nothing of a religion's scriptures, invite expansion of meaning, not merely new significance. Historical exegesis is a necessary control against arbitrary interpretations but what counts as arbitrary depends on contexts and reading communities' consent, as well as on linguistic conventions. It is agreement within the church as a reading community, not authorial intention, which demands and justifies the demand for readings of scripture which speak of God.[48]

If, for good theological reasons, one holds that the 'reading community' which is the Church, is constituted, shaped and sustained by the Holy Spirit, then this is, in fact, to say something quite strong about the 'expansions of meaning' that may happen as it reads. As we have had cause to note in the previous chapter, there is a powerful patristic legacy of arguments for a Spirit-led exegesis of Scripture – in the 'reading community' of the Church – which does not so much accept as *insist* that old texts will release

---

[46]Allison Jr. 2005.

[47]Ibid., 63.

[48]I quote a paper entitled 'Letter and Spirit: Four Types of Modern Biblical Interpretation' delivered in the University of Bonn in September 2007. A later version of the paper – though without this exact passage included – has now been published: see Morgan 2013, 47–73.

new meanings when circumstances are opportune. Thus, Gregory of Nazianzus (330–89/90) writes:

> [We cannot accept] that the slightest actions were treated for mere vanity by those who wrote them down and committed them to memory even up till the present, but [they were preserved] in order that we might have reminders and lessons from the examination of similar things, *if ever the right time came* [my emphasis], so as to flee certain things or choose others, following like norms (*kanosi*) or models (*tupois*) the patterns (*paradeigma*) set before us.[49]

This is a very patristic warrant for a theological use of reception theory. As Ben Fulford has suggested, it asserts that the narrative meanings of scriptural texts already intend lessons for the later reader, although the reader must supply imagination to make the analogy.[50] In the terms of Gregory's account, the 'coming of the right time' will certainly not be a matter of sheer arbitrary occurrence. It will be a result of the activity of God the Spirit who sustains the *reading context* as much as that same Spirit provides the *reading matter*.

Admittedly, the patristic sense of two-way causality, and the simultaneity of two distant points in history, is something not all modern Christian commentators will find it easy to share. It is impossible to be certain just how fully *Carpaccio* really shared it when he put Job and Christ in the same pictorial space, though it makes for a remarkable painting. And as we have seen, the explorations of literary reception stemming from the Konstanz school have certainly stopped short of theological claims like that.

---

[49]Or. 2.105, 5–9. See Gregory Nazianzen, 1995, 225. The translation here is Ben Fulford's, in an unpublished paper called 'Gregory Nazianzen's Sacramental Hermeneutics', delivered at the Cambridge Divinity Faculty's Systematic Theology seminar in October 2005, p. 10. There is a similar translation (again, Fulford's) on p. 39 of Fulford's thesis ('Biblical Interpretation in Gregory of Nazianzus and Hans Frei', University of Cambridge, 2007).

[50]See Fulford 2013, 139–40: 'Gregory thinks of biblical narratives as intended, in their story form, to offer lessons for us in analogous circumstances . . . [we] appropriating the stories by reasoning analogically between their terms and our own circumstances . . . reading symbolically where necessary.'

But they *have*, nonetheless, been happy to speak of our common historicity, and our common worldedness (to recall the word I used earlier) as a ground for bringing the questions of different historical epochs into proximity, and for not being disabled by Lessing. John David Dawson articulates what may be a workable modern adaptation of the patristic legacy that is less alien to the terms of reception theory, and so more digestible by modern Christian readers:

> By making former things gospel, the gospel as the Word's arrival does not supply new content but unveils a "gospelness" already present in those former things; former things and events become more of what they already were, although in such a way that this becoming more themselves depended on the occurrence of the later event.[51]

It is not wild fancy to expect to find our questions following – sometimes quite closely – the contours of questions asked long before us. We can learn from them even if we disagree with their priorities or the answers they once received. We can even affirm the sort of ontology that says that texts (and works of art) have real potential to do more and give more when catalysed by things that happened hundreds of years later, because they were made in the same world, by people who lived in the same world, as the world where the new questions or problems arise that 'draw them out of their seclusion'.

Moreover, even if they are just as nervous of affirming strange causalities as any reception theorist might be, modern Christians will have special reasons to draw on a strong version of reception theory's claims in their interpretative endeavours, and will have good grounds for bringing *some* theological language into their uses of it (language that will often, so I have argued, be pneumatological language). This is quite simply because of the foundational importance for them of the event of God in Christ, and its effects on their reading of the inherited texts of the Bible. For, to use Origen's words, after Christ's coming 'the gospel, which is a New Testament, made the newness of the Spirit which never grows old shine forth' in places where it was not evident before. This newness of the

---

[51]Dawson 2002, 134.

Spirit, writes Origen, 'is proper to the New Testament, although it is stored up in all the Scriptures'. So echoing Paul's language, Origen contends that the Gospel did not replace the Old Testament, but instead (by the Holy Spirit) further illuminated it, revealing unexpected 'newness' within it.[52]

In short, the story of Christianity's very origins is a permanent reminder of what it is for former things and events to become more than what they were in the light of a later event. To recall Dawson's words again, 'the Word's arrival does not supply new content but unveils a "gospelness" already present in . . . former things'. It '[makes] former things gospel'. And it is this that can make sense of placing Job, with later Christians, at the eucharistic table which is the foretaste of the heavenly banquet.

In the final sections of this chapter, I wish to return, at somewhat greater length than the earlier passing references have permitted, to the thought of R. G. Collingwood. This will enable us to harness for the present project Collingwood's unusually comprehensive philosophical meditations on history and historical knowing (which Jauss's more particular concern with literary history has left relatively undeveloped). It will also return some of the themes of this chapter to a specifically British intellectual milieu, in continuity with the Coleridgean tradition, which will, in due course, help to frame the conclusion of this book as a whole. That said, Collingwood's position neither contradicts nor conflicts with the arguments of Jauss (or of Gadamer, on whom he draws). Indeed, Collingwood is a British counterpart – and forerunner – of Gadamer (and therefore of Jauss) in many of his central concerns.

A Collingwoodian coda

For the purposes of my argument, the principal attractiveness of Jauss's Gadamerian approach to reception has been the way it prompts a revision of how we recognize and relate to the intrinsic historicality of all of our interpretative processes *per se*. Jauss unearths the way that such intrinsically historical interpretative processes can specifically constitute a literary history. In doing so,

---

[52]Ibid.; quoting Origen's *Commentary on the Gospel of John* 1.36. See Origen 1989.

he generates valuable resources for thinking theologically about how canonical Scripture develops, how Scripture is interpreted in doctrine and in the wider cultural settings with which doctrine finds itself conversing, and how works of artistic production can themselves embody developing theological interpretations over time. But what a final turn to Collingwood permits us to do is to move from a concern with how histories of interpretation work, to a consideration of how the interpretation of history works. To what cautions might it need to stay alert, and what disciplines of modesty and circumspection would it do well to observe? Some of these virtues of an historical consciousness will be learnable in the school of reception theory, but their value extends much further.

History, we might say, following Collingwood, is only history when past events can be related to by thought, in understanding. There are some periods which are inaccessible to us in this mode – perhaps through a lack of surviving evidence that will help us relate sympathetically to them, or perhaps because of some alienness in the questions they asked and the answers they conjectured as compared with our own questions. In such cases, we cannot really claim to have a *history* of such periods.

When we *can* and *do* relate with sympathetic understanding to earlier times (and texts) – in other words, when it does seem possible to think of history as a *medium* – then we might well ask what frames the relation. It has seemed that for Jauss it is our common worldedness. On this account, we do not relate to earlier times by meeting our forebears in some sort of essentialized, pure, archetypal set of experiences (this would be an ahistorical move). It means that we remain irreducibly historical, and historically located, but have it in common with our forebears that we live in and negotiate a world of which there is only one, however diversely it may be interpreted. Jauss was in this sense a realist: believing that texts participate in a world that is not mind-dependent, and that our minds are in important ways world-dependent (to reiterate: 'works are variously permeable of events in historical *reality*, according to their genre or to the form pertaining to their period'[53]; my emphasis).

Collingwood is aware of how uninteresting and uninformative most data from the past are. Notwithstanding the rise since

---

[53]Jauss 1982, 12.

Collingwood's time of a historiography that is far more consciously
'from below', and in which aspects of the material culture and
everyday experience of ordinary people are used to critique the
idea that history is only about the deeds of 'great men', the fact is
that the sheer bulk of mundane experience has to be made eloquent
in relation to a project of interpretative historical insight before
it will be felt to be valuable. The innumerable acts of eating and
sleeping that populate the pasts of ordinary human beings will
often be unedifying in this regard. They may have a definite locus
in time and space, but they are not by that token *history*. No one
is sufficiently interested in them to remember or record them. They
have not acquired the interest and meaning that will make of them
an event in *thought* as well as in *fact*.

It is not only these repeated 'natural' acts that may find
themselves outside the parameters of the historian's normal field
of interest, but also data that seem peculiar or alien to her or
his present-day experience. These are slightly different in kind,
because they may well have had interest and meaning in their time.
They may once have been 'events in thought', but the thought
with which they were invested cannot be shared in, or judged in its
significance, from a later standpoint. This incomprehension may
not be a permanent state of affairs, but nevertheless may hold for
a span. For as long as they lie uncomprehended, these data too
become dead letters.

It may very well be, of course, that the failure to find these data
illuminating is simply a failure of imaginative sympathy on the part
of the historian. The devils once reputed to be in the mountains and
capable of hindering a man's passage from one side to the other
may seem to an historian of today like the figments of ridiculous
superstition, dealt easily with by 'the facts',[54] but 'the facts' of
history include facts of belief as well as facts of empirical evidence
(which in any case – as past facts – are no longer directly available
for testing), with the result that the devils – as 'events in thought' –
will have a right to refuse to be laid to rest. And if their clamour will
not for now be heard, and if for the time being they find themselves
dismissed from consideration by the historian, then this will more

---

[54]The image is Collingwood's – see Collingwood 2005, 317.

than likely be a loss to the present rather than a gain.[55] It will be a sign that the interpreters of the present have not been up to seeing their real meaning for those who once feared them. Their 'positive function in human history' as things with '[their] own proper value in [their] own proper place . . . coming into existence in order to serve the needs of the men who have corporately created [them]'[56] will go undetected. Collingwood sees analogies here with the way in which a certain sort of history labels some eras as 'good periods, or ages of historical greatness', and others as 'bad periods, ages of historical failure or poverty':

> [t]he so-called good periods are the ones into whose spirit the historian has penetrated, owing either to the existence of abundant evidence or to his own capacity for re-living the experience they enjoyed; the so-called bad periods are either those for which evidence is relatively scanty, or those whose life he cannot, for reasons arising out of his own experience and that of his age, reconstruct within himself.[57]

The pattern of light and dark in these cases is, in fact, an 'optical illusion'. It is not sound knowledge.

Nevertheless, regret it or not, it remains the case that there is much data from the past which cannot readily be treated as history by any single thinker or in any single era. Both the inconsequential natural acts of most people's daily existence, and old patterns of thought that resist contemporary appropriation, can alike end up as dead letters. And this is really just to make the point that the accumulation of data is not what history (as a mode of knowledge) is all about. Data will contain both living and dead material. Its exhaustive accumulation might appeal to what Collingwood

---

[55]He quotes sympathetically in this regard the challenge thrown out by Croce: 'Do you wish to understand the true history of a neolithic Ligurian or Sicilian? Try, if you can, to become a neolithic Ligurian or Sicilian in your mind. If you cannot do that, or do not care to, content yourself with describing and arranging in series the skulls, implements and drawings which have been found belonging to these neolithic peoples' (Croce 1921, 134–5; cited in Collingwood 2005, 199).
[56]Collingwood 2005, 77.
[57]Ibid., 327.

disparagingly calls the 'scissors-and-paste' historian, but, as Hercule Poirot would have pointed out, this sort of 'human bloodhound' is not capable of seeing beyond mere occurrence to actual meaning; he will not use his 'little grey cells'.[58] Collingwood's riposte to the bloodhounds is that '[t]he historical past, unlike the natural past, is a living past, kept alive by the act of historical thinking itself'. History, for Collingwood, has to do with 'the life of mind', and where no interpretative judgements are being made about the facts or data of past times that are based on the sympathy, interest and at least partial understanding of present thinkers, then those facts and that data are 'dry bones, signifying nothing'.[59] The Jaussian parallels here need little highlighting: Collingwood's 'historical thinking' in whose activity we see the 'livingness' of the past, is in its own way an activity of *reception*, by which an event (just as, in Jauss's narrower focus, a work) remains alive and capable of 'speech' in new situations.

There can be no doubt that this makes historical knowledge a frustrating form of knowledge. It does not readily yield anything that might justify the name of universal meaning. The New Testament scholar C. H. Dodd noted in 1938:

It is probably this uncertainty about the meaning and value of history that encourages the religious mind to turn either to mysticism and the inner life, or alternatively to nature as the field of a recognizable and definable order, which empirical history fails to show.[60]

Prompted by this, we may now ask the question that is at the heart of this final section: what is theology's proper relationship to historical knowledge? Can it identify certain modes of historical description as exemplary – exemplary either in the terms provided

---

[58]The human bloodhound 'crawls about the floor trying to collect everything, no matter what, which might conceivably turn out to be a clue'. Collingwood, standing shoulder to shoulder with Poirot on this one, states robustly that '[y]ou can't collect your evidence before you begin thinking' (Collingwood 2005, 281).
[59]Collingwood 2005, 305. He commends the Romantics in this connection for the fact that they are *so* sympathetic to the past of Greco-Roman antiquity; for the fact that they recognize it as *their* past (Collingwood 2005, 88).
[60]Dodd 1938, 167.

by history itself as a discipline with its own rationales and sets of practices, or in terms that theology brings to bear on history? Can history be expected to yield to theology helpful evidence in the justification of the ways (or presence) of God to humanity? Will theology allow itself to be held accountable to history's most disciplined descriptions, however tempted it might be to take shortcuts through the dense material of history in favour of showing quickly how the parts relate to that whole which is supposedly discerned by the believing eye?

My answer here builds on the pivotal admission that there is no God's eye view of historical process available to us. We are not capable of assembling all the relevant facts beneath our gaze and reading off from them a pattern of activity that is straightforwardly disclosive of God's purpose. Dodd puts it as succinctly as any when he remarks:

> The truth of God [cannot] be discovered by treating history as a uniform field of observation (like the "nature" studied by the sciences), in which it is possible to collect *data* from all parts of the field, and to arrive by induction at a conclusion.[61]

What it does allow for is what (following Dodd) I would want to call the recognition of an 'intensity of significance' in certain key points in history – a recognition that will need to be rehearsed and reappropriated from each new historical vantage point, but that can have a remarkable durability nonetheless. This stands in contrast to the God's eye view that supposes it can command all the facts. It accepts that it must try to feel and judge the significance of historical events from *within* the course of history. There are, once again, significant parallels here with Jauss's insistence that great works will assert themselves in their own and subsequent contexts as worthy of special attention only because of the illumination they (continue to) shed on (successive) situations, taking their place in canons and forming traditions of interpretation.

A commitment to seeking the legibility of the divine within history (not by trying to get outside or above it) can have genuinely theological warrants. Dodd is himself an advocate of the need to

---

[61]Ibid., 24.

search for something like a divine 'instress' in the events of history.[62]
He writes:

> It should be clear . . . that when we speak of history as the field
> of the self-revealing activity of God, we are thinking not of
> bare occurrences, but of the rich concreteness of events. Fur-
> ther, since events in the full sense of the term are relative to
> the feelings and judgments of the human mind, the intensity
> of their significance varies, just as in the individual life certain
> crucial experiences have a more than everyday significance. We
> can therefore understand that an historical religion attaches
> itself not to the whole temporal series indifferently . . . but to a
> particular series of events in which a unique intensity of signifi-
> cance resides. This selection of a particular series is not incon-
> gruous with the nature of history itself. The particular, even the
> unique, is a category entirely appropriate to the understanding
> of history . . .[63]

To find an example of how such 'intensity of significance'
might be discerned in salvation history, we may revert to the
covenant of the pieces in Genesis 15 (first examined in Chapter 3
in its connection with the Exodus narrative). One thing that
was immediately apparent in our examination of that narrative
sequence was that it did not give a God's eye view of things. It was
full of strangeness; crammed with allusions, hints and tensions.
Yet, as we began to see, both Jewish and Christian interpreters are
in a position to bring that episode (and thereby bring themselves)
into a dynamic interrelation with other 'event-series' narrated in
other texts of Scripture. They can bring it into a certain sort of
company. In this respect, their interpretation of Genesis 15 may
offer an analogy for the sort of reading of history from *within* that
Collingwood, Dodd, Gadamer and Jauss (in their different ways)
insist upon.

The encounter which issues in the covenant of the pieces is an
intensive encounter – one in which, to echo Dodd's words again,
an 'intensity of significance resides'. To look to such a concentrated

---

[62]This is a term used by Gerard Manley Hopkins. See my longer discussion of
Hopkins in Quash 2005, 198–206.
[63]Dodd 1938, 29.

event for evidence of the divine purpose, rather than seeking to infer a providential pattern from 'the whole temporal series' is, I think, what the biblical material commends consistently. Those who discern such intensities of significance are not 'seeing more' than others in the sense that they are in possession of more data than anyone else. The process of unfolding occurrences of which they are a part (which is often then handled by the form of knowledge we call history) is empirically the same for them as it is for anyone else; it is the same for believer and non-believer alike. And likewise, as I have been arguing here, they are not 'seeing more' than others because God has given them a means to step out of history and look at it from a sort of divine viewing platform. The *seeing more* that goes on when history becomes revelatory is more like the opening out of a greater depth *in* (but not *in addition to*) the occurrences themselves.

As I suggested in Chapter 3, the Genesis 15 covenant seems to invite a set of connections with other moments (or sequences of events) in the combined biblical witness. This is because, in a discernment informed by faith *and also* by experience, exegesis and liturgical practice, 'one deep calls to another', so to speak. This moment seeks out the company of moments that have a comparable intensity of signification. To make such connections is not to claim to have a fully worked-out salvation history to which all historical particulars can be assimilated; it is to claim that the revelatory significance of one intensive encounter with divine causality may have continuities with others.[64] These others may recapitulate earlier ones in the way they use the past to make sense of the present (this is in one sense, following Collingwood, what *all* history does). Meanwhile, in some cases, later event-series will be used to *reinterpret* earlier ones, such that past events will take on a new life in the mind of the interpreter, having perhaps lain neglected or uncomprehended. 'It is a familiar fact', writes Collingwood, 'that every generation finds itself interested in, and

---

[64]We may here anticipate David H. Kelsey's thought, which we will engage with in more detail in Chapter 8. He makes the point in the context of a trinitarian theological account of God's purposes in history that Christians may affirm but *only with great care* that history is meaningfully legible: 'affirmation of the triune God's eschatological blessing . . . allows a positive answer to questions about the meaning of history, but only a highly qualified positive answer' (Kelsey 2009, 478–9).

therefore able to study historically, tracts and aspects of the past' which to its predecessors were uninformative and 'dry'.[65]

In light of Jauss's theory of reception, this means asking not so much how Abraham's encounter in Genesis points *forward* to Moses, but instead what made the story of the covenant of the pieces live in the ongoing historical thinking of those who looked *back* from the Exodus, or from the promised land, or (indeed) from beyond even that – perhaps from the time of Ezra, or Jesus Christ. What was discerned in the depth dimensions of this piece of 'intensively significant' narrative that made it important in later times? What constituted it as a narrative to be rehearsed and reappropriated from out of the experience of the Exodus, from out of the experience of exile, and beyond?[66] What kept it current (or prevented it from going into 'seclusion')?

Perhaps one of the central answers to this question, when we look back at it with what, in Chapter 3, I called Exodus lenses, but also when we simply read the words of this chapter of Genesis with attention, is that it is a covenant without conditions. There are *none*. God does not say he will keep his promise if Abram does something in return; there is simply no 'if'. God promises a salvation he *will* deliver, and establishes a covenant he *will not* forget even with all the passing of the generations. Whatever the 'more' is that is seen in this particular event-series by its chains of interpreters, this perception is crucial to it, and for its interpreters it makes the event-series worth focusing on as they seek to discern God in history. It gains further significance over time, as it is tested by apparent counter-evidence but also reaffirmed in new moments of discernment (we may note Paul in Galatians referring to the fact that this covenant with Abraham is not annulled [Gal. 3.15, 17]).

Scholars of covenant ritual and all the arcane piety of ancient sacrifice have looked at this passage and have seen things they recognize. The cutting up of the menagerie of animals – heifer, goat and ram – is a ritual with pagan parallels. But there is something different here, something which shows that it is not just Abram

---

[65]Collingwood 2005, 305.

[66]It goes without saying that this looking *back* and identifying the significance of the episode may precisely reconstitute it as something that pointed (or, in the experience of a reader now, points) *forward*, so the two emphases cannot straightforwardly be contrasted.

being transformed, but the idea of covenant itself – and with it, the picture of the God who makes himself known in covenant. For the old purpose of this cutting up of animals into pieces was probably that it signified what would befall the one who broke the terms of the covenant.[67] The covenant made was, in other words, *highly* conditional. But in this new version, extraordinarily, the one who appears in among the pieces – in the place of the transgressor, it could be argued[68] – is God himself, in the fire and in the smoke. More than anything else, *that* is what tells us that this covenant will not be reneged on. God uses this ritual form to suggest that any failure to keep the terms of this covenant will entail neither Abraham nor his offspring taking upon themselves the fate of the animals, but God himself.

Read like this, in a way that inescapably reads 'along the beam' of history and in the light of later traditions, but which nevertheless finds warrants in the text – it appears that God is not only leading his people down this covenant corridor in strength. God is doing something more. He is making his own self the guarantee of safe passage. He is undertaking to give whatever it will take to make it possible for his people to pass through, and in this a new insight into the covenant character of God is vouchsafed. It is in God's steadfast covenant love – the divine '*hesed*' – that a genuinely unconditional covenant is made possible. Such covenant love is what gives ultimate intelligibility to the dealings of God with his people. It is a central part of the depth of meaning of the history of God and humanity.

Collingwood is a master instructor in how the passage of time generates for human experience a highly fragmented body of historical material. He teaches us that, faced with such a complex and fragmented body of material, what is required is not a foolhardy belief that the mere aggregation of more and more facts will answer those difficulties. But nor, he advises, can an imposed and superficial smoothing over of evidence be the solution. What is needed is a deeper entry into the fragments of history, though

---

[67]See Weinfeld 1970, 184–203; cited in Lipton 1999, 203.
[68]Diana Lipton, in her highly suggestive treatment of the vision in Genesis 15 (on which I have drawn a good deal) draws attention to the fact that the verb form used of God's passing between the pieces (whose root meaning is 'cross') is the same as that used of covenant transgression (Lipton 1999, 203).

with a discerning eye ('flight to the heart of the Host', as Hopkins might say[69]) in order to find what divine fire there might be in their midst.

As was hinted at the conclusion of Chapter 3, this may point Christians to another great covenant moment in their history: the eucharistic rite. The Eucharist is the rite in which the 'new' covenant in Christ's body and blood is sealed. As in their engagement with Scripture, so too in the Eucharist there is much for the Christian faithful to do – for Christians are genuinely to be covenant partners with God even in his unconditional covenant. In the Eucharist, each time they celebrate it, Christians prepare to meet God's self-offering with their own, and they ask God to strengthen their vocation as people who abide – in him and for him; in him and for others. But that said, the covenant remains – really – unconditional, and that means that although Christians are meant to be partners in it, it does not matter if they fail – even if they fail again and again. God has gone into the breach for his people. In the sacrament of the Eucharist, Christians can read Genesis 15 and the covenant of the pieces not just with Exodus lenses, but with Gospel ones. And although the great span of history may remain riddled with crises and losses and uninterpretable data, there will nonetheless be grounds for uttering an 'Amen' in light of this chain of covenant insight.

This was the conclusion of the distinguished Christian historian, Herbert Butterfield, who (as Page Smith has pointed out) did a great deal to wrest back from liberal and progressive interpretations of history the sense of history's '*ambiguity, complexity, paradox, mystery, irony, ambivalence*',[70] and who furthermore insisted that '[i]t is essential not to have faith in human nature'.[71] For he also affirmed at the end of his book *Christianity and History* that the Christian historian can acknowledge 'a principle which both gives us a firm Rock and leaves us the maximum elasticity for our minds: the principle: Hold to Christ [though you are] for the rest . . . totally uncommitted'.[72]

---

[69]The phrase appears in 'The Wreck of the Deutschland', Part the First, stanza 3. See Hopkins 1994.

[70]Smith 1966, 80.

[71]Butterfield 1950, 47.

[72]Ibid., 146.

In their constant reception of the broken pieces of the eucharistic host, Christians see the broken body of the sacrificial Lamb – God who did not just say he *would* become like the divided animals for us if he *had* to, but who really *did*. And the pieces of this broken body open for subsequent Christian interpreters of history a new covenant corridor. The way of salvation opened by Christ's body and in Christ's body – and received repeatedly in countless contingent acts of liturgical *anamnesis* – is made sure for all eternity. This way of salvation is the path along which the Spirit moves as the flaming fire of God's holiness – leading his disciples forward as the children of promise, the children of faith, the children of Abraham who believed and it was reckoned to him as righteousness.

PART THREE

6

'Truly the Lord is in this place and I did not know it'

(GEN. 28.16)

Introduction

Chapters 4 and 5 addressed the way that receptions can work in tradition. Our key concerns in those chapters were with continuity and transmission through history. To be sure, we noted instances where past ideas or works were forgotten, and lay dormant for a time; reception theory showed itself more than capable of acknowledging interruption and the decay of memory. But overall, its concern (and ours in thinking with its help) was with the way that the past may be drawn again and again into meaningful dialogue with the present, and helped to say new things as a consequence.

Chapters 7 and 8 are about a more future-oriented form of imagination and reasoning. To use our now-familiar typology, they are about cases where 'givens' seem more inaccessible or more radically challenged by 'found things' than in those cases that best illustrate reception at work. They are about cases where there is more than mere interruption and decay; cases where there is disruption or even rupture, or a stimulus to a more dramatic leap of conjecture. In such cases, the givens seem less capable of generating help than in normal circumstances (though they may well need to be 'settled with' in some way). There is a heightened sense that new questions cannot be dealt with simply by producing old answers.

It is important not to overstate this contrast between the more retrospective mode in which reception theory works and the more prospective mode we will be exploring in the pages that follow. As we saw in the Carpaccio painting on which we focused, and as we suggested in relation to the Book of Job's continued interest for modern readers of it, a 'classic' work may find new receptions precisely because it speaks in some way to questions about the future: about death and/or hope. Likewise, many of the resources for 'imagining forwards'[1] will come from mining the past, even when the need for a radical renewal of vision is provoked by some unexpected urgency or opportunity – or even trauma – that throws the past into question. So, the emphasis of the next two chapters should in many respects be read as a complement to the emphasis of earlier ones, while at the same time recognizing what is a significant difference of emphasis: an emphasis on how discontinuities with the past, discovered in the present, have effects on our relation to the future – as compared with an emphasis on how new findings in the present have effects on our relation to the past. The latter emphasis we explored with special help from theories of reception; the former we will in due course explore with special help from theories of abduction.

In both cases, however, we remain within the territory marked out in Chapter 1; in both cases, we are discussing the business of how to make sense of things analogically. Whether looking backwards to see how our present may be understood and shaped better in light of past shapes and schemata (while at the same time respecting the unique and unprecedented aspects of our present – its special integrity), or whether by looking forwards and trying to negotiate the future by incorporating what we thought we knew and what we have now discovered into a new vision – as richly and comprehensively as we can – we are in every instance making analogical connections; we are connecting things that have similarities without assuming in them an absolute identicality. The discipline in both cases is not to seek to make found things conform to some prior format that they do not quite fit. Such an endeavour will always tend to betray our findings in some way, to resist history, and to manifest a doubt that God has anything to bestow by that history.

---

[1] A concept given body by Walter Brueggemann in *The Prophetic Imagination*. Brueggemann 1992.

As we did in relation to our discussions of maculation and reception, respectively, this section of the book will begin with a case study. In this instance, our case study will centre on the seventeenth-century poet Henry Vaughan (1621–95), although it will also make various critical comparisons with the earlier figure of George Herbert (1593–1633) and the marginally younger figure of Thomas Traherne (c.1637–74).[2] The case study here shares elements with the Carpaccio case study in Chapter 4 in that it is primarily concerned with a self-consciously artistic medium as a context for the development of theological insight and ideas. But it shares elements with the case study that examined the translation of the Bible into English in Chapter 2 inasmuch as it is about the need to stretch an inherited linguistic idiom to make it capable of expressing new truths it has not expressed before. As a poet, Vaughan (like Traherne and Herbert) has things in common with Carpaccio – though Carpaccio worked in paint. As an artist in language, Vaughan has things in common with the Bible translators – though those translators were not beginning with a blank page as poets do.

It should be more than apparent by this stage that I regard the forms of artistic creativity we have examined in this book's case studies as instructive for theological method. Of course, to expect to learn from them as a theologian requires a full acknowledgement of the dissimilarities as well as the similarities of genre and intention that mark out – say – a lyric poem exploring very private concerns, or a painting commissioned to reflect a patron's personal interests, from a theological discussion or statement intended as a communal orientation point for Christians at a particular point in history. However, artists frequently practise 'virtues' for the creative habitation of history from which theology can and should learn. Central to these is the ability to make the sorts of analogical connections we have just mentioned: to explore affinities between things through echoes and recapitulations across time, and likenesses across geographical distance, that do not immediately seek a taxonomy of them, or a hierarchy, or their subjection to some sort of prototype. Moreover, and this is a related point, artistic modes of expression, in their various obligations to use concrete imagery

---

[2]Traherne was writing in a part of the world very near to Vaughan's (the Welsh Marches, on the border between England and Wales).

or material in some form or another, often have a developed sense
of the claims of the particular on the human witness, over and
above the supposedly ideal or generic type. To recall a previous
chapter, they 'name cats'. And finally, artistic modes of production
often evoke alternative ways to respond to our place and time – in
thought and in feeling – to those that are arrived at by the processes
of logical inference we call deduction and induction (more on those
in the next chapter). They manifest a freedom and a facility to intuit
or imagine things, which is, arguably, less tied to the given and more
exploratory of the found than more formulaic and regimented
kinds of ratiocination. That this may not necessarily make them
un-rational is a point we will also explore in this pair of chapters.

To revert briefly to a set of ideas that was initially opened up in
Chapter 2, much great art, in whatever medium, situates us more
fully in that world of human ambiguity, openness and responsibility
about which modal auxiliaries help us to be eloquent. This is
especially true of the sort of art which Dorothy L. Sayers called 'the
poetry of search' rather than 'the poetry of statement'.[3] Art that is
merely indicative or imperative in its intentions does indeed exist,
and in some cases has contributions to make to human flourishing.
But art which draws us to ask questions, which awakens desire or
fear or hope or commitment in us, which prompts our sympathetic
imaginations to project different possible ways of living, speaking
and relating, is art working in line with the 'coulds', 'shoulds',
'mays' and 'wills' of our language-freighted existence. It thereby
reconstitutes us (and equips us) as the historical beings we really
are, disciplining us against our habitual instinct to suppose that we
live in a fixed element.

And so to Henry Vaughan, who could have no illusion whatever
that he lived in a fixed element: too much in his lifetime was in revolution. He lived at the latter end of what we might call the 'founding trauma' of modern English Christianity (of which the Henrician
Reformation was the most obvious early stage): the time of the
Commonwealth (including, for a span, Oliver Cromwell's Protec-
torate) and of the Puritan ascendancy. It was a period of religious
and political rupture in which the Elizabethan settlement was
thrown into radical question again, and numerous fixed landmarks

---

[3]Sayers 1963.

(including the idea of England as a monarchy) were removed. Like Thomas Traherne, he would have been equally aware of another set of revolutions underway too: those of a new sort of science which was changing the way the world was henceforth going to be seen, understood and – to use one of Traherne's favourite words – 'enjoyed'. What both of these men show us – not only despite but also because of the revolutions they responded to in their writings – is that disruptions can release unusual imaginative energy and awaken exceptional creative resources. 'Found things' – even traumas – can precisely *found* things, generating the bases for new settlements and new theological thought.

In what follows, I will begin by outlining some features of the disruption that Vaughan, in particular, underwent, and how this is registered in the darker and more agonized aspects of his poetry. It accounts for a good deal of the tone of his poetry taken as a whole – but not all of it, for Vaughan is often also celebrated as a poet of wonderment. In this respect, he can be aligned very naturally with Traherne even though Traherne's work is not nearly as dark. The apparent paradox is signally important, and I will take it as an invitation to look for a relation between the two dominant features of his work: the trauma and the wonder. Acknowledging the extent of the former can, I will suggest, help with an appreciation of the latter.

Henry Vaughan's founding trauma

And God heard the voice of the boy; and the angel of God called to Hagar from heaven, and said to her, "What troubles you, Hagar? Do not be afraid; for God has heard the voice of the boy where he is. Come, lift up the boy and hold him fast with your hand, for I will make a great nation of him". (Gen. 21.17-18)

This is the Genesis account of the child Ishmael's banishment by Abraham into the wilderness with his mother. He is deprived of his inheritance and of his place in the house of Abraham; but alone under one of the bushes, he is sustained in his isolation by the particular attentions of God.

Vaughan too was in a sense banished. The episcopally led Church of England – his mother church – was illegal at the time he wrote his major collection of poetry *Silex Scintillans*[4]; it had been 'sent into the wilderness' by the Puritans. Consequently, Vaughan was a man in retreat, writing in the remote surroundings of his Welsh home, and nurturing his faith in relative isolation, deprived of any corporate underpinning for it. Vaughan describes with pain the fragmentation he sees: the proliferation of sects, and their diverse claims to the truth. He expresses his sorrow vividly and accusingly in his poem *The British Church*, using the scriptural image of Christ's seamless garment:

> The soldiers here
> Cast in their lots again,
> That seamless coat
> The Jews touched not
> These dare divide, and stain.

> (*The British Church*, ll. 6–10)

This mood is common in his body of work as a whole; his poems are very frequently those of a man weeping on account of his isolation, fearful of his spiritually barren environment, and longing to be lifted up out of his situation. His poetry, in other words, consistently bears the marks of his enforced, Ishmael-like retreat.

Vaughan's association with Ishmael is an unusual one. Medieval exegetes regarded him as a type of the reprobate or heretic.[5] Vaughan, on the other hand, finds himself sympathizing with the situation of what Barbara Lewalski calls the 'weeping, thirst-wracked' condition of the boy.[6] Indeed, Vaughan adopts the stance of Ishmael's 'correlative type' – not so much regarding himself as the fulfilment of the Old Testament figure (his antitype) as instead recapitulating the experience of that figure. He continues to look for the water that brings life, rather than resting assured of his deliverance. He prays that on his way through the desert his bottle may be filled with the tears of his repentance (*The Timber*); he complains of God's coldness to his cries, whereas of old 'thou didst hear the weeping Lad!' (*Begging (II)*, l. 12); and in *The Seed growing Secretly*, he cries

---

[4]See H. Vaughan 1976.
[5]Barbara Lewalski notes this in her *Protestant Poetics and the Seventeenth-century Religious Lyric*. Lewalski 1979, 492, note 39.
[6]Lewalski 1979, 329.

out as a new Ishmael for the dew of grace from heaven: 'O fill his bottle! thy child weeps!' (l. 16). This is an alignment to which we will return, because it is in my view the key axis between the lament and the wonder that we find in Vaughan's poetry. The adoption of an Old Testament perspective, in which themes of unfulfilment and wandering can be explored, is by the same token the adoption of a perspective of expectation, to which themes of promise and discovery are just as appropriate.

Recapitulating the experience of Ishmael, Vaughan's feeling of separation from God takes the view (in the poem *The Retreat*) that life is a period of exile. Here, he casts himself in the form of a child, and looks back as though at the beginning of a journey '[w]hen yet I had not walk'd above/A mile or two from my first love' (l. 7–8), and imagines he 'could see a glimpse of his bright face'. As a man, the child must journey successfully through life before being able to return to that 'first love'. It may be a long journey. As described in the poem *Man*, 'ever restless and irregular' this now-grown child must 'run and ride' about the earth, like a shuttle that winds and quests through the looms of earthly existence:

> He knows he hath a home, but scarce knows where.
>
> (*Man*, l. 19)

We have seen a hint already of Vaughan's governing sense of his church's decline. In *Religion*, a closely related vision is conjured, and one in which a longing look over the shoulder also plays its part. Vaughan evokes with nostalgia the familiarity of heaven in the time of the patriarchs:

> I see in each shade that there grows
> An Angel talking with a man . . .
>
> (ll. 3–4)

He continues with a certain intensity:

> . . . is't so, as some green heads say
> That now all miracles must cease?
>
> (ll. 25–56)

Then he expands unexpectedly from octosyllabic lines into a full
iambic pentameter, concluding with the impassioned cry:

> Look down great Master of the feast. O shine
> And turn once more our water into wine!

(ll. 51–2)

The sentiments of this poem are not uncharacteristic of the whole
of *Silex Scintillans*. Vaughan's spiritual experience is continually
characterized by 'his painful awareness of the veils, clouds and
darkness which shroud mortal existence, and his longing to escape
to life and light through the recovery of the purer days of childhood
and of the patriarchal ages, through release of the soul in death, or
through the apocalyptic renewal of all flesh'.[7]
The Church for George Herbert had been less ambiguously the
place of fulfilment. Typological symbolism is absolutely central to
his poetic vision. This is true both within individual poems, and also
of the structure of *The Temple* as a whole, each section of which
corresponds symbolically to the New Covenant version of some
Old Covenant 'site'. The 'Church Porch' is the antitype of the Outer
Court; the 'Church' is the antitype of the Temple itself; and the
'Church Militant' is the antitype of the wandering Ark. There is an
overwhelming sense of a new order rounding out and completing
an old one. For Vaughan, the typological equation means very little;
his sense of the progressive decay and corruption of the Christian
religion is too great. His preoccupation with mists and darkness
suggests that he is not happy with the Pauline proclamation that
the veil of the Old Law has been replaced with the clear glass of
the Gospel (2 Cor. 3.13-18). Rather, he rests with Paul's other and
complicating assertion in 1 Cor. 13 that 'now we see through a
glass, darkly; but then face to face'.[8] This projects the burden of
fulfilment forward onto the Second Coming, rather than backward
onto the historical events of Christ's earthly life. Vaughan seems
to expect the great antitypical fulfilment of all promises and types
at the end of time or in the next world, and the historical person

---

[7]Ibid., 321.
[8]1 Cor. 13.12; I have used the King James Bible translation here, rather than the
NRSV, as it would have been Vaughan's text.

of Jesus figures less in his poems than the glorified visitor of, for example, *The Dawning*.

The implications of this stance are not to be underestimated, for they suggest a complexification of the 'given fact' of the incarnation, which sets Vaughan very definitely apart from other Protestant poets. In Lewalski's words, 'whereas Herbert found in Christ a man, a friend, a person to meet in a relationship', Vaughan did not.[9] Christ for him was someone more elusive, to whom he related more in hope than in accomplished intimacy; one to whom he looked to deliver a union with the divine that was not yet achieved.

The interplay of voices woven into Herbert's poetry shows what substance the incarnation has for him, and what substance it gives his poetry. The divine voice is presented directly as an interlocutor or commentator on many occasions – directing, aiding or rebuking the speaker – and often resolves the speaker's poetic problems:

As when th'heart says (sighing to be approved)
O, could I love! And stops: God writeth, Loved.[10]

(*A true Hymn*, ll. 19–20)

A substantial indication of Vaughan's unsuccess with the historical person of Christ, meanwhile, comes in *The Search*. I acknowledge here that, in many ways (and as I have written elsewhere), this poem is a celebration of Vaughan's local landscape as a 'Bible-landscape', in a way that makes it a precursor of some of the visions of Bunyan and Milton. The drama of pursuing God is as intense in the Usk Valley in Wales as it might have been in the Sinai desert. God is capable of 'heavening' any place – not just the established places of worship to which Vaughan now has restricted access.[11] And yet, there remains a sharp, poignant note of frustration in the poem. The entire first section is devoted to recounting disappointed attempts at visualizing Christ in the context of biblical sites and in situations gleaned from scriptural

---

[9]Lewalski 1979, 319.
[10]See Herbert 2004.
[11]See my discussions of this aspect of Vaughan's vision in Quash 2012, 68–71, and Quash 2013, 104–6.

accounts. These are attempts at making his presence reassuringly concrete. The speaker tells us he

> . . . enquired
> Amongst the doctors, and desired
> To see the Temple, but was shown
> A little dust, and for the town
> A heap of ashes.

He visits Bethlehem and Calvary; garden, wilderness and tomb, only to be prompted:

> Search well another world; who studies this
> Travels in clouds, seeks manna, where none is.[12]

> (*The Search*, 3: 95–6)

Simply, Vaughan does not straightforwardly engage with a person, or experience the direct encounters and developing relationship with God in Christ that are so important to Herbert. He is caught in what seems at times to be a state of chronic flux, consumed in anticipation of a relationship yet to come.

This in turn adds a profoundly complicating strain to Vaughan's encounter with the natural world, and here too we may discern the traumatic effects of his ecclesial deracination. Vaughan wants another way to be intimate with God in the absence of traditional rites and sacraments, but in his encounters with nature – as in his meditation on Scripture – this intimacy seems once again to elude him. He meets the 'skin, and shell of things' (*The Search*, l. 81), and while in other times such surfaces might have been purely delightful, in Vaughan's circumstances they are sometimes a source of grief: an obstacle.[13] Although he will not say they are evil in themselves, he sometimes wants them to drop away. Sometimes, the earth (and even his own body) feel like shackles to his desire to partake of God's glory, and this desire is such an impassioned one that the restraint of the shackles is all the more keenly felt. 'Oh that I were

---

[12]N.B., part of what this may be expressing is not so much the inaccessibility of Christ *per se* as the unavailability of 'Temple' and 'City'.
[13]'Skin', whose etymology links it with the verb 'shine' and the idea of appearance or manifestation, can also be called 'hide' and associated with concealment.

all soul!', he exclaims in *Cheerfulness*. In *Distraction*, he talks of himself as he sees humanity, 'that am crumbled dust', and his life on earth (in *Ascension-Hymn*) as 'mere glimmering and decays' in this 'world of thrall'. In *The Ass*, he bemoans:

> These bonds, this sad captivity,
> This leaden state, which men miscall
> Being and life . . .

> (*The Ass*, ll. 54–6)

The paradox of this situation, as Vaughan knows, is that the created order speaks of God's nearness, even if at the same time it appears to be the obstruction to any grasp of God. It is a view that has been recounted in theological tract as much as in art.[14] But Vaughan has none of the theologian's analytical coolness when depicting humanity's bounded condition; he is intensely frustrated:

> How do I study now and scan
> Thee, more than ere I studied man,
> And only see through a long night
> Thy edges and thy bordering light!
> O for thy centre and mid-day!

> (*Childhood*, ll. 39–43)

Many of the poems show the intensity of Vaughan's longing to be free of the world's fetters in terms of a wish to die. Obviously, his impulse towards consummation in God – union with God – is the motivating force behind this wish: a yearning to shake off mortality and gain celestial brightness ('One everlasting Sabbath' [*Day of Judgement*, l. 69]). Nevertheless, there is something distinctly unsettling about the emphasis Vaughan places on death's attractions, when compared, for example, with Herbert's more moderate desire

---

14   [T]here is no proportion at all, between that which is infinite, and that which is bounded and limited, and we can go no farther in comprehending that which is incomprehenable, than to know it to be incomprehenable. But God having made man, not to be comprehended of him, but yet to be known notwithstanding, and adored in the government of this world, hath given him a soul indeed with understanding, which may attain as it were to the borders and skirts of his Majesty, having for his object this goodly theatre of the world above and beneath. . . . (Beza 1587, 29)

for a submissive heart and a quiet faith. I believe this, too, can be read as an index of the trauma that marks his historical experience (and that will also feed his capacity for amazement and discovery, as we shall see shortly). In *The Mutiny*, we hear a typical echo of the weeping of Ishmael which refers cryptically to death:

> . . . I know thou hast a shorter cut
> To bring me home, than through a wilderness.
>
> (*The Mutiny*, ll. 29–30)

And it is quite usual for Vaughan to clothe his longing for death in the most heightened rhetoric, woven with images of light and lustre. We see this in *Cock-Crowing*:

> . . . make no delay
> But brush me with thy light, that I
> May shine unto a perfect day,
> And warm me at thy glorious Eye!
>
> (*Cock-Crowing*, ll. 43–6)

We also meet it in the apostrophe of *They are all gone into the world of light*:

> Dear, beauteous death! The jewel of the just,
> Shining nowhere, but in the dark;
> What mysteries do lie behind thy dust;
> Could man outlook that mark!
>
> (*They are all gone into the world of light*, ll. 17–20)

Here too we see an example of Vaughan's tendency to put faith less in the redemption already achieved by an historical Christ's passion than in the apocalyptic release yet to come.

To reiterate, then, Vaughan regularly feels that his created surroundings are (relatively) a wilderness. For Vaughan, they are a wilderness not only in comparison with a world forfeited, but also in comparison with a world to come, the promise of which only a divine intervention will fulfil. Vaughan questions and strains after a goal as yet unrealized, and certainly unattainable in his own strength. This above all is what accounts for the marked preference we have noted already for identifying himself with Old Testament figures (Jacob, Israel wandering in the desert, Isaac and especially and most unusually Ishmael), rather than patterning himself opposite them. This tendency shows Vaughan most at home in a posture of anticipation and expectation rather than of fulfilment.

But in this lies the seed of another, and far more affirmative, relationship with the natural order, as well as a more hopeful relationship with time. For the frustrations and pain of Ishmael and his fellows are also readable by Vaughan (at times, perhaps, when the trauma seems less intense) as stages on a journey, and invitations to read the gifts of creation not just as veils but also as tokens of favour and of promise (even as something like sacraments).

In making this turn, I do not intend to explain away the paradoxes and contradictions in the different statements that Vaughan makes: a body of poetry is not a system of thought, nor should it be measured as one. The laments and the groaning, when they occur, are, I think, authentic expressions of Vaughan's spiritual state at certain times. But they are not a complete picture. For to be in a posture of anticipation and expectation – even of painful longing – is at the very least not to have despaired utterly, and at best it is to be wide open to a future from which grace may come.

Wonderment, hope and creature meditation

Even if it is only in order to sustain him for as long as his journey through the wilderness demands, Vaughan recognizes that God gives him 'water' from the resources of his creation. That there is something still better beyond it remains an awareness with which (as we have seen) Vaughan is constantly in touch:

> As birds robbed of their native wood
> Although their diet may be fine,
> Yet neither sing, nor like their food,
> But with the thought of home do pine.
>
> (*The Pilgrimage*, ll. 17–20)

Creation only 'temper[s] the Light' (to borrow the words of Bernard of Clairvaux) 'to the weakness of the eye and prepare[s] the eye for

the Light itself',[15] and this certainly means that the Light is a greater
wonder than any lesser thing it may infuse – this is why Vaughan
cannot ever wholly overcome his impatient desire to peep beyond
the wonted forms into glory. And yet, creation is at the same time –
rightly – an object for wonderment, and when Vaughan is disposed
to wonder at it, he wonders beautifully.

In itself, Vaughan's readiness to read God in the Book of Nature
does not make him exceptional for his time. As Samuel Bethell
points out of the period, its 'intense intellectual curiosity' meant that
'expression of the plenitude of creation was particularly stressed'.[16]
Thomas Traherne – a close contemporary of Vaughan – is one of the
best exemplars of this curiosity and this sense of plenitude. He was
interested in *all things* ('things' being one of his favourite words[17]);
indeed, one of the headings in his *Commentaries of Heaven* is
actually – unabashedly – 'All Things'.[18] He embodies in his own
day a polymathic range of interest for which modern university
scholars are being encouraged (or goaded) to reach once again, as
'interdisciplinarity' is increasingly feted. Traherne's encyclopaedic
interests have a quality of insatiability (something like Gregory of
Nyssa's *epektasis*[19]) in which science, poetry, politics and religion are
all alike meet subjects about which (and in which) to praise God.
Even if one cannot be confident in one's power comprehensively to
understand – or even to know of – 'all things', one can nonetheless,
according to Traherne, at least say that there is *no single* 'thing'
unworthy of one's expectant attention. The lowliest creature – in

[15]See Bernard of Clairvaux 1937, 139.
[16]Bethell 1951, 42.
[17]See, for example, his poem *Ease*:

> Things fals are forcd, and most Elaborate,
> Things pure and true are Obvious unto Sence;
> The first Impressions, in our Earthly State,
> Are made by Things most Great in Excellence.

(Ease, ll. 5–8)

See Wade 1932, 37.
[18]See Traherne 2007, 407–14.
[19]The concept of *epektasis*, or perpetual progress, is explored in, for example,
Gregory's writings on Moses. See, Gregory of Nyssa 1978. For a concise description
of *epektasis* with a bibliography, see Mateo-Seco and Maspero 2010, 263–8. For a
more modern discussion of *epektasis* in Gregory of Nyssa, see, for example, Bentley
Hart 2003.

each of its accidents – can show itself to be *capax infiniti* in the way that the matter of the Eucharist is for a sacramentally minded Christian of the sort that Traherne (and, indeed, Vaughan) was.

Judged by the conventions of much literary endeavour, it will be no great surprise to find flowers, or fruit, celebrated in this way:

> Apples, Citrons, Limons, Dates, and Pomgranates,
> Figs, Raisins, Grapes, and Melons,
> Plumbs, Cherries, Filberts, Peaches,
> Are all thy riches; for which we praise and bless thy Name.[20]
>
>   *(Thanksgivings for the Glory of God's Works*, ll. 64–7)

But the insatiable Traherne is just as capable of delight in insects – and perhaps of even more sustained attention to them because of the greater surprise that they hold in store, being less a part of the poet's usual armoury:

> The creation of Insects affords us a Clear Mirror of Almighty Power, and Infinit Wisdom with a Prospect likewise of Transcendent Goodness. Had but one of those Curious and High Stomachd Flies, been Created, whose Burnisht, and Resplendent Bodies are like Orient Gold, or Polisht Steel; whose wings Are So Strong, and whose Head so Crownd with an Imperial Tuff, which we often see Enthroned upon a Leaf, having a pavement of living Emrauld beneath its feet, there contemplating all the world. That verie Flie being made alone the Spectator, and enjoyer of the Universe had been a little, but Sensible, King of Heaven and Earth. Had some Angel or Pure Intelligence, been Created to consider him, doubtless he would hav been amazed at the Height of his Estate . . . The Infinit Workmanship about his Body, the Marvellous Consistence of his Lims, the most neat and Exquisit Distinction of his Joynts, the Subtile, and Inperceptible Ducture of his Nerves . . . the stupendous union of his Soul and Body the Exact and Curious Symmetry of all his Parts . . . the vigor of his Resentments, his Passions, and Affections, his Inclinations, and Principles, the Imaginations of his Brain, and the Motions of his Heart, would make him seem a Treasurie wherein all Wonders

---

[20]From *Centuries, Poems and Thanksgivings*. See Traherne 1958, 245.

were shut up together, and that God had done as much in little there, as he had done at large in the whole World. Having a life far greater then his Body, he can feel a Remote object. He is able to exceed him self, and to be present there, where his Body is not. In spirit he is every where and filles the World with sense, and Power. The Universe hath a Temple in his Understanding: He is Surrounded with the Rayes of his Knowledg, as the Sun is with the Glory of its Resplendent Beams. All Visible and Material things find themselves alive in his Intelligence: His Ey is the Throne of Beauty . . .[21] (*The Kingdom of God*)

Theodore Beza wrote in 1587 that:

[M]an is not only bound to give God thanks for that which he hath received from him, in himself, but also for all the gifts which God hath bestowed upon all other creatures for man; which are as it were preachers of the glory of God unto men (Psalm 19) and if they had understanding and mouths would cry with a loud voice, both above and below, saying, "Ye men, for whom we are made, thank God for us, glorify him in us".[22]

This demonstrates how Vaughan is part of a tradition in feeling intensely the potential for creation to witness to a divine presence. The idea perhaps excited him with its promise of a rich variety of experience, communicating a God more immanent to him now than either the historical (but exalted) person of Christ or his collective Body the Church might have seemed capable of delivering to his senses. Certainly, Vaughan shows a particular awareness of the way in which other creatures are related to God, and respond to him by instinct according to natural laws. He joins in the long Christian tradition – maintained and respected, on the whole, by English Protestants – of 'creature meditation'.

But, as so often, Vaughan distinguishes himself by operating within this common tradition in an uncommon way. An Ishmael among Protestant poets, he likes to walk unconventional paths, and will frequently eschew the established paradigms and images advocated by Beza and others. Protestants had mocked 'Popish'

[21]See Traherne 2005, 422–3.
[22]Beza 1587, 34.

tales of St Francis preaching to birds, beasts and stones as though they had 'sense',[23] but Vaughan's really does seem to resemble a Franciscan sensibility in the intense feeling with which he suffuses his meditations on natural objects:

> My fellow creatures too say, Come!
> And stones, though speechless, are not dumb.
>
> *(The Day of Judgement*, l. 15)

Elsewhere, he urges an almost hermetic idea of the fellowship of all created things, a 'tie of bodies',[24] binding the created order to God, and allowing it to be sustained along invisible lines of influence. It intrigues and excites him:

> And do they so? Have they a sense
> Of aught but influence?
> Can they their heads lift, and expect,
> And groan too?
>
> *(And do they so?*, ll. 1–4)

Vaughan clearly envies the constancy of the creation around him, for he exclaims in the next stanza of the same poem:

> I would I were a stone or tree,
> Or flower by pedigree,
> Or some poor high-way herb or spring
> To flow, or bird to sing!
>
> (ll. 11–14)

He makes a familiar distinction between the human being – who although made in God's image and the recipient of grace is, nevertheless, the victim of a rebellious will – and the rest of creation, which although subject to the same natural and physical laws as man, is yet tied more strongly to God, because it is free from the interference of wilfulness. Although it is a familiar distinction,

---

[23]Beza, it may be noted, says '*if* they had sense' (my emphasis) when meditating on flowers (Beza 1587, 207).
[24]See H. Vaughan 1976, 185.

Vaughan feels the difference acutely, and longs to experience the immediacy of the creatures' apprehension of God.

Vaughan, in sum, makes himself very dependent on what the created order seems to promise. The tenor of his poetry implies a strong and genuinely felt attraction to created things. We have seen already the constraints and qualifications under which that response is compelled to operate, but it is fundamentally, a generous response. In the same vein as Donne's admission that:

My creation is a holy wonder, and a mysterious amazement[25]

Vaughan states that, for man:

> . . . all the vast expense
> In the creation shed, and slav'd to sense
> Makes up but lectures for his eye and ear.
>
> (*The Tempest*, ll. 18–20)

Indeed, the wonderment at nature, which has a pervasive influence on his poetry, cannot simply be contrasted with his fascination with the miraculous manifestations of God in former ages. It shares much with it. For it is to nature that Vaughan frequently (and not always frustratedly) looks in order to regain that sense, which he believes the patriarchs had, of a God gloriously manifest. His evocations of angels, it should be noted, are frequently set in groves or under trees.

The poem *Vanity of Spirit* shows wonderment poised with longing in precisely the relationship which informs the great part of Vaughan's poetry; it is the sort of poem to which his meditative and contemplative nature lends itself:

> I begged here long, and groaned to know
> Who gave the clouds so brave a bow,
> Who bent the spheres, and circled in
> Corruption with this glorious ring . . .
>
> (ll. 3–6)

There is tremendous intensity in Vaughan's 'groaning', which is symptomatic of his heightened sense of God in creation. But this

---

[25]Donne 1839, 193.

poem goes further to illustrate Vaughan's characteristics, for it is interesting to see how the inspiration (the wonderment) comes only after Vaughan has turned away from two things:

> Quite spent with thoughts I left my cell; and lay
> Where a shrill spring tuned to the early day

(ll. 1–2)

Clearly, he has first abandoned the 'cell' of indoors, in order to be exposed to the influence of God in nature. But he has also left aside 'thoughts' that have exhausted him. This is not to say that Vaughan's mind is not active. Rather, the thoughts he abandons are those of a more ratiocinative, a more analytical frame of mind. He was not an analyst in the way that Herbert or Donne were analysts. He did not frame careful arguments, neither did he take the same amount of time and effort generating metaphors and conceits as part of a more self-conscious process of 'manufacturing' wonder. Dennis Quinn states, with reference to Donne, that:

> The more we wonder at the newness of a thing, the more earnestly we observe it; and the more carefully we consider it the more fully we come to know it.[26]

This is true more generally: wonder is a means to an end for all these poets – a means of engaging readers with subjects using the lure of curiosity and admiration. But Vaughan shares a wonder he cannot help but feel, while Donne (in, for example, the novelly contrived imagery of *A Valediction: Forbidding Mourning*) is deliberately provoking it. Vaughan communicates the wonder with which he himself wonders; he does not engineer it for the benefit of others. Wonder for him is not the result of an intellectual exercise, and not a mechanism or tool. One feels he communicates a more virgin experience, respecting its integrity where possible, and disdaining to mould or manipulate it for argument or art's sake. Vaughan's poetry, and the fuel for that poetry, are the products of a response more credulous than rationalizing. Ultimately, he would prefer to

---

[26]Quinn 1969, 631.

respond with the 'shrill spring' of *Vanity of Spirit*, and, like it, 'tune to the early day', if only this were possible.

A common object for creature meditation was the flower. Beza claimed that among all the creatures 'there is none more admirable', and Herbert went further and applied this object of nature to himself as a symbol of his spiritual growth, showing how he received the same nurture and protection as the flower. In this way, like many other Christian writers, he illustrated the effects of divine grace.

Herbert, in other words, fingered a familiar descant on an acknowledged and traditional theme. But Vaughan's exercises in the same tradition have a significantly different timbre. We see this in the poem that begins:

> I walked the other day (to spend my hour)
>   Into a field
> Where I sometimes had seen the soil to yield
>   A gallant flower . . .
>
>   I digged about
> That place where I had seen him to grow out
>   And by and by
> I saw the warm recluse alone to lie
>   Where fresh and green
>   He lived of us unseen.
>
> Many a question intricate and rare
>   Did I there strow
> But all I could extort was, that he now
>   Did there repair
> Such losses as befell him in this air
>   And would ere long
> Come forth most fair and young.

(I walked the other day, ll. 1–4, 16–28)

The difference lies, characteristically, in the richly experiential texture of the poem's meditation. It has been made very personal; full of details. Vaughan contemplates what we feel to be an actual flower; he wonders at its powers of recovery; and he then, and only

then, finds in it something of himself and his own relation to God –
and consequently, also, the substance for his poem.

In such moments, Vaughan sees the immaterial shadowed forth by
the material – he senses the unseen in the seen when he exclaims in
wonder at nature, for there he sees signs of God; a divine semiosis:

> There's not a spring
> Or leaf but hath his morning hymn; each bush
> And oak doth know I AM.

(Rules and Lessons, ll. 14–16)

Vaughan's view of creation can only reinforce the argument that
he does not stick to conventional Protestant pathways when dealing
with the incarnation. He is something of a maverick in his approach,
rarely displaying an unquestioning confidence in benefits already won
by Christ. We might say that he instinctively – or even deliberately –
introduces a much more open and anticipatory concern with what
must still be searched out (and, he hopes, found) to complement what
some of his fellow Protestants claim to know already (as given). This
emphasis on the yet-to-be-searched-for complements that possessed
'knowledge' of Christ and of his benefits which is so central to some
of the strands of Protestant theology we explored in Chapter 2. But it
also, perhaps, offsets or counterbalances it. To put it another way, he
inclines to a more pneumatological sensibility which has effects on
his appropriations of Christology.

It needs to be admitted, of course, that the models of assurance
which Vaughan eschews are in their own way pneumatological: in
them, the Spirit functions to confirm the reliable truth of what is
felt and thought by the person of faith.[27] So it is not that Vaughan
is pneumatologically focused while mainstream Protestant tradition
turns its back on the Spirit. It is more that his pneumatology
gears itself around what we earlier called an 'additive' dynamic,
in which significant discovery still occurs for the Christian seeker,

---

[27]This can be seen in a classic Puritan text like John Owen's *Pneumatologia or, a
discourse concerning the Holy Spirit. Wherein an account is given of his name,
nature, personality, dispensation, operations, and effects.* The text was first published
in London in 1674 and is most easily available online (accessed 15 August 2013)
at http://www.ccel.org/ccel/owen/pneum.toc.html. A version abridged by George
Burder was published in London by Richard Baynes in 1835.

and the meaning of Christ continues to be amplified as successive historical moments unfurl. Pneumatology does not function as an epistemological rubber stamp for Vaughan, making received knowledge official and trustworthy; it helps him to articulate a living presence diffused though creation and active in 'making more' of what is given in Christ. The following words are from his poem *Resurrection and Immortality*:

> . . . a preserving spirit doth still pass
> Untainted through this mass.

> *(Resurrection and Immortality*, ll. 31–2)

They echo the writings of his twin brother Thomas at about the same time: '[f]or God breathes continually, and passeth through all things like an air that refresheth'.[28]

Elsewhere, in *The Night*, Vaughan compares his own encounter with Christ to that of Nicodemus. But one is struck by the fact that Nicodemus met and spoke with an earthly Jesus, while Vaughan, alone in the darkness, strives for 'commerce' with 'light' (Nicodemus's former experience being unrepeatable: 'what can never more be done'). Because of this, the Christ in the poem seems deliberately presented not so much as the concrete historical personage whom Nicodemus encountered, but rather more as the diffused presence of *Resurrection and Immortality* – an impression that is enhanced by images drawn from nature:

> So rare a flower,
> Within whose sacred leaves did lie
> The fullness of the Deity.

> *(The Night*, ll. 16–18)

Vaughan learns a form of 'looking beyond bodies' perhaps above all from the fact that he is forced to look for something *beyond the body* of the *Church*. In *The Night*, he seems to acknowledge the insufficiency of outward forms, ceremonies and ordinances. The ostensible reference is to the Ark of the Covenant, but knowing how often Vaughan identifies himself with the figures of the earlier

---

[28]T. Vaughan 1650, 56.

dispensation, it would be easy to extend its range of reference to include ecclesiastical structures too:

> No mercy-seat of gold,
> No dead and dusty Cherub, nor carved stone,
> But his own living works did my Lord hold
> And lodge alone.

(ll. 19–22)

The Lord must, and perhaps even *should*, be sought in 'living works', in the present activity of a God who is known in history.

This is not an easy path. Vaughan's pneumatological emphasis on the divine presence 'findable' in-and-through nature, for example, causes him many difficulties. The diversity and variety of the creatures that offer themselves to the one who seeks God make any response to nature a selectively interpretative one, and any pursuit of discernment in the 'found' things of the world potentially a 'narrow, private path' (*The Timber*). The God thus intuited is hard to pin down. For Vaughan, this God is always just behind, or beyond, or inside material creation, continually intimated but rarely felt at first hand. This accounts, surely, for much of his frustrated experience – feeling God as a secret to be unlocked, at once immanent and transcendent, but never fully yielded as either. 'What little light he has' is little enough to make him often feel, again like Ishmael, an outsider. Frank Kermode's words, used to describe the 'radiant obscurity of narratives',[29] serve equally well to describe what, for Vaughan, is the 'radiant obscurity' of creation, and the frustration of trying to apprehend God's presence. Nature, like a text for Kermode, has 'latent mysteries, intermittent radiances'[30] (or, in Vaughan's words, 'traces and sounds of a strange kind' [*Vanity of Spirit*, l. 16]); it seems to engage in 'simultaneous proclamation and concealment'.

Nevertheless, Vaughan is undeterred. Louis Martz compares his approach to creature meditation – his evocation of intuitions of the divine through the ladder of created things – to that in Bonaventure's *Itinerarium Mentis in Deum*,[31] and as we have observed, Vaughan

---

[29]Kermode 1979, 47.
[30]Ibid., 122.
[31]Martz 1954, 150–2.

attributes sense to non-human nature in a way that other Protestant critics would have scorned. With astounding virtuosity, he takes even a piece of dead wood and imagines its obscure antipathies, 'feeling his way into its life'.[32] So, if Vaughan is highly aware of the precariousness of his position (as a seeker, and as an outsider kept from full understanding), nevertheless, unlike Kermode's seeker after meaning, he does believe in the possibility that there may be a divine authentication of his initially very private attempts at understanding. Kermode talked of parables as dark sayings, open to manifold interpretations. For Vaughan, the created order is similarly dark, but there are repositories of light wandering in it; retreatants like Ishmael, favoured by God. Vaughan seems sometimes to hope that he may be one of them. He acquiesces in a kind of wager as he finds himself forced to practise a faith that involves walking alone with God – largely among his works rather than in his Church. Choosing to take all creation as his material (and not just traditional emblems from it), Vaughan accepts the inevitable selectivity and uncertainty that will be involved whenever he adopts examples from it to express his beliefs. But he seems content to accept the demands this makes on his own private, interpretative actions. This, in turn, implies he has faith in God's power and willingness to justify such imagery.

That's best/which is not fixed, but flies and flows

Significantly, it is not particularly to Scripture, as the Word of God, that Vaughan turns for his justification. This is yet another way in which he rearranges traditional Protestant priorities. When it came to the poetic art, Beza, like many other Protestant commentators, could be found calling for poetry that echoed Scripture; that echoed:

> . . . those songs . . . of which sort we have a great number made and uttered by the Holy Ghost. With this harmony therefore the Bridegroom tuneth his song, and inviteth his spouse keep therein

---

[32]Bethell 1951, 151.

like time and accord with him. And what is this voice of the
spouse but his holy word?[33]

The turtle's mate in the Song of Songs, he points out, *echoes* the
song of the turtle.

Lewalski writes of *Silex Scintillans* that 'biblical texts are an
integral part of most of the poems in this volume'.[34] 'Integral' strikes
me as an inappropriate word in this context. Scriptural texts are
generally cited or quoted in a headnote or an endnote by Vaughan to
create a frame for the poem, but they are hardly integrated. Vaughan
prefers to leave the Bible to speak for itself, allowing it to comment
on the poetry without extensive intervention or manipulation by
the poet himself. But by the same token, he gives the poetry its
own domain too; one in which it does not merely echo but also
makes proposals. By permitting the Bible a certain independence,
he thereby releases his own poetry to an equivalent extent. In fact,
some of the appended texts bear only very loosely on the substance
of the poem, as in Vaughan's apostrophe *To the Holy Bible*, which
concludes vaguely:

> Glory be to God in the highest, and on
> Earth peace, good-will towards men.
>
> (*To the Holy Bible*, ll. 37–8)

Vaughan is generally free of Herbert's often excruciating concern
with the appropriateness of his art to divine praise. His poems
seldom treat at length the problem of how to write religious verse.
Committed primarily to private, meditative verse, he is not overawed
by scriptural precedent. This is not to say that he finds his art easy, or
that he denies his need of God:

> . . . to write true, unfeigned verse
> Is very hard! O God disperse
> These weights, and give my spirit leave
> To act as well as to conceive!
>
> (*Anguish*, ll. 13–18)

---

[33]Beza 1587, 266.
[34]Lewalski 1979, 343.

He affirms that God's grace is necessary; his verses must spring
from appropriate spiritual emotions. But it is grace he calls for as a
guide, not specifically Scripture. Even Lewalski must concede that
'poems of that classic Protestant kind, meditations upon a biblical
text' are few in Vaughan's corpus.[35] Of course, many meditations
have been prompted by texts – obviously Vaughan is imbued with
the Bible like any Christian writer of his day – but this does not
mean that the meditations are *on* the text. The story of Nicodemus
in *The Night* is hardly the poem's central preoccupation; it is more
a point of departure from which Vaughan goes on to consider his
own mystical experience. *The Water-fall* is a meditation on the
sacramental significances of water (this 'useful Element and clear'
[l. 23]) and an intimation of God's nearness, but it is a meditation
that admits guidance by the Spirit more than by Scripture. It resists
Calvin's assertion that the Book of Nature can only be read by the
light of the Scriptures.[36]

Open-ended in his employment of Scripture (loosely attaching
biblical texts to his poems rather than weaving them tightly in),
Vaughan also displays a certain openness in the poetic forms he
adopts. He is not as anxious in his use of language as Herbert –
we do not find ourselves trying constantly to make such strenuous
connections across lines. His poetry spreads itself more, and this
can be liberating. He can achieve a buoyant momentum, as though
he 'as quick as light/Danced through the flood' (*Regeneration*,
ll. 57–8). The forms of his poems are the springboards from which
he hopes to peep into glory; they require the fluidity to 'hurl' a
reader's sensibilities unexpectedly, and send them winging:

> . . . that's best
> Which is not fixed, but flies and flows.
>
> (*Affliction*, ll. 25–6)

Vaughan's best poems are the least tightly formed, and (because
strict metric regularity tends to feature more in public than in
private and meditative verse) they are best when least public. One
of Vaughan's very rare hymns is *Easter-Hymn*. Its trite language and

---

[35]Ibid.
[36]See Calvin 1960; cited in Lewalski 1979, 494, note 57.

images, and its sing-song regularity, seem to betray Vaughan's true qualities:

> Death, and darkness get you packing,
> Nothing now to man is lacking
> All your triumphs now are ended,
> And what *Adam* marred, is mended;
> Graves are beds now for the weary,
> Death a nap, to wake more merry.
>
> (*Easter-Hymn*, ll. 1–6)

This is far from the glories of *Disorder and Frailty*, when the language becomes noticeably richer in quality:

> O is! But give wings to my fire,
> And hatch my soul until it fly
> Up where thou art . . .
>
> (*Disorder and Frailty*, ll. 46–8)

Or *The Dawning*:

> Shall these early, fragrant hours
>   Unlock thy bowers?
> And with their blush of light descry
> Thy locks crowned with eternity . . .?
>
> (*The Dawning*, ll. 9–14)

Silex Scintillans in general, so Lewalski points out, 'does not approach [Herbert's] *The Temple* in the range of kinds and forms of verse' it uses: poems like *The Dawning* are in couplets; there are many more in quatrains, and in 'variously patterned stanzas in which lines of uneven length are linked in regular rhyme schemes'.[37] Vaughan does not struggle to fit his sentiments to strict patterns or structures. He aspires to greater self-expression by a more idiosyncratic application of form.

Ishmael was cut loose to wander, deprived of a fixed state. Fluidity suits Vaughan far better as an image than fixity. If this is true in

---

[37]Lewalski 1979, 332.

Vaughan's use of metrical and stanzaic form, it also characterizes
his use of landscape – 'sometimes the real Welsh countryside (as in
the opening lines of "The Showre", or "The Water-fall"), sometimes
emblematic (the scales on the mountain in "Regeneration"); often
biblical (the groves in "Religion" [where the patriarchs wandered])'.[38]
Often, the landscape is a shifting 'fusion of all these elements'.[39]
Vaughan reminds us that their coherence depends on his unifying,
interpreting activity. His inclination towards eclecticism in the
forms, themes and traditions he adopts for self-expression may also
cast light on his choice of pilgrimage as a unifying metaphor for
Silex Scintillans,[40] rather than the more solid construct of Herbert's
The Temple.

The Vaughan who makes less of Scripture and less of structural
form than Herbert (on whom he modelled himself in so many other
ways) must inevitably make more of the guidance of grace and the
inspiration of the Holy Spirit. To be justified in our understanding,
'God must "give us eyes to see" (Psalm 146:8), "ears unto our
heart to hear" (Psalm 40:8), in a word "we must be taught of him"
(Isaiah 54:13)'.[41] This, more than anything, prompts all Vaughan's
meditative and artistic endeavour: the craving for understanding
imparted by the Spirit. This is what gives Vaughan the confidence
to ignore Beza's assertion that all sacred poetry should merely echo
Scripture. He admits that worthy praises, like the renovation of the
heart, must be essentially God's doing ('of my Lord's penning') –
but interprets this to mean only that the praises must spring from
a heart endued with grace. Such an attitude allows for originality.
Vaughan is confident that he is equipped for praise, because he is a
repository of light in a dark world:

> I have one pearl by whose light
>   All things I see
> And in the heart of earth, and night
>   Find heaven . . .
>
> *(Silence and stealth of days,* l. 29)

---

[38]Ibid., 331.
[39]Ibid.
[40]Lewalski 1979, 327.
[41]Beza 1587, 101–2.

Typically, and as in his relationship with figures like Ishmael, Vaughan did not see himself as the antitype of the biblical *poets* anymore than of the Old Testament wanderers and exiles who so fascinated him. He was confident enough to see himself as *their* correlative type, too, identifying himself as a fellow 'hagiographer', or sacred writer, with David and Solomon as much as with Donne and Herbert. Dudley Fenner (1558–87), the Protestant commentator, had diverged from Beza (who attributed the very style of the Song of Songs to the Holy Spirit) and allowed some scope for Solomon's own art:

> Solomon was indued not only with a great measure of spiritual understanding, necessary for the matter, but with the knowledge of the natures of all creatures: whereby so great and heavenly mysteries might be made more easy and plain to our understanding, when similitudes are aptly drawn from them, and with the special grace of songs, which he attained by great practice: by all which gifts he was able to frame such a song as the grace whereof might work in our hearts a most heavenly melody.[42]

This was ground which, surely, Vaughan saw himself occupying, with the assistance of God's grace. The knowledge of creatures and an ability to write 'songs': both are self-confessed priorities of Vaughan's. He seems to imply that he, also, has received 'a measure of spiritual understanding necessary for the matter', and – with Solomon – he looks ahead to future glory.

Vaughan, the night visionary

Vaughan was forced to cope with attachment to a denomination denied its ordinances and public ceremonies, yet one of the consequences of this trauma was a stimulus to searching reflection, and enquiry after God in unwonted places. Such meditations became, in turn, a brace to Vaughan's passage through the world. Anything that is valuable along the path is discerned and appropriated by his energized (and often troubled) imagination. Disrupted

---

[42]Fenner 1594; cited in Lewalski 1979, 236.

and questioning, he contemplates nature and is enraptured by
the promise of future glory in *Vanity of Spirit* or *The Dawning*.
Disrupted and questioning, he formulates his understanding of
sacramental significance in the created order, nourished by a
tradition of natural theology insofar as it provides a basis for his
innovative readings of subjects personally selected and experienced.
The ultimate justification of his art he links to the intimation that
he – in a rare gift – has been given the grace to conceive and write
truly, in the manner of former inspired sacred poets, and not simply
to rehearse their words. This is because he, like them, is a wayfarer
and a pilgrim, as styled by Paul in 2 Cor. 5.1.

Although this path is 'solitary', it is also 'fair'.[43] It is on this
disrupted and questioning path that Vaughan's 'findings' are
vouchsafed to him – his poetry's occasional, partial, impassioned
intimations of God. In the light of these 'findings', Vaughan sees
himself as a longing Ishmael, a lily among thorns and also a lamp
shining in the darkness of the world. He recognizes in the bleakness
of an historical experience that initially seems to lead nowhere in
particular – an arbitrary and meaningless spot distinguished only by
the contingent fact that he finds himself 'thrown' there – something
akin to Jacob's vision when exhaustion makes him pick a random
stone and use it for a pillow: 'the Lord is in this place'.

> This little Goshen, in the midst of night
> And Satan's seat, in all her coasts hath light,
> Yea, Bethel shall have tithes (saith Israel's stone)
> And vows and visions, though her foes cry, None.
> This is the solemn temple sunk again
> Into a pillar, and concealed from men.
> And glory be to his eternal Name!
> Who is contented that this holy flame
> Shall lodge in such a narrow pit, till he
> With his strong arms turns our captivity.
>
> (*Jacob's Pillow and Pillar*, ll. 31–40)

This chapter has done its work in establishing Vaughan's poetic
practice as a mode of boldly inventive, deeply devout theological

---

[43]It is in his poem *Righteousness* (l. 1) that Vaughan talks of his 'Fair, solitary path'.

speculation. Several things mark it out: the immense significance of historical (and personal) experience in setting the terms for its quest for knowledge of God; the role of an actively contemplative imagination in that quest; the willingness to break with many of the well-worn tropes that were being used by other spiritual writers to convey their pious thoughts and lessons, experimenting instead with more unconventional alternatives (as well as confessing their failure when they led nowhere); and – perhaps most of all – Vaughan's positioning of himself, as a Christian seeker, so as to share more fully the perspective of Old Testament expectation. This latter, above all, has as its consequence a remarkable forward-orientation; a passion for the future, which does not at all seem like a betrayal of Christ, but rather a full embrace of Christ's promise of the Spirit who will lead into all truth.

The set of directions that Vaughan pursues is complex and sometimes disconcerting – and it is hard to give any sort of theoretical account of what he is doing such that it can be transmitted and in some way reappropriated (non-identically) in later theological work. What the next chapter will propose, however, is that there is something to be gained from theorizing Vaughan's (and also, in their own ways, Herbert's and Traherne's) leaps of theological imagination, made under the pressure of intense ecclesiastical crisis, with the help of the idea of *abductive reasoning*.

7

Abduction

Introduction

The previous chapter gave us a window onto how the religious controversy of Vaughan's day intensified his need to forge for himself some alternative to the forms of corporate faith that had been denied him; to respond creatively to the trauma of having his 'givens' taken away from him by a new exercise of his poetic and religious imagination. It seems that he felt a commission to foster new sources of illumination while in retreat from the world. Without a sacramental channel for his relationship with God, he turned to other sources: to dreams, visions, nature, Scripture and his sense of his own mortality.

In his own words, Vaughan had to 'outlook the marks' that had previously defined the limits of his sight. He used this image in relation to death, but it can appropriately be extended to many of the other fixed points that he found himself questioning. He is a searching poet, a night visionary looking to find whatever things 'shine' in his darkness, and to discern the 'mysteries' that lie behind the world's 'dust'.[1] And although this questing can at times seem like a desire for escape from the burdens of his material existence –

> Search well another world; who studies this
> Travels in clouds . . .[2]

– nevertheless, ultimately, Vaughan is not a Manichee but a sacramentalist. The 'clouds' are more typically the place he *begins*

---

[1] *'They are all gone into the world of light!'*, ll. 17–20.
[2] *The Search*, ll. 95–6.

to read, and in them to find the intimations of the greater mysteries they signify. The immaterial is shadowed forth by the material, and it is in the 'heart of earth, and night', and not by flight from them, that he most often seeks to 'find heaven'.[3]

This chapter is about the legibility of experience, and about the value of thinking about such experience in terms of signs. Its main conversation partner will be the semiotician and pragmatist philosopher C. S. Peirce (1839–1914), because of the elegance and insight with which he develops his account of how human thought and action unfold as a form of sign-reading. More specifically, it will be interested in his account of how such sign-reading involves creative steps – even leaps – of imaginative inference on the part of the human reasoner whenever she is faced with a challenge to her fixed 'marks'. Peirce's is, as Peter Ochs has shown better than anyone has,[4] a philosophy of foundness. In this respect, he provides an extraordinarily apt theoretical language both for the interpretation of our case study (Henry Vaughan's religious poetry) and for the wider issues we are seeking to explore through that case study, namely, how theological interpretation must work in full and sensitive responsiveness to historical experience. The most useful feature of all (among many) in his philosophy is his account of that mode of logical inference he calls 'abduction'.

In what follows, I propose to outline some of the key aspects of C. S. Peirce's theory of abduction as a mode of logical inference. His discussion of this theme is spread across numerous essays and lectures, spanning several decades from the mid-nineteenth century until the early twentieth century, and these works evidence various modifications, qualifications and changes of emphasis over time. My intention here is not to spend very much time discerning and evaluating the significance of the differences between the earlier and the later writings, and the questions his theory may or may not leave hanging. Rather, my intention is to make heuristic use of Peirce's extraordinarily suggestive discussions of abductive modes of reasoning for my own theological (and, more particularly, pneumatological) ends. In my view,[5] they represent a set of conceptual categories that are

[3]*'Silence, and stealth of days!'*, ll. 29–32.
[4]Ochs 1998.
[5]As also in the view of Dan Hardy, on whose theology I will increasingly draw in the closing stages of this book.

especially illuminating when put to work for a theology of the Holy Spirit, and (under that broad rubric) for a theological account of the task and function of Christian imagination as well.[6]

However, before turning specifically to Peirce's treatment of abduction alongside the other modes of logical inference, it will be useful to give our investigation some context in Peirce's thought more generally.

Some key principles of C. S. Peirce's thought

Peirce supposes that all human language about 'being' or about 'the real' can only be language about what human beings are able to *cognize*, and therefore also *experience* in some fashion. This is because whatever we cognize is based upon 'percepts', which is to say *conceptions about* the world that have an inalienable experiential grounding to them, and are thus rooted in *perceptions of* the world. Concepts, in other words, are never *a priori*. They are consequent upon experience, and are forms of distillation of what is learnt in experience (often via abstraction from it, but never in such a way that such abstractions do not remain answerable to the experiences out of which they are developed). He writes in an early essay entitled 'Questions Concerning Certain Faculties Claimed for Man' (1868):

> [A]ll our conceptions are obtained by abstractions and combinations of cognitions first occurring in judgments of experience. Accordingly, there can be no conception of the absolutely incognizable, since nothing of that sort occurs in experience.[7]

And he goes on to add, on the basis of this principle, that:

> In short, *cognizability* (in its widest sense) and *being* are not merely metaphysically the same, but are synonymous terms.[8]

---

[6]Peirce himself, it should be noted, was aware of the ways in which his philosophy (and especially his philosophy of triads, which we will come to shortly) bordered on theology.
[7]Peirce 1992, 24.
[8]Ibid., 25.

In these and similar statements, Peirce reveals that in key respects he is using an empirical method not unlike that of a natural scientist. Knowledge begins from observed (or 'perceived') data.

Peirce develops a sophisticated account of signs (a semiotic theory) to accommodate his claim that all reality is cognized, or mental in some way. Material objects in the world are signs, but so are human persons and human thoughts, and even human emotions.

> [W]henever we think, we have present to the consciousness some feeling, image, conception, or other representation, which serves as a sign. But it follows from our own existence . . . that everything which is present to us is a phenomenal manifestation of ourselves. This does not prevent its being a phenomenon of something without us, just as a rainbow is at once a manifestation both of the sun and of the rain.[9]

Why signs? Because we do not have experiential access to 'things in themselves'. We only know things as they are *mediated* to us in subjective experience; in other words, as they *signify something to us*. This much is granted to Kant. '[T]here is no thing,' writes Peirce, 'which is in-itself in the sense of not being relative to the mind, though things which are relative to the mind doubtless are, apart from that relation.'[10]

What Peirce proposes by contrast with Kant, however, is a relation to truth via reason which is far more historicist, and which eschews the idea of necessary or timeless truths of reason. The conceptions which are signs in a long succession of signification are not finally anchored in a suprahistorical domain of transcendental categories. They are constantly being re-inferred in new circumstances as what has already been thought encounters what is now being newly experienced. If there is anything stable and unchanging at all in this process, it might (debatably) be said to be the laws of logical inference in themselves. But even these (in Peirce's account) allow plenty of room for contingency and error, as we shall see later, and even these are only laws insofar as they are

---

[9]'Some Consequences of Four Incapacities' (1868), in Peirce 1992, 38.
[10]Peirce 1992, 52. But Kant's continued positing of 'things in themselves' (as things whose formal existence reason can assert *apart* from sensory experience) is not granted by Peirce.

laws *for* someone (or many someones) in an historical process of thinking. '[L]ife is a train of thought,' writes Peirce, in which 'men and words reciprocally educate each other; each increase of a man's information involves and is involved by, a corresponding increase of a word's information.'[11]

This, for now, gives a sufficient outline of the way Peirce thinks, to have prepared us for his important discussion of the three main modes of logical inference – three modes of reasoning – which are deduction, induction and abduction (the latter sometimes also being called 'hypothesis'). An analysis of these modes of reasoning is of recurrent interest to him, and the theoretical clarification Peirce gives to the third of them will be of particular use to this book. This is because abduction is a mode of inference whose occasion is almost always something newly 'found' (something surprising), and whose method requires an unusually *imaginative* response by contrast with the modes of deduction and induction, as will become clear. This interplay of foundness and imagination is, of course, utterly central to the concerns of this book, and – as I am arguing – finds a positive Christian articulation in the form of an understanding of the Holy Spirit's ongoing work in history. In this respect, abduction has a close relationship too with the 'eventual' (which we will discuss later) in its openness to development, change and indefinitely unfolding insight.

Three modes of inference

Deduction

The classic example to which Peirce turns in order to describe the three modes of inference, and to distinguish them from one another, is that of beans being drawn from a bag. I will follow him here in using the bag of beans example.

It will also be helpful in what follows to keep in mind the three parts of every inference, whose relation to one another is nonetheless different depending on whether the inference is deductive, inductive or abductive. The three parts of every inference, as Peirce deploys them, are the *Rule*, the *Case* and the *Result*.

---

[11]Peirce 1992, 54.

In deduction, the *Rule* is always known in advance. A *Case* is then adduced that falls under the Rule, and the *Result* can then be concluded with certainty. So, for example, it is *known* in advance that all of the beans in the bag are white (this is the *Rule*). The *Case* is that a particular handful of beans is drawn from that bag. The secure *Result,* or conclusion, that can be inferred from this is that these beans are white. No new knowledge is added that is not already contained in the *Rule* and the *Case.* The conclusion is simply 'analytic', which is to say that it articulates a truth already fully present in the premises.

Peirce sets out the deduction as follows:

DEDUCTION

Rule. – All the beans from this bag are white.
Case. – These beans are from this bag.
∴ *Result.* – These beans are white.

Induction

We can turn to the example of the bag of beans again to help us in relation to induction. In this case, by contrast with deduction, no *Rule* is yet known about the colour of the beans that are contained in the bag. There are only *Cases* to go on. Induction puts Cases and Results together to infer a *Rule.* Each act of drawing a white bean out of the bag is a *Case,* or example. The ever-growing pile of white beans is the cumulative *Result* of these Cases. At a certain point, with some confidence, the *Rule* may be inferred that the bag contains only white beans. In other words, induction proceeds by the accumulation of examples or of evidence that progressively point to the probability of some particular truth being so. (Sometimes, of course, a probability or theorem is already in an experimenter's mind when she or he begins to accumulate evidence, and the inductive method is used specifically as a strategy to test the strength of that theorem.[12])

In more complex forms, induction is therefore the mode of reasoning typically used by insurance companies, as Peirce points out in his 1869 essay 'Grounds of Validity of the Laws of Logic'. Let us imagine a bag with two *different* colours of bean in it, black as well as white. The more beans are drawn out of the bag, the more

---

[12]Peirce notes this in Peirce 1998, 216.

accurately will it be possible to gauge what the overall proportion of black to white is. The exact ratio will never be known absolutely until the bag is empty (at which point the reasoning is no longer inductive), but it can be reasoned with increasing confidence 'in the long run', as bean by bean the bag gets emptier:

> [I]t cannot be said that we know an inductive conclusion to be true, however loosely we state it; we only know that by accepting inductive conclusions, in the long run our errors balance one another.[13]

Elsewhere, Peirce says of induction that it might well be called 'statistical argument'.[14]

Unlike a deduction, which is 'analytic' because the third part of the syllogism (in deduction's case, the *Result*) is entirely contained already in the first two parts, an induction is 'synthetic' because the third part of the syllogism (in induction's case, the *Rule*) is *not* wholly contained in the first two parts. It is simply implied by them as a probability (though it is sometimes placed 'in front' of them as a hypothesis to be tested), and the shortfall of certainty, so to speak, has to be 'made up' from somewhere else.

But let us return to the initial example, in which there were only white beans in the bag in order to show Peirce's formal way of setting out how induction works, by contrast with deduction. The induction can be set out as follows:

INDUCTION

Case. – These beans are from this bag.
Result. – These beans are white.
∴ *Rule.* – All the beans from this bag are white.

Abduction

We turn finally to abduction, which shares with induction the fact that it is a synthetic and not an analytic form of reasoning. (In the essay we have principally been drawing on so far,[15] Peirce calls it

---

[13]Peirce 1992, 79.
[14]'Some Consequences of Four Incapacities' in Peirce 1992, 33.
[15]'Deduction, Induction, and Hypothesis' (1878) in Peirce 1992, 186–99.

'hypothesis', but it is clear that it has the same features as what he elsewhere calls 'abduction'.) This form of inference has to do even more 'synthetic work' than induction does, however. We might say that the shortfall of certainty is greater, and that more 'gaps' have to be filled in. If induction is the inference of a *Rule* from putting *Cases* and *Results* together, then abduction (or hypothesis) is the inference of a *Case* from putting a *Rule* together with a (usually peculiar) *Result*. Peirce writes:

> Hypothesis is where we find some very curious circumstance, which would be explained by the supposition that it was a case of a certain general rule, and thereupon adopt that supposition.[16]

Its use in the context of natural-scientific research (which, as we have noted, is one of Peirce's main interests and influences) should be clear from this. Abductive reasoning is concerned to address the challenge of what appear to be anomalies in the predicted behaviour of something by coming up with a better hypothesis – by adducing other rules that it might fall under along with, or instead of, the rule that it was initially supposed would apply. A new *Case*, or explanatory context, is supplied.

Peirce uses the bag of beans example as follows to illustrate abduction. This time, the example takes on a more Sherlock-Holmes-like feel; a greater sense of narrative context is offered to make the illustration work:

> Suppose I enter a room and there find a number of bags, containing different kinds of beans. On the table there is a handful of white beans; and, after some searching, I find one of the bags contains white beans only. I at once infer as a probability, or as a fair guess, that this handful was taken out of that bag.[17]

Or, in a more stripped down format:

HYPOTHESIS

Rule. – All the beans in this bag are white.
Result. – These beans (found outside the bag) are white.
∴ *Case.* – These beans are from this bag.

---

[16]Peirce 1992, 189.
[17]Ibid., 188.

The additional narrative content that Peirce finds himself needing to supply in order to explain just how hypothesis works is an important indication (i) of what we have already noted, namely, that a greater *quantity* of gap-filling is required in abduction than in induction but also (ii) that in many cases a different type or *quality* of material needs to be part of the explanatory synthesis. Or, to put it another way, the boundaries of what counts as relevant need to be widened further in abductive reasoning than in inductive. Peirce says in his 1903 essay 'The Nature of Meaning' that '[a]bduction . . . is the only logical operation which introduces any new idea.' Yet, 'if we are ever to learn anything or to understand phenomena at all, it must be by abduction that this is to be brought about'.[18] Indeed, 'every single item of scientific theory which stands established today has been due to abduction'.[19]

An example that Peirce gives which helps to illustrate this point is that of fish fossils being discovered far in the land-locked interior of a country. (The point has even more force if we add something to Peirce's description of it, and say that it is the first time such a discovery has been made: let us imagine we are a Victorian hill-walker with an eagle eye and a small pickaxe.) This is, in the formal terms we have been using earlier, a *Result*, which in conjunction with a *Rule* (viz. that fish live in water) requires a *Case* to be hypothesized in order to deal with it. The hypothesis or abduction, which cannot be directly, empirically proven, might be that once upon a time the sea washed over this piece of land, but that shifts in the configuration of the earth's surface over millennia have now placed the sea far away.[20] This is a more elaborate exercise than that involved in induction, at least as Peirce characterizes it, because it is not that there are numerous instances from which to build towards something that can be concluded to be true of a whole class (not at least until more discoveries of inland fish fossils are made). An induction will conclude that 'facts, similar to observed facts, are true in cases not examined'.[21] The unearthing of fish fossils is an *odd* circumstance that is as yet too tenuously related to any recognized class of things to be readily related to such a class. It is not a fact 'similar to observed facts'. Because there

---

[18]Peirce 1998, 216.
[19]Ibid., 217.
[20]Peirce 1992, 189.
[21]Ibid., 194.

is no existing class to which to appeal, a greater *quantity* but also a different *quality* of explanatory material needs to be supplied than is typical of inductive reasoning. This material will be supplied by some sort of imaginative conjecture, which can open up the question of what the prehistoric movements of seas and continents might once have been in their relation to this particular piece of territory.

We might say that abduction very often has to operate in moods that – in English – make heavy use of the modal auxiliaries. In particular, it will tend to move from interrogative to subjunctive and even optative modalities (although the optative is more clearly discernible in Samuel Taylor Coleridge's version of abduction than in Peirce's, as we shall see), for these are the moods of speech and thought that best suit adventurous imaginative thought. They are especially oriented to future finding. Givens, of whatever sort, can be expressed without them, as Peter Ochs points out in his discussion of certain pneumatologically resistant theologies:

> [W]hen representations freeze into idols they tend to display only indicative and imperative moods . . .[22]

So, we have found it necessary to introduce the *qualitative* difference in the material treated by abductions as compared with inductions, alongside the *quantitative*.

> By hypothesis, we conclude the existence of a fact quite different from anything observed, from which according to known laws, something observed would necessarily result.[23]

If – prior to the discovery of the inland fish fossils – there had been no existing theory of the movement of continents and seas, then something more than the introduction of *additional information* to the problem would have been going on. A fact not yet in accordance with the 'known' would find itself being surmised. An inference would be going on from 'facts of one kind to facts of another', by

---

[22]Ochs 2011, 217.
[23]Peirce 1992, 194.

contrast with induction's inference from 'one set of facts' to 'another set of similar facts'.[24]

A second example that Peirce gives helps to illustrate this point about *qualitatively* different material even more vividly. By the same token, it gives us a second occasion to feel ourselves in a detective story – specifically, to attend to aspects of conjectured narrative and intentionality. This, unsurprisingly given what has been said so far, will contrast significantly with what goes on in an induction.

A sheet of handwritten paper is found, which has had a small piece torn out of it. The small piece is missing but the finders have some intuition or clue about who might have written on the sheet they now have in their possession. So they go to that person's house, and are enabled to search his desk (to which no one but he normally has access). There they find a torn piece of paper that in size and irregular shape fits the sheet they have already found. Their conclusion is that the sheet of paper really was – as they had guessed – authored by the man whose desk they have just searched. This, says Peirce, is more than an induction not just because of the breadth of context that has to be invoked to come up with an inference, but because of the ambition of the inference itself. Inductive reasoning would serve very well in the delimited task of analysing the torn piece of paper in relation to the sheet as a whole. It would start to aggregate the ways in which it seemed to fit: a colour match, a match of this angle here and that angle there. With the rapid build-up of such evidence, its inductive conclusion would be that the whole class of edges, corners, colourations, etc., would be likely to fit; even the minor irregularities would match because so many of the major ones have been shown to match. But this would be an inference only at the level of the paper and its properties. The ambition of the larger *abductive* process is manifest in the way that the matching of the pieces of paper is considered within a far broader context in which the ownership of that piece of paper is being speculated about and then tested. The *Case* that is conjured up in relation to the *Result* and the *Rule* is, so to speak, more 'three-dimensional' than the narrow issue of whether one flat piece of paper was once attached to another flat piece of paper. Of course, to say it is more 'three-dimensional' is really to speak metaphorically of the human and narrative dimensions of the

---

[24]Ibid., 198.

inference – both what stimulates the desire to make the inference in the first place, and the quality of the inference itself.

Case, Peirce seems to imply, is a name for 'context'. An abduction is the supplying of a context in which a *Result* will make sense as evidence of some sort of *Rule*. Both the quantity of additional evidence appealed to in an abduction, and the qualitative variety of this evidence (what I have just called its 'three-dimensionality'), set it apart from the other kinds of reasoning that Peirce examines.[25]

Artistic abduction

It is possible to assemble from various places in Peirce's discussions of it, three distinct aspects of abduction that may be of use in a theological discussion of its value to a Christian pneumatology. These are its interrogative character, its intensity and (perhaps overlapping with the first two) its similarity to what goes on when

---

[25]The relation of the three kinds of inference is, of course, more complex in practice than this scheme allows. The diagrammatical forms that I set out earlier, following Peirce, are relatively neat, and have the advantage of assisting a clear comparison of the formal differences between the three kinds of inferential reasoning. However, what it does not show is how these three forms of inferential reasoning habitually interrelate and interact *with one another*. According to Peirce (1998, 216), what happens in practice is that the progression towards a new insight (in particular, a new scientific insight) begins with an abduction (the hypothesization of a possible 'Case') which is then adopted provisionally *as if* it were a 'Rule', ready to perform the role of the first term in a deductive syllogism. An inductive process then tests it, not with the aim of ever coming up with an absolute and irrefutable proof of it, but in the service of increasing the accuracy of our power of predicting how singular events may relate to a general pattern (this Peirce calls the 'mode of being' of a 'law'). The regularities it perceives enable inductive reasoning to attribute a 'value' to these singularities. Thus, although Peirce lists the three kinds of inference in the following order (with an implication of a sort of descending hierarchy among them):

> Deduction proves that something *must* be, Induction shows that something *actually is* operative, Abduction merely suggests that something *may be*. (Peirce 1998, 216)

he, in fact, leaves room for a bold claim that (in the blink of an eye) raises abduction to a very high status, by adding that:

> [I]f we are ever to learn anything or to understand phenomena at all, it must be by abduction that this is to be brought about. (Peirce 1998, 217)

a creative artist makes art. An examination of these three will afford us an opportunity to turn back to Vaughan's poetry, to see whether some of the key features of that poetry are well-described in Peircean terms.

I have just remarked that the 'three-dimensionality' of abductive inference sets it apart from other kinds, but it also, as Peirce observes, makes it far more precarious. 'As a general rule', writes Peirce, 'hypothesis is a weak kind of argument'.[26] It involves taking 'bolder and more perilous' steps than are taken in induction.[27] And one of the corollaries of this is that it should habitually adopt an interrogative mode, as is suited to something involving a high degree of conjecture:

> The hypothesis should be distinctly put as a question, before making the observations which are to test its truth.[28]

There will therefore always be a degree of provisionality, or revisability, about abductive inferences, in the light of the many new *Results* that may manifest themselves unexpectedly, this in its turn being the result of the many aspects of the context (or *Case*) that retain the status of conjecture.

So, the interrogative character of abduction is one of its key aspects (consequent upon which, as we have suggested, will often be a subjunctive mode of proposing 'solutions' to the questions asked). Second, it will have a quality of what Peirce calls 'intensity' about it. This is something to do with the heightened synthesizing that – as we have noted – goes on in an abduction. It has to do with thinking things in a more ambitiously comprehensive way (notwithstanding the fact that it also thinks them interrogatively). Induction may assemble lists of potentially relevant data around a particular subject. Abduction (or hypothesis) goes further.

> Hypothesis substitutes, for a complicated tangle of predicates . . . a single conception.[29]

---

[26]Peirce 1992, 189.
[27]Ibid., 192.
[28]Ibid., 193.
[29]Ibid., 198.

And in this ambitious and complicated synthetic act – which Peirce calls 'a single harmonious disturbance' – a certain set of sensuous or emotional phenomena are generally present:

> Now, there is a peculiar sensation belonging to the act of thinking that each of [a tangle of] predicates inheres in [a particular] subject. In hypothetic inference this complicated feeling so produced is replaced by a single feeling of greater intensity, that belonging to the act of thinking the hypothetic conclusion.[30]

I take Peirce here to be describing a sort of 'eureka' moment, not wholly susceptible to explanatory analysis in itself, by which 'everything comes together', and the penny drops. However, once again, this 'coming together' will have aspects of the subjunctive about it: it may convince, but as a 'could be', or a 'may be', or a 'might be' that is recognized to be open to further exploration.

The third aspect of abduction to which Peirce adverts and that is of interest to this present project is the analogy he sees between its function as a mode of logical inference (especially in science) and the way that creative artists operate synthetically to draw out a unity or connectedness in things which delivers a greater insight into those same things. As with the work of the scientist, though in a different medium, this activity is in the service of displaying the 'intelligibility' of things, in the richest possible sense that can be given to that word. To jump back for a moment to the seventeenth century, maximizing such intelligibility will engage the affective as well as the analytical faculties of the human enquirer; it will show the mutual implication of feeling and forensic skill in uncovering and displaying the deepest essence and purpose of things in their interrelation with all other things. It may even depend upon a certain sort of prayerfulness, which relates those things to the God 'who made and loves them all'.[31] Traherne might have called this something like *felt thought*, and in the same context would have asserted that a failure to love the found things of the world is by the same token a misapprehension of them; their intelligibility is lessened when love is absent from

---

[30]Ibid., 198–9.
[31]I refer deliberately here to Samuel Taylor Coleridge's *Rime of the Ancient Mariner*: 'He prayeth best, who loveth best/All things both great and small'. ll. 661–2 (1798 text); ll. 618–19 (1817 text). P. H. Fry 1999, 74–5.

the relation. Misapprehension, to extend the point, could even be a name for sin.[32]

Peirce's third category of artistic insight plays its role in that 'highest kind of synthesis' by 'introducing an idea not contained in the data, which gives connections which they would not otherwise have had':

> The work of the poet or novelist is not so utterly different from that of the scientific man. The artist introduces a fiction; but it is not an arbitrary one; it exhibits affinities to which the mind accords a certain approval in pronouncing them beautiful, which if it is not exactly the same as saying that the synthesis is true, is something of the same general kind.[33]

In the previous chapter, we saw all these aspects of what Peirce calls abduction amply manifested in the poetic work of Henry Vaughan: the interrogation, the intensity of synthesis and the (fitting) imaginative leap. It was evident, for example, in *Vanity of Spirit*, in which we saw Vaughan quit his cell and lie outdoors gazing heavenward. The indoor environment that constrained him is abandoned, but as we noted in the last chapter Vaughan additionally leaves aside the 'thoughts' that have exhausted him. And yet, as we also saw, *this does not mean that Vaughan's mind is now inactive*, for there is *intense* activity in the sudden burst of speculation that takes place as he gazes up at the sky. He asks a series of ambitious questions about the world's origins and the providence that may or may not govern it; he tells us how he 'summoned nature', and:

> pierced through all her store,
> Broke up some seals, which none had touched before . . .
>
> (*Vanity of Spirit*, ll. 9–10)

---

[32]Francis Bacon – more forensic than either Vaughan or Coleridge – read a similar instinct in Franciscus de Verulamio in his view that 'the human intellect was the author of its own difficulties by not applying calmly and opportunely the right remedies which lie within Man's power – whence comes manifold Ignorance of Things, and from the Ignorance of Things countless disadvantages – he thought that every effort should be directed to seeing how the commerce between the *Mind*, & *Things* . . . could be restored, or at least improved'. Bacon 2004. For Traherne, as for Henry Vaughan, this commerce between 'Mind and Things' could not be a full commerce without love.
[33]Peirce 1992, 261.

We concluded in the previous chapter that the 'thoughts' he first abandoned were those of a more abstractly analytical frame of mind. But to put it in the way we have been developing in this chapter, we may now say that he has moved from the securer forms of inference (symbolized, perhaps, by the fact that they were pursued 'indoors') into the activity of abduction.

If, in *Vanity of Spirit*, Vaughan is gazing at the sky, it is water that preoccupies him in another of his great poems: *The Water-fall*. The complex dynamics which characterize abductive reasoning in Peirce's account of it are expressed equally well here; it affords rich examples of Vaughan's fascination with nature's 'signs' (in this case far more than mere obstructions to knowledge). I reproduce it in full:

The Water-fall

With what deep murmurs through time's silent stealth
Doth thy transparent, cool and watery wealth
   Here flowing fall,
   And chide, and call,
As if his liquid, loose retinue stayed
Ling'ring, and were of this steep place afraid,
   The common pass
   Where, clear as glass,
   All must descend
   Not to an end:
But quickened by this deep and rocky grave,
Rise to a longer course more bright and brave.
Dear stream! dear bank, where often I
Have sat, and pleased my pensive eye,
Why, since each drop of thy quick store
Runs thither, whence it flowed before,
Should poor souls fear a shade or night,
Who came (sure) from a sea of light?
Or since those drops are all sent back
So sure to thee, that none doth lack,
Why should frail flesh doubt any more
That what God takes, he'll not restore?
O useful element and clear!
My sacred wash and cleanser here,
My first consigner unto those
Fountains of life, where the Lamb goes?

What sublime truths, and wholesome themes,
Lodge in the mystical, deep streams!
Such as dull man can never find
Unless that Spirit lead his mind,
Which first upon thy face did move,
And hatched all with his quickening love.
As this loud brook's incessant fall
In streaming rings restagnates all,
Which reach by course the bank, and then
Are no more seen, just so pass men.
O my invisible estate,
My glorious liberty, still late!
Thou art the channel my soul seeks,
Not this with cataracts and creeks.

Here, as in *Vanity of Spirit*, intensity gives way to interrogation, which in turn (and more successfully than in *Vanity of Spirit*, which ends in frustration) gives way to a glimpse of the divine conditions for the earthly forms at which Vaughan gazes so intently. The poem opens with a characteristic contemplation of nature, in which lies a reassurance of divine presence. However, as the meditation develops, a new awareness emerges that is of something in excess of the given form; something that is pointed to but not captured by that form:

O my invisible estate
My glorious liberty, still late!
Thou art the channel my soul seeks
Not this with cataracts and creeks.

(*The Water-fall*, ll. 37–40)

Vaughan comes to realize that, although the stream is part of the natural universe, and is therefore good, there is a beauty and a reward that exceeds it. This realization is similar to the intimation of a 'greatness beyond' (a greatness nature can only occasionally reveal) that we saw infusing the rapturous poem *The Dawning* in the previous chapter:

Shall these early fragrant hours
Unlock thy bowers?

And with their blush of light descry
Thy locks crown'd with eternity . . .?

(The Dawning, ll. 9–12)

The waterfall points Vaughan beyond itself – 'giving more than it has', to recall the phrase of Jacques Maritain's.[34] Indeed, Vaughan's awareness that the water drops are creatures that have a special power to return heavenwards helps him to direct his thoughts to the 'invisible estate', which is his own ultimate inheritance. The sacramental and liturgical associations of baptism are explored too, and they also inform the richly theological character of the abduction:

My sacred wash and cleanser here,
My first consigner unto those
Fountains of life, where the Lamb goes . . .

(The Water-fall, ll. 24–6)

Of immense significance for our enquiry is the fact that Vaughan grounds the actual *activity* of abduction (and not just its insights) in theology. More specifically, he grounds the activity *pneumatologically*. If there is one thing, more than any, that prompts all of Vaughan's meditative and artistic endeavour, it is the craving for understanding imparted by the Spirit. Here, in this poem, that fact is as transparent as the 'cool and watery wealth', 'clear as glass', which the poem celebrates:

What sublime truths, and wholesome themes,
Lodge in thy mystical, deep streams!
Such as dull man can never find
Unless that Spirit lead his mind,
Which first upon thy face did move,
And hatched all with his quickening love.

(The Water-fall, ll. 27–32)

---

[34]'Things are not only what they are. They constantly pass beyond themselves and give more than they have . . .'. Maritain 1953, 127. This is discussed in Williams 2005, 26.

The Holy Spirit is the 'leader' of the abductive mind, and is, moreover, equipped to do this by its special role in the primal origination of the whole created order; its shaping of the terms of the world's very existence.

The Spirit's role in establishing and sustaining the world ('hatching' it, in Vaughan's image) is one to which we will return in a moment. First, however, a technical question about the extent of the applicability of Peirce's model to Vaughan's activity needs clarification. What is the oddity, or surprise, or interruption of a given state of things which provokes this abduction?

Above all, it is the painful historical situation, which we described in the previous chapter as Vaughan's 'founding trauma'. As we have seen, not only this poem, but also a vast array of Vaughan's poems are galvanized by this break-up of the fixed marks (or, in Ochs's words, the 'frozen representations') by which he had previously set his course. How is he to read water in an untroubled way as part of God's gentle beneficence (and sacramental provision) when the order of things in which that signification was 'natural' is no longer in place? This need to *interrogate* (the first of Peirce's three marks of abduction) is a key part of what creates the occasion, or stimulus, for the poem.[35] His founding trauma is likewise what

---

[35]There are good counterparts to this in Herbert's work, with interrogation emerging from disruption. Poems dealing with experiences of illness, despair or a sense of abandonment illustrate this especially well. In *Affliction*, for instance, Herbert writes:

Yet lest perchance I should too happie be
          In my unhappinesse,
Turning my purge to food, thou throwest me
          Into more sicknesses.
Thus doth thy power crosse-bias me, not making
Thine own gift good, yet me from my wayes taking.

(*Affliction I*, ll. 49–54)

To be 'crosse-biassed' (with the pun that that contains) is to be sprung from one's reassuring givens ('me from my ways taking') and made more ready to find afresh. It involves realizing that one is, as Jacob was in the desert, in a wholly new place that previously had no special meaning but is now a place in which God is to be newly discovered:

Now I am here, what thou wilt do with me
          None of my books will show . . .

(George Herbert, *Affliction I*, ll. 55–6)

gives Vaughan the *intensity* which is the second of Peirce's three
marks of abduction. In part, this intensity is the heightening in
him of a desire for a personal, experiential relationship with
God. We see this heightened desire throughout all of his poetry.
But Peirce means more than intense feeling when he talks about
intensity; he means a power to perceive a deeper 'singleness' in
apparently tangled experience. Vaughan shows us this too, at
certain moments. It arises from his native instinct to look hard and
long at things, to observe small details which may not fit a stock
analogy, and which thereby make him reason in a deeper and more
ambitiously synthesizing way. Part of the stimulus to his abduction
is a sense that his thoughts have not been *adequate* to the world
he looks at. And finally, Vaughan undertakes *imaginative leaps* of
some daring (Peirce's third mark), when he conjures images of the
heavens which are both the true depths of creatures and at the
same time absolutely beyond them. This sense of another world is
a common element in all of Vaughan's poetry, and he experiments
with what Peirce calls 'fictions' (which are not necessarily untrue
in Peircean terms just because they are hypothesized) in order to
explore that elusive but embracing context for what is known in
this world. His fictions, as we have seen, are remarkable: although
sharing so much with earlier Protestant poets in England – Donne
and Herbert, for example – Vaughan is at his most interesting
when he diverges from recognizable tradition, and becomes both
more private and more idiosyncratic; when he presses beyond the
established themes and forms of his predecessors to a sense of
glory which we feel to be very personal. Both by nature and by
circumstance, Vaughan is a poet whose meditative habits express
themselves in unpredictable terms which combine the orthodox
and the innovatory in a frame of reference that is distinctively his
own. To recall a point we made in the previous chapter, his poems
are often *springboards* from which he hopes to peep into glory. In
turn, they offer their readers an opportunity to leap too. In their
abductive experimentation (just as in the fluidity of their metrical
forms), they have the power to send the reader's sensibilities
winging unexpectedly heavenward.

I hope that to some extent the usefulness of the Peircean theory
of abduction to a fuller understanding of this religious poet of the
seventeenth century will have emerged by now. We have also begun
to see its compatibility with the idea of spirit-led abduction, of the

sort that Vaughan hints at (though he would not put it in such terms!). In the section that follows, I want to push a little further with that idea, looking at two wider aspects of Peirce's theory of signs (i.e. two aspects of the theoretical context in which he sets his theory of inference) to identify 'pneumatologically friendly' features of these too. One aspect might be called, a little artificially perhaps, ontological; the other, temporal.

Being and time in Peircean terms

The ontology of signs: *Thirdness*

The key thing about signs, for Peirce, is that they have a threefold function, and this opens onto what is a central commitment of Peirce's philosophy as a whole: the idea that all healthy thought will be alert to what he calls 'Thirdness'.

The threefold function of signs recognizes, first, that they signify *to* someone or something. Some subject, or interpreter, receives the sign. This subject or interpreter thereby represents the element of Firstness in the process of cognition. Second, signs signify something by standing *for* that something (which may, in fact, be a previous sign in a chain of cognition, as that sign is thought anew). This referent of the sign represents the element of Secondness in the realm of cognition. From the point of view of the interpreter (in her or his Firstness), this Secondness will often be experienced as otherness, or over-againstness. So far, we seem to have a version of the classic subject–object distinction, which so much Western epistemology worries over. But Peirce introduces Thirdness at this point in his discussion of how signs work. He says:

> 3d, it is a sign, *in* some respect or quality, which brings it into connection with its object.[36]

Signs are signs in a *medium of relationship*, which the idea of over-againstness fails to describe or to account for. In this medium of relationship, signs are 'brought into connection' with one another,

---

[36]Peirce 1992, 38.

ensuring a participative encounter between knower and known object; between knower and knower in their knowledge of objects; and between known object and known object in their meaning for knowers. Signs have a quality of connectedness, or relation, which Peirce's Thirdness helps to articulate; Thirdness is the medium in which things exist coherently and intelligibly together, and can trustingly be related to by knowers (who also participate in this medium). It is what Henry Vaughan might have called the 'tie of bodies' (*Sure, there's a tie of bodies!*), which also 'ties' the thoughts and sympathies of sentient creatures to the things they know.[37] It is a sphere in which the language of generality can also make sense; in which it is possible responsibly to relate to the objects one encounters as more than discrete and atomistic units. There is some affinity here with Samuel Taylor Coleridge's account of 'logos', as he develops it in various of his works, including most importantly the *Opus Maximus*. Logos is a principle of intelligence at work both in human reasoning and also in the ordering and life of non-human nature, such that when a human mind attends to non-human nature, it encounters something it recognizes as jointly part of its own rational medium. (In Coleridge's view, creative art could bring this recognition out especially.) 'Logos' is something in which both the human cognizer and the-things-that-humans-cognize are together participants. Or, in the words that Peirce uses in a footnote to his essay 'Some Consequences of Four Incapacities' (1868), '[J]ust as we say that a body is in motion, and not that motion is in a body we ought to say that we are in thought, and not that thoughts are in us.'[38] Elsewhere, Peirce talks as Coleridge would have talked about 'Nature' as a repository for the laws of relation between things (the laws of relation being another name for what he calls Thirdness). Nature has 'intelligibility'; it is 'reason objectified', and this is what 'makes thirdness genuine'.[39] It permits 'the consciousness of synthesis' which is 'the consciousness that binds our life together'.[40]

---

[37]In this respect, Peirce's account of Thirdness stands also in contradiction of Frank Kermode's pessimism about the consistency and intelligibility with which objects in the world can be meaningfully interpreted and collectively experienced.
[38]Peirce 1992, 42.
[39]'A Guess at the Riddle' in Peirce 1992, 255.
[40]Peirce 1992, 261.

And, like Coleridge,[41] Peirce is not averse to allowing his account of Thirdness (and the Firstness and Secondness that Thirdness brings into relation through time) to have theological resonances; this is something we noted a little earlier. In particular, Peirce's account of Firstness, Secondness and Thirdness is given a highly theological direction in the fragments of 'A Guess at the Riddle': a book manuscript that would never reach its full realization. 'Guess' is Peirce's most ambitious attempt at a full-scale speculative philosophy treating all major branches of knowledge. In it, he writes that:

> The starting-point of the universe, God the Creator, is the Absolute First; the terminus of the universe, God completely revealed, is the Absolute Second; every state of the universe at a measurable point of time is the third.[42]

The temporality of Thirdness is something to which we will turn more explicitly in the following section; for now we may simply note how compatible is his idea of the connectedness of 'every state of the universe' as it is displayed progressively through 'measurable points in time' with the analogical logic we set out in Chapter 1, through analogies with Milbankian 'pleonasm', English common law tradition, the Gospel descriptions of Jesus going from town to town and so on. This, as Chapter 1 argued, is fittingly read with the help of scriptural images of how the Holy Spirit works as 'unfolder' of Christ's truth, post-Pentecost. This unfolding-in-connection binds absolute origin with absolute end, in the life of a Godhead that enfolds rather than opposes difference and time.

There is also a quasi-theological aspect to Peirce's account of how abduction – uniquely – delivers something one can genuinely call 'understanding' of the world, rather than the tautologous self-confirmation of hermetically sealed thought processes that is more typical of deduction. He asserts his conviction that when human enquirers are faced with as-yet-unexplained circumstances, and try to explain them, the surmises they come up with are far more frequently near the mark than can be accounted for by the laws of chance. This, for him, is the result of a certain ability to 'divine'

---

[41]For 'logos' is unavoidably a term with Christian associations.
[42]'A Guess at the Riddle' in Peirce 1992, 251.

the ways of Nature, which is to imply in turn a medium of relation between instances of things and knowers of things (between what he calls Secondness and Firstness) which facilitates in the human being 'a certain Insight'. This 'Insight' is:

> [N]ot strong enough to be oftener right than wrong, but strong enough not to be overwhelmingly more often wrong than right. [It is an "Insight"] into the Thirdnesses, the general elements, of Nature. . . . This Faculty is at the same time of the general nature of Instinct . . . in its so far surpassing the general powers of our reason and for its directing us as if we were in possession of facts that are entirely beyond the reach of our senses.[43]

Admittedly, this is a contestable claim in strictly empirical terms, but it is one which can claim to have on its side a great weight of support from those parts of the Christian theological tradition which speak of the eloquence of creation in speaking of God to humanity, and the attunement of a humanity (when undistracted by reductionist materialist narratives about nature[44]) to hear this speech – or, to put it another way, to discern the coherence and benevolence of the created order, and the fact that all things 'come from God and go to God'. It can be read as a quiet vote for the pneumatological idea that our human knowing can be inspired; that the Spirit can give insight into the deep things of God and God's creation:

> "What no eye has seen, nor ear heard, nor the human heart conceived . . ." – these things God has revealed to us through the Spirit; for the Spirit searches everything, even the depths of God. . . . [N]o one comprehends what is truly God's except the Spirit of God. Now we have received not the spirit of the world, but the Spirit that is from God, so that we may understand the gifts bestowed on us by God. And we speak of these things in words not taught by human wisdom but taught by the Spirit, interpreting spiritual things to those who are spiritual. (1 Cor. 2.9-13)

---

[43]Peirce 1998, 217–18.
[44]A humanity which has also uniquely been given the power to *name* created things, by knowing them in love.

Such knowing in the Spirit means knowing God's creation (and God) without either 'madness or rational certainty', as Peter Ochs puts it.[45] It is a form of knowing to which the imaginative powers of the human mind are intrinsic. These are ideas with which the poetical divines of the seventeenth century would have been quite comfortable.

Incidentally, a pneumatological take on such ideas, of the sort I have proposed with the help of 1 Corinthians 2, may also allay any fears that by using Peirce's theories (to which *human experience* is so fundamental, in his arguments that the 'real' is necessarily mediated by 'percepts'), Christian theology would have to abandon a doctrine of divine revelation. Doctrines of revelation are often opposed to theologies drawn from experience, the former frequently emphasizing divine initiative and the latter human construction. But the free ability of God to reveal or conceal that which 'no eye has seen, nor ear heard, nor human heart conceived' need not necessitate the claim that such things cannot by the work of the Spirit become 'percepts': meaningful signs for human beings. As Paul's words indicate, such spiritual things can become 'interpretable', and can take on the form of human 'understanding'. A revelation so wholly other that it was never mediated by experience would not be revelation at all. 1 Corinthians suggests that such revelation is disclosed by the 'searching' Spirit who is generous in sharing the 'findings' that are consequent upon this search with those who are ready to receive (i.e. ready also to 'find' in the Spirit).

The temporality of signs: The eventual

The historicist nature of Peirce's account of truth may have the initial effect of making one afraid of its relativism. If there is no fixed point from which to evaluate the validity of inferences, and one is confined (immanently) within the series of such inferences, then surely a truth is only as good as the present moment in which it seems to hold. There will be time-local truths that barely merit the title 'truth' at all. The 'real' will be 'an *ens* relative to private inward determinations, to the negations belonging to idiosyncrasy',

---

[45]Ochs 2011, 186.

as Peirce puts it. But Peirce believes there to be a robust (though not suprahistorical) alternative to such truths. This alternative is safeguarded by *community*, which his confidence in the connectedness and shareability of the medium of thought ensures is a strong principle in his philosophy. The continual transmission and testing of conceptions over time and in new circumstances give increased surety to those conceptions, and increased assurance to those who espouse them. The '*ens* belonging to idiosyncracy' can give way to 'an *ens* such as [can] stand in the long run'. He writes:

> The real, then, is that which, sooner or later, information or reasoning would finally result in, and which is therefore independent of the vagaries of me and you. Thus, the very origin of the conception of reality shows that this conception essentially involves the notion of a COMMUNITY, without definite limits, and capable of an indefinite increase of knowledge.[46]

We have had cause to note the highly personal nature – bordering on idiosyncracy – of Henry Vaughan's experiments in religious thought. There is an obvious risk in such experiments – clear, too, in any claim to have received some private illumination from the Holy Spirit; it is a risk that they are at best a form of misapprehension, and at worst a form of narcissism. How is one to distinguish one adventure in interpretation from another (as we remarked in Chapter 5 on reception aesthetics, the issue has similarities to the question of how one is ever to adjudicate between the merits of different interpretative receptions of a text)?

Peirce's solution to this potential problem involves time, in which the experiments of one person can be tested by others. Here, the idea of abduction can very naturally be reintroduced into the picture, for abductions are precisely experiments: experiments in thought, prone to idiosyncracy and in need of communal testing over time.

Let us imagine the stimulus to an abduction, which, as in Vaughan's case, might be a trauma (something that Peter Ochs synecdochically calls 'a cry'). Each such cry 'marks the irrefutable

---

fact that something has happened and things are not now what they were':

> We do not, however, know clearly what the mark signifies, what gave rise to it, what will result from it, or what to name it. We simply know that something has changed, and we know that the change has called us to attention.[47]

What follows is that individual respondents will try to account for the fact that 'things are not now what they were', and yet to re-establish some relation between what they were and what they are now (between the given and the found). But the success of such attempts will require time and community. Ochs writes:

> Abduction is . . . of the cosmos and of God, but also fallible: not because it may have been performed errantly, but because abduction is always of the creature as well as of God, and the creature is always fallible. . . . Abductions must be tested. In this case, testing means engaging in the all-the-more-creaturely activities of institutionalizing one's abductive recommendations . . .[48]

Individuals may hazard proposals, but they are validated when 'institutionalized'. Ochs is working through the implications of Peirce's thought here with particular reference to religious communities, and with Christianity as his case in point. As such, it seems very apposite to the seventeenth-century crisis that we have been using as our main illustration:

> To receive [reparative] guidelines [from Scripture; though perhaps also, we may add with Vaughan and Traherne in mind, from Spirit-led observation of nature] is not a matter of cognition or of individual study alone. It is a consequence of being formed into reformational practice through the presence of the Word and the work of the Spirit in sacrament [and, we may add, nature], in lives of imitatio Christi, and in communities of reformational enquiry.[49]

---

[47]Ochs 2011, 199.
[48]Ibid., 194.
[49]Ibid., 262.

Henry Vaughan does not think everyone is condemned to sit alone in his or her own little patch of darkness. He interprets boldly believing in the possibility that there may be a divine authentication of his initially very private attempts at understanding. The very fact that he commits his private musings to the communicative medium of poetry is, perhaps, a sign that he does not wish them to remain his alone. They take a step towards 'institutionalization' in the sense that they become available for others to imagine and feel with; to be received or rejected as helping to fit one to a 'new world'.

At this point, we may return to Peirce's own writings. Peirce says that in the process of testing one's conceptions of reality in community, two 'series of cognitions' separate out from one another and become progressively clearer, under the names of 'real' and 'unreal'. The former consist of those which 'at a time sufficiently future, the community will always continue to reaffirm'; and the latter consist of those which 'under the same conditions, will ever after be denied'. These series of cognitions separate over time.[50]

Even here, however, at any projected 'end' of this collective train of thought which is 'life', there is a certain indeterminacy at work; there is an 'indefinite' moment in which, although truths will be held more certainly, they will still never be held statically. Indeed, it is not clear that it is appropriate to talk of an 'end' to the historical process at all in Peircean terms. This would, of course, constitute a point of significant difference from Vaughan's outlook, in which ideas of eschatological consummation are appealed to constantly. And yet, at another level, the built-in indeterminacy of Peirce's projections forward has a great deal in common with Vaughan's acute sense of 'unrealization' – his future orientation; his close alignment with Old Testament figures; his adoption of a perspective in which themes of unfulfilment and wandering can be explored.

---

[50]Rather as (in the terms used by the First Letter of John) the children of light are progressively separated out from the children of darkness, as the fruit they bear is proven (or not):

> If we say that we have fellowship with him while we are walking in darkness, we lie and do not do what is true; but if we walk in the light as he himself is in the light, we have fellowship with one another ... (1 Jn 1.6-7)

In other words, community 'proves' the light.

Moreover, the indeterminacy that marks the future destiny of Peirce's process of thinking seems to mirror the indeterminacy that marks its past. The origins of the initial sign-thoughts in that train of thinking which is 'life' are likewise inaccessible to the rational enquirer; they are, so to speak, lost in the mists of time.

Nonetheless, according to Peirce, it is not to be supposed that there is an infinite regression of inferences. That there is an origin of *some* kind is a surd fact for him. And that there is a 'real' which is an 'ideal state of complete information' is also a surd fact. The point is that at no stage can this be uncoupled from the fundamental medium of community, in which meaning resides or else is nothing at all. '[W]hat anything really is, is what it may finally come to be known to be,' insists Peirce, thereby orienting truth to a historical future in which its fullness lies. It is drawn forward, in something resembling a process of 'final causality', in an Aristotelian sense.

> [T]hought is what it is, only by virtue of its addressing a future thought which is in its value as thought identical with it, though more developed. In this way, the existence of thought now, depends on what is to be hereafter; so that it has only a potential existence, dependent on the future thought of the community.[51]

This is to give a very high status to the 'eventual', and to its adverb 'eventually' – one which Peirce uses on several occasions when discussing this theme of progressive community-based insight.[52] In past writing, I have considered the importance of the notion of the 'while' to Christian understandings of historical existence.[53] The discussion was prompted by the farewell discourses in the Gospel of John, in which Jesus says to his disciples that he is going away for 'a little while', but that after 'a little while' they will see him again.[54] The vagueness of this evocation of a time period is part of its interest; it dispossesses the disciple of mastery of her or his time, perhaps with the effect of ensuring a more genuinely dramatic dwelling within time, in which she or he will be more ready to

---

[51]Peirce 1992, 54–5.
[52]See, for example, 'Ground of Validity of the Laws of Logic' (1869) in Peirce 1992, 64.
[53]Quash 2005, 220.
[54]Jn 16.16. See also Jn 7.33.

receive the gifts of 'complete joy' that Jesus promises to those he is leaving behind. If that suggestion is accepted, then a similar thing might in turn be concluded about the idea of the 'eventual', as Peirce uses it. 'Eventually' and 'a little while' have a good deal in common in their quality of vagueness and yet assurance. The entry into all truth will, surely, come, but there is no overview of the historical process which will deliver it such that the timescale of its coming can be measured and the stages of its advance plotted. The Holy Spirit keeps such knowledge in reserve, and is thus the safeguard of the 'eventual'.

This, once again, reinforces an association between pneumatology and Peirce's characterization of abductive inference. Abduction's way of orienting one to the future is both vague *and* worthy of trust, in that it is premised on a principle of extendability (unfolding), which – as an analogical mode of reasoning – insists on the meaningfulness of 'generalities' but is suspicious of the short circuit frequently represented by an appeal to 'universals' (which are favoured by deductive modes of reasoning). As Peirce says, deduction's medium is 'necessity', while induction's is 'probability' and abduction's is 'expectability'.[55]

Indeed, might one use a term even stronger than expectability? Might one say *hope*? Abductive generalizations in Peirce's terms can be read as a mode of hopefulness; and they are a mode of hopefulness because as well as heightening 'expectability', they account for this expectability with reference to an 'ideality' that is the condition for all thinking, even though the full form of that ideality remains vague for now.

Hoping for what we do not see

One of the most sustained and important pneumatological passages in the New Testament comes in Paul's Letter to the Romans, and it is all about hope. The account Paul gives of Christian hope is strikingly compatible with a Peircean account of expectability – conditioned by a future that is both sure and nonetheless vague. Moreover, in English translation, it is littered with the modal auxiliary 'will'. Temporal coding is as essential to Paul's account

---

[55]Peirce 1998, 233.

of the Spirit's role in human redemption as the modal auxiliaries are essential to how the English language captures the ambiguous nuance of human activity in history: 'will' can mean both what we commit our wills to and also a futurity with some 'objective' reality independent of ourselves:

> I consider that the sufferings of this present time are not worth comparing with the glory about to be revealed to us. For the creation waits with eager longing for the revealing of the children of God; for the creation was subjected to futility, not of its own will but by the will of the one who subjected it, in hope that the creation itself will be set free from its bondage to decay and will obtain the freedom of the glory of the children of God. We know that the whole creation has been groaning in labour pains until now; and not only the creation, but we ourselves, who have the first fruits of the Spirit, groan inwardly while we wait for adoption, the redemption of our bodies. For in hope we were saved. Now hope that is seen is not hope. For who hopes for what is seen? But if we hope for what we do not see, we wait for it with patience. (Rom. 8.18-25)

The future orientation of this passage is intense, expressed as it is through the metaphor of labour pains – a powerful image in which a chain of events in which the human being is wholly invested (in body, mind and emotion) at the same time unfolds with its own 'independent' and certainly unstoppable momentum. An awareness of the unstoppability of the process may be what underwrites Paul's use of the language of predestination a little while later in this passage:

> For those whom he foreknew he also predestined to be conformed to the image of his Son, in order that he might be the firstborn within a large family. (Rom. 8.29)

But the dominant imagery that Paul uses, and that frames this statement, does not commend complacency of the sort we explored in some historical strands of Calvinism in Chapter 2. You cannot be complacent in labour pains. The human will is (usually) maximally engaged in the act of giving birth even if, simultaneously, not in control. And Paul says that Christians must 'wait' for the redemption they hope for in just this manner: not in some loitering, heel-kicking passivity, as for something 'foregone'; rather, in a momentous giving over of the self, to which eagerness, longing and (possibly painful) openness are fundamental. This degree of self-investment revolutionizes most normal meanings of the word wait.

There are cognitive elements to this: an epistemology which, like abductive reasoning itself, is constituted by the imaginative conjecture of shapes of future fulfilment and their energetic (though provisional) embrace. Meanwhile, the greatest threat to such Spirit-led modes of knowing is 'a spirit of slavery', which is wholly determined by the presently existent or by the past. To use Paul's language, it takes the form of 'falling back'.

> So then, brothers and sisters, we are debtors, not to the flesh, to live according to the flesh—for if you live according to the flesh, you will die; but if by the Spirit you put to death the deeds of the body, you will live. For all who are led by the Spirit of God are children of God. For you did not receive a spirit of slavery to fall back into fear, but you have received a spirit of adoption. When we cry, "Abba! Father!" it is that very Spirit bearing witness with our spirit that we are children of God, and if children, then heirs, heirs of God and joint heirs with Christ—if, in fact, we suffer with him so that we may also be glorified with him. (Rom. 8.12-17)

One of the ways in which a certain sort of 'theology of the given' is comparable with *deductive* (rather than abductive) reasoning[56] is in its ability to work in a hermetically sealed way. In other words, it can quite easily bracket out – or abstract itself from – certain more ethnographically or empirically grounded measures of its own adequacy. As Peirce puts it:

> Among the characters to which we pay no attention in this mode of argument [i.e., deduction] is whether or not the hypothesis of our premises conforms more or less to the state of things in the

---

[56]Becoming thus a problematic version of what Peter Ochs identifies in an American post-liberalism, that has relinquished its virtuous and creative relationship to tradition, and has tipped over into a narrow 'tautologism'.

outward world. . . . Our inference is valid if and only if there really is such a relation between the state of things supposed in the premises and the state of things stated in the conclusion. Whether this really be so or not is a question of reality, and has nothing at all to do with how we may be inclined to think. . . . If the entire human race were unable to see the connection, the argument would be nonetheless sound, although it would not be humanly clear.[57]

But this eclipsing of the human – indeed, of the whole 'outside world' – in service of a closed system of self-ratifying supposition is well described as 'slavery'. It is also, in Paul's terms, a denial of the God who 'searches', and by whose own instructive activity of intercession (an activity in which those who wish to know how to pray are invited to join) human beings also are oriented towards the world, and opened up to *find* things in it:

Likewise the Spirit helps us in our weakness; for we do not know how to pray as we ought, but that very Spirit intercedes with sighs too deep for words. And God, who searches the heart, knows what is the mind of the Spirit, because the Spirit intercedes for the saints according to the will of God. (Rom. 8.26-27)

Temporal process is not bypassed in the working out of God's purposes towards the full glorification of all things: this is not in question for Paul, and it is in his own way (and in pneumatological form) the presence in his theology of an equivalent of Peirce's 'eventually'. We see it most clearly in his statement that 'all things work together for good' (Rom. 8:28), which is a wager on what the future will confirm to have been true, even in the face of what is as yet unassimilable to a necessary, or even a probable, explanation.

It is time to draw to a close this discussion of the ontology and the temporality of Peirce's model of how reason negotiates the world of which it is part. No doubt because of his huge influence on the thought of some of the key thinkers whose ideas we engaged with in Chapter 1 (and especially on Peter Ochs), Peirce's model

---

[57]Peirce 1998, 212.

has proved very sympathetic to the idea of analogical reasoning (reasoning through generalized particulars rather than through universal concepts) which we set out in that first chapter. Indeed, this book has championed such analogical reasoning in each of its case studies, and has found versions of it in each of its theoretical sorties.

The resources offered by theories of maculation, reception and abduction help articulate the ways in which one may harness a 'powerful generalizing force' from certain sorts of attention to historical particulars, even when individual interpreters 'do not have the power on [their] own to foresee what the next example will look like'.[58] Like Jacob, who was only *after the fact* able to exclaim 'Truly God is in this place and I did not know it,'[59] it is often the case that the next analogue will be something we find by surprise. Or perhaps by providence. In a Christian account – and as Ochs states – '[t]he Spirit alone discloses the analogue[s]' by which we may see the knowledge of God that we have (mediated, for example, in the forms of practice and belief of our own religious tradition) coming into meaningful dialogue with new insights gleaned from attention to the world (including, incidentally, other religious traditions, and apparently 'secular' forms of life). Our part is to wait with eager longing, with a heightened openness to the found and what will be disclosed in it.

That said, the 'flow' is not all from the given towards the found. To recall another important point from Chapter 1, but now with the assistance of Peircean language, the conjectures (or abductively generated '*Cases*') which are a mode of our active waiting, by which we participate in the world of Thirdness, and anticipate the ideality which is to come, do still have inherited shapes against which we can measure the adequacy of what we think we have found. In other words, we need there to be givens in order in a meaningful way to find anything at all. We may never know exactly what will come next as we interpret historical experience, but for something we find to be known and incorporated as an analogue of preceding cases when it *does* come (and not simply an arbitrary occurrence), there remains a role for '*Rules*'. Here, as

---

[58]Ochs 2011, 189.
[59]As Peter Ochs observes: Ochs 2011, 189.

noted before, we see the interrelation of the pneumatological with the christological.

To put it in Peircean terms, there are limits to what abduction can conjecture. Even though its distinctive mode is to generate *Cases*, it is still, after all, regulated by the need to affirm a *Rule* to account for a *Result*. Peirce points out that 'quite new perceptions cannot be obtained from abduction'.[60] The point may be transposed into Christian theological terms as follows: Christ is a *Rule* whose authority the *Cases* generated in the Spirit seek to establish and re-establish. Christ imparts some form to the *Cases* that may be conjectured. This is not to say that the *Rule* remains untouched by the unfolding progression of *Cases* that seek to incorporate it in actual, humanly meaningful situations. To recall again our analogy with the English Common Law tradition, the *Rule* lives though the *Cases*, and becomes more nuanced and effective in each new particular application of it to a *Case*. Or, to put it in yet another way that we have developed, there is an 'additive' logic to the way that *Rules* work themselves out in *Cases*.

For a final time in this chapter, Paul's Letter to the Romans seems to confirm a pneumatological-christological nexus as a theological counterpart to this model of abductive reasoning. The 'Spirit' (or 'Spirit of God') is at the same time the 'Spirit of Christ'. The found things that are encountered as a consequence of being 'in the Spirit' prove lively, generative and life-giving (and therefore genuinely 'spiritual') when 'Christ is in you'. In other words, when the form (or the *Rule*) of Christ and the activity of negotiating new experience in the Spirit (or the *Cases*) correspond in the believer, then there 'is life because of righteousness':

But you are not in the flesh; you are in the Spirit, since the Spirit of God dwells in you. Anyone who does not have the Spirit of Christ does not belong to him. But if Christ is in you, though the body is dead because of sin, the Spirit is life because of righteousness. If the Spirit of him who raised Jesus from the dead dwells in you, he who raised Christ from the dead will give life to your mortal bodies also through his Spirit that dwells in you. (Rom. 8.9-11)

---

[60]Peirce 1998, 231.

Peirce said that 'pragmatism . . . allows any flight of imagination, provided this imagination ultimately alights upon a possible practical effect'.[61] Abductive reasoning is, for him, the key mode in which imagination takes flight in service of new insights and the new forms of life that follow from them. They enact the human yearning for a fuller participation in the true, relational, communicative reality of the world.

In a Pauline vein, it might be said that the business of searching (and finding) in the Spirit likewise legitimates 'any flight of imagination', provided this imagination ultimately alights upon a *sanctifying* effect. The test of whether an effect is indeed a sanctifying effect (and whether the flight of imagination that led to it is therefore to be endorsed) is whether it manifests a transformation of persons in appropriate conformity with Christ (that 'appropriate conformity' being something importantly distinct from the identical repetition of Christ's words and action).

Peirce's insistence on the indispensability of community to the process of discernment when faced with these 'flights of imagination' – and, in turn, to the embedding in shared forms of life of the insights gained from them – is well-suited to a Christian theology of how the Church tests every 'spirit' in the power of the Holy Spirit. The Church affirms that the Holy Spirit is the Spirit of community, and looks to see whether greater communion (or fellowship) flows from the newly proposed 'findings' that are presented to it. The corporate patterns of the Church's life, the mediums of exchange within the Church, the strength of the bonds of love which hold the Church together, the instruction in the virtues that make the Church what it is, are one and all attributed to that Spirit who guarantees fellowship. That which does not pass the test of whether it serves communion in the Spirit becomes a victim of the 'eventual', and becomes, in time, associated with unreality.

Thomas Traherne's as yet unpublished manuscript *The Ceremonial Law* includes an extraordinary discussion of the burning bush in Exodus. After an exquisite passage in which he characteristically combines scientific observation with theological interpretation to talk of how this bush (which is a trope of the Church) weeps for

---

[61]Ibid., 235.

her sins,[62] he goes on to describe how the fruits of this bush are fivefold:

Hope, Patience, Glory, faith & Charity
Within the Splendor of her flames we see . . .

This is a powerful image with which to end the present chapter on abduction. Faith, hope and charity have been celebrated by the Church as the 'theological virtues' – the Pauline triad, which together abide into eternity, and are the vital gifts that animate Christians' discipleship of God. They are given and sustained by the Spirit, and they build up the community of Christians. But by adding two more to them – patience and glory – Traherne has done an arresting thing.

He has, first, embedded an enhanced sense of the importance of relating well to the 'eventual' by adding to hope a further virtue (or 'fruit') which is patience. The provisionality, the openness to the future, the readiness to wait (and often to try things again in another way) are fundamental features of an abductive approach to discerning God in the world. Peirce, as we have noted, remarked on how risky abduction is as a form of inference. It is as though, here, Traherne recognizes that anything as risky as 'thinking towards God' is bound to need patience as well as hope.

But the rewards of such risks, as Vaughan too knew, are a glimpse of the divine glory which is the first and final cause of All Things, and this glory is a fruit of the Church as well as an attribute of God in that (communally, and *through* their patience) Christians are made participants in it, by the operation of the Holy Spirit.

---

[62] It is not meet that she should Barren be,
Since she's inspird, O Lord my GOD, by Thee
As burning Wood doth at the Ends express,
A Weeping Moisture, & it self confess
An Enemy by nature to the fire
In whose Embrace it doth or Expire,
Or is Transformd: So doth thy church confess,
Her Enmity, & it in Tears express.

(Thomas Traherne, *The Ceremonial Law*, 8a [unpublished manuscript]; I am grateful to Elizabeth Dodd for this transcript of the text.)

Abduction is both patient and glorificatory; both painstaking and transfiguring. This is why, as Peter Ochs says, it can be not only 'scientific reasoning', but also 'worship'.[63]

> And yet, as Angels in some brighter dreams
>   Call to the soul, when man doth sleep:
> So some strange thoughts transcend our wonted themes,
>   And into glory peep.

> (Henry Vaughan, *They are all gone into
> the world of light!*, ll. 25–8)

---

[63]Ochs 2011, 193.

PART FOUR

8

Vertiginous at-homeness

Introduction

Abduction, says Peter Ochs, 'is science, but not positivism'.[1] This is because abduction supposes the reality of states of affairs that it cannot always demonstrate empirically (though it can test them experientially), and that sometimes it will have to revise.

There are some abductions which must be assumed very *strongly* to be real in order for a whole series of other forms of thought and action to be sustainable. They are what we might call 'founding' abductions. Peirce once designated foundational forms of thought of such a kind 'A-reasonings', by contrast with the 'B-reasonings' which they invisibly facilitated and could sometimes repair.[2] He seems to be talking about something very like these A-reasonings when elsewhere he refers to 'an extreme case of abductive inferences' which differ from the majority 'in being absolutely beyond criticism'.[3] In other words, there is a group of reasonings that have a constitutive relation to the appreciation of 'generality' by which we negotiate our lives from day to day, and without which we could not live at all. This does not exempt these A-reasonings/ extreme-case abductions from being 'extremely fallible' (they are 'beyond criticism' only while in use, generating and sustaining productive forms of life), but it *does* relate them to our instinctive sense that we can live confidently in the world in a way that is not perpetually afflicted by scepticism (or, to put it another way, that

---

[1] Ochs 1998, 193.
[2] Hartshorne et al. 1958, §189.
[3] Peirce 1998, 227.

we can be 'at home' in the world). They seem to have something of the character of religious faith about them: faith is not typically an object of direct perception or analysis in itself, but more a lens by which the world is seen and negotiated. B-reasonings have more to do with the activities that are consequent upon having such a lens; they do not typically examine the lens as such. B-reasonings, by the same token, present themselves far more explicitly to our conscious mind than A-reasonings do, and we can analyse how they interrelate, and say how one follows upon another. (B-reasonings *are*, therefore, 'subject to criticism'.)

That said, there are some adventurous forms of thought which do from time to time seek to make observations about the conditioning suppositions or intuitions (the extreme-case abductions, or A-reasonings) in which our other activities are grounded, and on which they seem to depend. These adventurous forms of thought are frequently philosophical or theological in character – although, as I hope to have demonstrated in this book, they often take a literary or visual form too. They are, we might say, *non-extreme abductions* (because they are conscious and cognized) about the character and sources of our *extreme abductions* (which are usually precognitive). As we have noted, and as Peter Ochs has argued in far greater detail, such adventurous explorations of the usually invisible are very often a consequence of a crisis, in which our habitual B-reasonings do not seem to work any longer. We saw a version of this in Vaughan's need to ask again how God was present to him in the world when his liturgical and sacramental order ceased to function. But at other times, perhaps, such adventurous thought might simply be the result of an intense desire to relate more fully to the mysteries of creation; to see the sum of 'All Things' as a sort of divine dictionary, capable of teaching us the language of the Holy Spirit.

In *Another Reformation*, Ochs relates the exploration of extreme-case abductions to pneumatology in just such a vein. He first writes:

> [T]he bases of our actions lie in conditions that precede and ground our capacity to think and conceptualize. These conditions are therefore "precognitive" but not unknowable. Knowledge of them is simply of a different sort from direct perception or rational inference. It is a posteriori the way that empirical

science is a posteriori: reasoning from effect to cause, it offers us probable knowledge of such laws of creation as gravity or the speed of light.[4]

The precognitive conditions of our day-to-day thought are at one level, as we have indicated (following Peirce's lead), another sort of 'reason'. They are precognitive (extreme-case) abductions that in turn make it possible to make intentional abductive inferences. But Ochs suggests that in seeking a greater understanding of our precognitive (extreme-case) abductions, our intentional abductions may then go one stage further, and speculate abductively about what is the condition of *those* abductions. What, in other words, is the source and goal of even the extreme-case abductions, which are, in their turn, the condition of intentional thought? To pick up again the analogy between extreme-case abductions and religious faith, this would be to ask (abductively) not only how faith is the condition of certain sorts of knowing and action, but to ask what the condition is for faith itself coming into being. Here is where pneumatological language enters explicitly into Ochs's account, for these abductions will be:

> [A]*bductions* – probable, nonnecessary, but testable observations – about the characteristics of Spirit as ground and presupposition [and, I would suggest, *goal*] of our actions. Such abductions enable us to "see" the Spirit, not face-to-face but through the "shadow" or "back" of our visible behaviors . . . inferring by hypothesis and then reconceiving in response to new experience.[5]

In what follows, I want to return to the thought of Daniel W. Hardy, whom we first met in Chapter 1, and look especially at his method of discerning divine 'operative conditions' in the particulars of the world. As Ochs asserts, Hardy's method is a form of richly theological abduction. I deem it to be in a tradition that stretches back – at the very least – to Vaughan and Traherne.

As Ochs also asserts, these pneumatological forms of abduction are forms of abduction that correspond very closely indeed to the activity of worship. As a consequence, part of this chapter will test

---

[4]Ochs 1998, 176–7.
[5]Ibid., 176.

the idea that Christian liturgical worship is a mode of making the divine operative conditions of the world as fully present as possible, so as to live in the fullest possible relationship to them.

In saying that Hardy stands in a tradition that stretches back to Vaughan and Traherne, it is necessary to add that he does so by way of the mediation of one very important figure (both literary and theological in his output) whom we have examined only in passing so far: Samuel Taylor Coleridge. In this final chapter, our initial examination of Hardy's thought will, therefore, open out onto a consideration of Coleridge too. This will actually amplify the discussion of how theological abduction corresponds to worship, for Coleridge's own account of how abduction works (as Hardy realized with admiration) is fundamentally linked to the idea of attraction towards God. In this regard, Coleridge – though a precursor of Peirce in his development of the idea of abductive reasoning – goes further than Peirce does in the extent to which he is prepared to give ontological and theological body to the dynamics of abduction.[6]

The whole of the present chapter's enquiry is framed by the idea that there is a quality of *vertiginous at-homeness* to human life in the world that is radically open and comprehensively truthful; a quality to which abduction does better justice than many more artificially constrained, and often reductionist, modes of rational enquiry. Why vertiginous at-homeness? The phrase captures the paradox of a sense of dazzled wonderment, of the kind we have seen in the seventeenth-century divine poets, in which the self finds great vistas opening up – opening up in the sheer multiplicity and diversity of created things, and simultaneously in the infinite detail and depth that characterize each one. In being related to God, this profusion of and profundity in things becomes all the more dizzying. At the same time, the activity of abduction is intrinsically affirmative of the bonds between things, and of ourselves (who are also part of the world of things) as likewise bonded to what we see, know and love. This was what underlay my use of the phrase 'being at home in the world' earlier in this chapter, in relation to how A-reasonings serve fruitful negotiation of the world rather than paralysing scepticism about it. So abduction throws wide – as wide as thought itself – the

---

[6]Though, as Ochs points out, Peirce is pretty theological too, despite Hardy's misgivings; see Hardy et al. 2010, 72, note 9.

sphere of its attention and interest (as we observed in the previous chapter, the boundaries of what counts as relevant for an abduction can be massively greater than those for an inductive inference); and yet, at the same time, abduction is premised on a confidence in the connectedness and shareability of the medium of thought.

Operative conditions and worship

It was in a short but penetrating introduction to the theology of Karl Barth that Dan Hardy deployed the notion of operative conditions to account for the structure of the *Church Dogmatics* and the way that its different parts rest upon (or, perhaps better, *open onto*) one another.[7] In looking at the notion here, I am more concerned with how the idea sheds light on Hardy's own way of articulating the dynamics of theological knowledge than with its accuracy as an account of Barth (though I happen to think it is a very good tool for interpreting Barth).

Fundamental to Barth's project was how the 'movement of God' in history could be 'accessible through participatory, personal knowledge' even when 'beyond access' by empirical investigation.[8] The *logic of Christian dogmatics* must work with this distinctively constrained (and liberated) form of knowledge, which bears many of the hallmarks of what, with Peirce's help, we have been calling abduction.

The pattern that Hardy sees in the *Church Dogmatics* as a whole is, he says, like 'a chain of dialectical unities: if it is to be more than human practice or concept, the "lower" in each case must rest on the *operative condition* of the "higher," without which it falls out of its relation to God into the kind of "distance" of which Barth spoke so passionately in his commentaries on the Epistle to the Romans'.[9] Thus, with Barth as his case study, Hardy summarizes the logic of Christian dogmatics as follows:

The purpose is to identify the *operative condition* by which [Church proclamation] *is* proclamation (or the church *is* the

---

[7]Hardy 2005, 21–42.
[8]Ibid., 24.
[9]Ibid., 28–9.

church) as distinct from something else, that is the *Word of God* as attested in the preached, written and revealed Word of God. Next, we find that the Word of God thus found has its *operative condition* in that it is God's *actual speech* to humanity; and the *operative condition* for that is then also found, etc. This "chain" of "operative conditions" is at the heart of [*Church Dogmatics*]. Dogmatics, as a theological science distinct from testimony and service, is to be the self-examination of the church to find whether, at each level of assertion, its operative condition is in place. To put it differently, Dogmatics is to examine the agreement of human speech or concept with its operative condition: uncovering truth as the agreement of the two is the task of theology. But if the *operative condition* for human speech is other than Word of God/God's Speech/God's Self-Revelation/etc. – as appropriate to the level of examination – then whatever is said is simply human speech or concept and, from a theological viewpoint, untrue.[10]

This is the reason that Barth writes the volumes on the doctrine of the Word of God before he writes the volumes on the Doctrine of God. Preaching opens onto its own legitimating and animating condition in Scripture; Scripture opens onto its own legitimating and animating condition in God's speech (above all in Christ); God's speech opens onto its own animating condition in God's life as triune. In Christian theological terms, this is a demonstration on a grand – even vertiginous – scale of what earlier we saw Peter Ochs describe as *a posteriori* enquiry: working back from the things we know to enquire about the conditions for the things we know. ('[T]he bases of our actions lie in conditions that precede and ground our capacity to think and conceptualize,' as we heard Ochs put it – and even though these operative conditions cannot be perceived directly they are not thereby absolutely off-limits for knowledge, for it is possible to '"see" the Spirit, not face-to-face but through the "shadow" or "back" of our visible behaviors'.[11]) Importantly, these conditions though *a posteriori* in epistemological terms (in other words, arrived at later than their effects by our processes of knowing) are at the same time 'higher'. Understood in these terms, says Hardy, '[t]he *operative condition* that makes human speech

---

[10]Ibid., 28.
[11]See p. 239 above.

and life *actually proclamation and church* is the *Word of God'*, and 'if it does indeed rest on the operative condition' that it should rest on then 'it is indeed the speaking of God, the God who is free to be – and to reveal himself in – Jesus Christ'.[12]

As I have said, this way of expressing what Barth is up to functions just as well, in many ways, to shine a light onto Hardy's own theological approach. What he appreciated in Barth, and summarized so succinctly, is comparable with what he sought to do in his own work. In one of the moving conversations recorded by his friends and family in the months before his death, Hardy spoke as follows of the 'fundamental impulses' he recognized in himself:

> [T]o go deeper and deeper into things, for myself and with others; . . . to find greater depths which are found again to be the depths of God. This is about my *almost insatiable* concern for God, not just for knowledge about God but a more insatiable thirst again than that . . .[13]

Here, as in Barth, there is a vertiginous sense of depth (which is also a sense of that which is 'higher'), and at the same time a recognition that one's ownmost need – one's home in God – lies in these depths. One is only oneself (and oneself-with-others) in relating well to these depths. Though expressed in a somewhat different register from his account of the dynamics of Barth's *Dogmatics*, we nonetheless find here in Hardy's theological method a parallel concern with 'operative conditions'.

But the 'somewhat different register' is also a sign that there are important differences between Hardy and Barth, and that there is a limit to how far Barth's thought can be 'Hardified'! As Hardy will go on to say in the same essay, Barth's theology risks underappreciating the contribution of human growth-in-historical-process to the knowledge of God. And while, yes, the 'task of theology' may be 'to examine the agreement of human speech or concept with its operative condition', and identify 'truth' whenever such agreement is 'uncovered', this can suggest a more narrowly cognitive concern with correspondence than is suggested by Hardy's reflections on the

---

[12]Hardy 2005, 29.
[13]Hardy et al. 2010, ix.

almost 'maternal' intensity of those operative conditions of human life which theology is invited to search.[14]

Hardy is more open than Barth is to what may be learnt from historical experience and observation of the natural world. He has a theophanic account of the created realm that, as I have hinted already, has much in common with the seventeenth-century Anglican spirit. It is put relatively soberly by Thomas White in his *Method and Instructions for the Art of Divine Meditation*:

> . . . Meditation is a serious solemn thinking and considering of the things of God, to the end we might understand how much they concern us, and that our hearts may be raised to some holy affections and resolutions.[15]

And it is put relatively ecstatically by Thomas Traherne in writing about 'Accidents' in his *Commentaries of Heaven*:

> I am taught to look for all Glory & Delight among Accidents. . . . Hony with out its Sweetness is but Yellow Mire. Gold without its Yellowness and Consistence is a Shadow, & without its Price a Stone. What would a Rose be without its Redness, an Ey without its Sight, a Star without its Splendor? Accidents are the very Robes of Glory.[16]

Hardy's approach nearly four centuries later has features both of the solemn and of the ecstatic. It is open to beginning its 'divine meditations' – its search for the operative conditions of All Things – not only with the practice of Church proclamation, but also with any of the accidents of the world. Take, for example, his description of the 'accidents' of water as he encountered them in a renewal of baptismal vows during a pilgrimage to the headwaters of the Jordan river, and the way these accidents opened for him onto the divine depths which were their (and the pilgrims') operative conditions:

> I became aware of distinct elements of the pilgrimage after I became aware of distinct elements from the baptism: the elements

[14]Ibid., 23.
[15]White 1655, 5–6.
[16]Traherne 2005, 111–12.

of head, water, hands. I also became aware of specific actions, such as extending the hand forward. But the defining moment of awareness was of a physical sensation: "It is cold! It is more than just water. It seems to be alive." The waters poured into an impressed area by the cave, so that when the area was filled, I was surrounded by waters full of life, so I was filled as well by the most vivid sense that, when I reached in to draw a handful, what I touched was not merely H_2O, but also a regathering of the life that is within the waters.[17]

It is hard not to be reminded here of Henry Vaughan's meditation on the waterfall ('What sublime truths, and wholesome themes,/ Lodge in thy mystical, deep streams!/Such as dull man can never find/Unless [the] Spirit lead his mind'). In both cases, there is a pneumatological opening out from accidents to depths, proving the accidents to be robes of glory. Hardy continues his account by making a different (though, as we shall see, not unrelated) literary connection:

> In Coleridgian terms, what I sensed was a concentration of thought occurring there. Before the [renewal of] baptism, the idea of pilgrimage was only cognitive for me, without any attention to the affections. I had anticipated pilgrimage in a "cool way", my thoughts "independent" of desire. But through that moment of scooping up the baptismal water, what had been merely thought became an instrument of desire. The enactment of pilgrimage meant an awakening of the affections.[18]

The Trahernian language of (and fascination with) accidents – which seems in this context so apposite to Hardy too – is a reminder of another important way in which Hardy's enquiries into operative conditions differ from Barth's. They are more sacramental. Or, at least, they want to give an account of how we learn about God by looking into the operative conditions of sacramental practice and materials as much as we do by looking into the operative conditions of proclamation (which is Barth's principal

---

[17]Hardy et al. 2010, 43.
[18]Ibid.

concern).[19] In Traherne's context, the language of accidents could not but have continued in some measure to carry the freight of associations with Reformation battles over eucharistic presence, even as (at the same time) they were a useful term for analysing the objects of a wave of new scientific investigation. Traherne's Anglicanism, like Hardy's, does not lead him to a forensic or institutionalized account of real presence in the Eucharist, in which accidents have a highly prescribed meaning, but it does permit a rich doctrine of presence to which accidents are essential. Material things in such an account are, as we have said in an earlier chapter, *capax infiniti*, and their outward forms are not so much 'hide' (which conceals) as 'skin' (which shines), if viewed and enjoyed aright. Their operative conditions announce themselves in them.

The Eucharist's importance for Hardy's theology is repeatedly emphasized by those who have written about his thought. In David Ford's words:

> For Dan one of the most powerful signs of hope for the fulfillment of God's desire for the deepest communion with all humanity and creation was the Eucharist; it is the main everyday locus of attraction to God . . .[20]

And as Hardy himself writes in *Finding the Church*:

> The Eucharist is an embodiment of all the dimensions of human existence in the world; biological, physical, historical circumstance, personal participation, social relations, political configuration, economic exchange, and cultural formation – in a forward trajectory anticipating the good of all people and things. . . . The Eucharist is . . . a comprehensive event or performance of social meaning. . . . It preserves the characteristic dynamics of God's relations to the world in exemplifying them, not by stating them as if we were outside of them observing them.[21]

---

[19]One way of handling this is, of course, to admit that sacramental practice is itself a sort of proclamation, but there is always a risk in this of substituting its drama with theological and/or homiletical propositions.
[20]Hardy et al. 2010, 117.
[21]Hardy 2001, 244.

Incidentally, and to recall the discussion of the Eucharist in Chapter 1,[22] it is precisely the conviction that the Eucharist is such a 'comprehensive event' while always also being an historically and temporally highly particular event, and perforce a tradition-specific one, that makes it not so much a problem as a resource when engaging with other religious traditions. If it is held to offer a window onto the operative conditions of all human sociality (and the constitution of the non-human world too), then it is *relevant* to an understanding of other religious traditions (if you are a Christian, and sometimes also if you are not) even if it is not the universal practice of all religious people. Other religious people may have their own practices that also open onto such ('abduced') operative conditions for human well-being; the potential value of these ought not to be denied in advance. In this we see a good exemplification of the principle of reasoning by analogy, which we established in Chapter 1. By believing in its comprehensive relevance not as a universal concept but as an enacted dynamic, it is possible to generalize from the Eucharist in such a way that one becomes more alert to other possible (analogous) windows onto divine operative conditions than one was before.

In its own way, the performance of Christian sacraments like the Eucharist (and, I suggest, other liturgical rites too) are *themselves* a sort of abduction, inasmuch as they take something immediately present to one's experience (the act of scooping water with one's hands, for example, while in the company of other pilgrims) and through it open up a vertiginously more profound (or 'comprehensive') hinterland of meaning, giving us not just the thing as such, but communicating the way in which that thing (in the company of all other things) comes from God and goes to God, in a chain of complexly stacked and related operative conditions. Thus, the operative conditions for our liturgical activity can be seen as the shape of a new and redeemed humanity offered to us in Christ (and unfolded continually by the Spirit); the operative conditions for that humanity the desire of God to make, redeem and fulfil us; the operative conditions for that the dynamics of the triune life itself.[23]

---

[22]See p. 21.

[23]An extra link might be added to this chain in that our liturgical formation might in its own turn be seen as providing the operative conditions for our ethical practices.

For Hardy, worshipping practices both *preserve* and *exemplify* 'the characteristic dynamics of God's relations to the world'. Like abductions in the realm of inferential reasoning, they provide a picture of a bigger kind in which the objects of our immediate concern make better sense.

Liturgical abduction of this kind, as Peter Ochs points out, 'discloses the creative and reparative activity that animates the cosmos as well as the triune life and therefore doubly obligates the believer to hope for and participate in this cosmic and divine work of repair'.[24] In other words, liturgical abduction both shows us something and instructs us in something; it tells us what the world we belong to is really like, and in doing so equips us to belong to this world even better than we presently do. To know it at all well is to know one ought to participate in it; to know it better is to know one ought to participate in it better. In Hardy's words, '[t]o confess to the light is to acknowledge you've strayed: the light reveals both the grace and the disgrace of creation'.[25] So enquiry into divine operative conditions, with the help of liturgy and sacrament, is not just a matter of acquiring more knowledge; it is a form of getting involved with God, because it is itself a joining in with the work of the Spirit (who, *as* God, searches among the deep things of God).[26] And in this involvement with a God who seeks to repair the world (to make all things new), we learn more about just what repair is needed and – it could be – become *part* of that repair.

In this approach, as Hardy puts it, human social meaning is 'infolded' through worship and sacrament with God's infinite meaning. A celebration of the Eucharist can never, therefore, be conceived adequately as simply the manifestation of 'an already-complete action of God in human life in the Church'[27]; or, in our terms, a simple 'given'. On the contrary, '[w]hile the Eucharist always brings to light the mutual involvement of the drama of human life with God's work, this is *always as history* . . .'.[28] It is always open to finding. Unlike some eucharistic theologies which emphasize the

---

[24]Ochs 2011, 193.
[25]Hardy et al. 2010, 21.
[26]See Ochs 2011, 183.
[27]Hardy 2001, 246; cited in Ochs 2011, 181.
[28]Hardy 2001, 247; cited in Ochs 2011, 181.

completeness of the Eucharist either as an ecclesially possessed ideal form (a more Roman Catholic and Orthodox tendency) or as an accomplished historical action (a more Protestant tendency), Hardy's Anglican habit of mind inclines him to emphasize how the Eucharist's abductive performance of social meaning in the Spirit 'does not lose its character as fragile, incomplete, and forward-moving even as it is drawn by God toward the eschatological finality of God's work'.[29]

The sense of a guaranteeing finality is clearly present in Hardy's model, as the preceding quotation attests. However, the finality that guarantees is at the same time something that awaits our finding. The language that dominates Hardy's frequent reversion to these issues is the language of attraction. The life of Christian discipleship (which has as its operative condition the fundamental orientation of creatures to God) 'is about recognizing how much more there is than we have ever seen before and about being attracted by it and lifted up to it'.[30] This is Hardy's own version of the *desiderium naturale visionis Dei* (and thus another point at which he parts company with Barth, who questions the 'naturalness' of any such desire):

> Creatures have a seed of perfection in them antecedently: a capacity for benevolence, for being attracted and thus for being brought into relation with their creator.[31]

This informs the 'inherent sociality of all creation', and it is our powerful attraction to God (the operative condition of sociality) that makes human 'sociopoiesis' work. Refusal of or immunity to that attraction is what frustrates social life (after all, as Augustine knew, a society is nothing without common objects of love, and those objects of love have to be worthy ones if the sociality they underwrite is to be durable).

Hardy approves of Richard Hooker's idea of a 'divinely infused rationality', seeing the compatibility of this idea with the idea of the fundamental attraction of the human creature into more intensively

---

[29]Hardy 2001, 246; cited in Ochs 2011, 181.
[30]Hardy et al. 2010, 104.
[31]Ibid., 49.

realized social life. The typical activity of such divinely infused
rationality is, in Hardy's view, abduction, inasmuch as it is a mode of
'[reasoning] through attraction to others and to God'.[32] Abduction
is a 'capacity to turn away from self-engagement'[33]; it 're-opens the
self-absorbed human being to [primordial] attraction'.[34] Abduction
'does not therefore quiet the appetites; it transforms them into
desire for God and thus desire for the other's wellbeing'.[35]

All of this leads Hardy to make the claim that '[t]owardness is
even more basic than creation and redemption':

> [T]owardness . . . is the direction of creation. Creatures are
> created to move toward God. When creatures somehow lose
> that towardness – becoming obsessive at some point, separating
> from the whole of things and serving only themselves – then the
> creation loses its order.[36]

At this point, I want to pause, and turn to some of the pneumatological proposals made by David H. Kelsey in his monumental
recent work on theological anthropology, *Eccentric Existence*. The
prompt for doing this is precisely Hardy's appeal to a preposition
('toward') to help characterize the relation of certain doctrines to
one another. Prepositions are something that Kelsey makes use of
in a similarly constructive way, though a little differently. But the
more substantial purpose of this venture into Kelsey's thought is
that he very helpfully sets out a model in which the eschatological
orientation of human life is more fundamental even than its need
of redemption. This both confirms and amplifies Hardy's abductive
outlook, and also my larger agenda in exploring a theology of the
found.

Last but not least, Kelsey sketches a central role for the theological
imagination, which will prepare us for an examination of Hardy's
debts to, and affinities with, Coleridge's thought in the closing
sections of the chapter.

---

[32]Ibid., 50.
[33]Ibid.
[34]Hardy et al. 2010, 53.
[35]Ibid., 51. Importantly, one of the key forms of behaviour such abductive activity
should issue in is *care*, a precious part of the Church's vocation both collectively and
individually. See Quash 2012, Chapter 3.
[36]Hardy et al. 2010, 47.

David H. Kelsey: Being drawn to consummation

Kelsey's project is an example of what he calls 'secondary theology', in the context of which it is proper and, indeed, productive to operate in a 'hypothetical mode'.[37] This is, in the language we have been developing, a sort of abductive theology, very much open to what is found in the context of new cultural and historical situations, and ready to conjecture larger contexts in which to relate the newly apparent to the previously inherited. Kelsey writes:

> [E]nactments of the practice of secondary theology . . . provide analyses of the relation between received – that is, traditional – theological formulations and relevant features of the current culture of the ecclesial community's host society that show in what ways and why the former are inadequate in that cultural context.[38]

They do so not necessarily to condemn and discard previous formulations, but often in order to re-conceive and often re-receive such formulations, knowing that sometimes new life is activated in them through their critical encounter with 'current culture' (these were issues we looked at in Chapter 5). Kelsey is far from being a theologian who is against tradition. On the contrary, he seems to share Oliver O'Donovan's view that '[t]hose who have difficult vocations to explore need the tradition to help the exploration'.[39]

---

[37]Kelsey 2009, 9.

[38]Ibid., 24.

[39]O'Donovan 2009, 108. He writes too:

> No element formed by tradition can claim absolute allegiance. But the right to revise traditions is not everybody's right; it has to be won by learning their moral truths as deeply as they can be learned. . . . And if it should really be the case that [one is] summoned to witness on some terra incognita of "new" experience, it will be all the more important that [one's] new discernments should have been reached on the basis of a deep appropriation of old ones, searching for and exploiting the analogies they offer. No one who has not learned to be traditional can dare to innovate.

> This is an important caution to the theological approaches being explored and often commended in this book – and a valid one, whose test the 'innovators' I have examined in my case studies do, I think, pass.

But in his emphasis on taking seriously the challenges of the found, I regard Kelsey's work as very sympathetic to the core aims of the present book. He is helpful in a more specific way too. With great care, Kelsey delineates the ways in which the dynamic of God's relation to the world for the sake of its eschatological consummation is formally distinct from (and not reduced to or made dependent upon) the dynamic of God's relation to the world for the sake of its reconciliation. Kelsey is anxious to avoid any suggestion that the operations of any one of the three persons of the Trinity can be divided from the operations of the others. They are indivisible. However, he sees the usefulness of certain distinctions within this unity, partly because of the fact that the canon of Scripture offers what he discerns as three distinguishable 'stories' about how God relates to the created world, and – furthermore – offers these three 'stories' in forms that can be appropriated to the three persons of the Trinity, respectively. Like a triple helix (an image Kelsey himself adopts), the three stories are interconnected in a complex and generative way, but there is an irreducible threeness to them. They are stories of creation, eschatological consummation and reconciliation. He explores the persons of Father, Holy Spirit and Son, respectively, as the ways in which God is most properly active in these three stories.

What is striking about Kelsey's next step is his insistence that (i) a doctrine of creation does not in any way entail a doctrine of reconciliation, nor indeed of eschatological consummation (there is something 'complete' about creation that does not require it to be construed as a prelude to some further divine project); and (ii) that a doctrine of eschatological consummation is not just an extension of a doctrine of reconciliation. There is a sheer gratuitousness about God's (equally primordial) decision both to create and to eschatologically consummate human creatures; the non-necessity of the latter simply expresses God's perpetual love of doing *more than before*, as we might rather inadequately put it.[40] But this enables one to say (formally, if not in historical fact) that eschatological consummation can be understood as part of God's project

---

[40]Kelsey writes of our eschatological transformation that: 'Such enhancement does not entail that [human creatures] cease having limits. They remain finite creaturely powers, and God remains beyond human powers to comprehend God. But eschatologically enhanced, those powers are capable of knowing and loving God more deeply, not only more deeply than they could as fallen, but more deeply than they could as created' (Kelsey 2009, 40).

'apart from' the Fall. Had humanity never sinned, eschatological consummation would still have been bestowed, as a further and non-necessary supplement to creation.

And this, in turn, means that accounts of the Spirit's work (for it is the Spirit with whom this second story is most properly associated, just as it is the Father with whom the first story is most properly associated) must not construe it as a simple 'extension' of the Son's reconciling work.[41] Kelsey acknowledges the way that in our appropriation of these three stories an overemphasis on any one of them can have the distorting effect of 'bending' the others towards itself. This is especially evident in the way that sanctification has often been seen as a mere follow-up to justification – like the progress of liberating troops across a country once the decisive military victory has already been won. But this distorts the fact that humankind is (gratuitously) destined by God for glory *anyway*. The Fall – adventitiously, as Kelsey puts it – means that the work of eschatological consummation in fact has to deal with the consequences of sin (which is why the Spirit appears so engaged with this task in the story Scripture tells about the Spirit), but it is not the need to deal with the consequences of sin that provides the most basic rationale for the story most properly associated with the Spirit. In Kelsey's words:

> [S]tories of God relating to consummate creatures eschatologically are logically independent of stories of God relating to reconcile estranged creatures. Nothing about the stories of God drawing creatures to eschatological consummation entails that creatures must also be in need of reconciliation.

This is despite the fact, noted earlier, that:

> [A]s narrated, God's reconciling of creatures does seem to be partly dependent on God's drawing them to eschatological

---

[41]Although the story that tells mainly of the Spirit's work is also intimately *bound up* with the story that tells mainly of the Son's work; indeed, they are dialectically related: '[W]hile the claim that God draws us to eschatological consummation can and must be distinguished from the claim that God also reconciles us, the relation between the two claims is so dialectical that each may serve as part of the background of theological explanations of the other. Focus on how God relates to us to reconcile us requires, rather than supplants, claims that God also creates and eschatologically consummates us' (Kelsey 2009, 58).

consummation. If God is drawing creatures to an eschatological consummation that is a creaturely participation in the divine life, marked by holiness, and if those creatures are in fact alienated from God and are thus unholy, then drawing them to consummation does entail reconciling them. In concrete actuality, the "ifs" do obtain.[42]

The prepositions Kelsey uses to characterize the governing orientation of God to human beings in each of the three stories are, respectively, 'to' (for the orientation in creation), 'between' (for the orientation in eschatological consummation) and 'among' (for the orientation in reconciliation).

In creation, God's concern is directed in self-sufficiency to the making of something that is not-God, and the creation (which is not-God) is wholly in receipt of its being from beyond itself. This freedom of God in relation to a creation made *ex nihilo* is well characterized with the preposition 'to', says Kelsey.

In reconciliation, the incarnate God comes to abide in the midst of fallen creatures, to reshape them by his example, his teaching and his entry into personal relationships, which are grace-bestowing. This gracious intimacy-in-relation is well characterized with the preposition 'among', says Kelsey.

The Spirit, who draws us to eschatological consummation, is 'circumambient'. Kelsey points out that this makes it harder to speak of the Spirit as a 'Who' (in other words as somehow a distinct object of our regard or address) than it is to speak of Son or Father in this way.[43] To recall Ochs's phrase once again, the Spirit is known 'through the "shadow" or "back" of our visible behaviors'; or, in that powerful New Testament image, the Spirit is like the wind, discerned not directly but through the effects it has:

> The wind blows where it chooses, and you hear the sound of it, but you do not know where it comes from or where it goes. So it is with everyone who is born of the Spirit. (Jn 3.8)

The Spirit is the 'operative condition' for the life of transformation in holiness, as the wind is the operative condition for the movement

---

[42]Kelsey 2009, 122.
[43]See Kelsey 2009, 526.

of leaves, let us say, or the rise and fall of breakers on the shore. The Spirit may be known by a sort of abduction from what our direct experience presents to us: in this respect 'earthly things' can help us to understand 'heavenly things'.

But very often we will fail to 'receive their testimony' (Jn 3.11-12), and when we do succeed, the Spirit has to be operative in that understanding – not only as (on occasion) the '*object*' of our understanding but also as its '*medium*'. This sort of abductive knowledge of the Spirit from heaven – a Spirit elusive as well as highly intimate – is not just the result of reflection upon the life of transformation in holiness; it is itself an aspect of the life of transformation in holiness. For the same reason, although we have used an 'object'/'medium' distinction to articulate, respectively, the *what* and the *how* of knowledge of/in the Spirit, 'object' language is actually wholly inadequate here, for such knowledge is participatory at every level, and we cannot stand over against the Spirit.

The circumambient Spirit, argues Kelsey, empowers in us a 'vitality ordered to wisdom'.[44] Here is where a complicating strain enters his heuristic allocation of prepositions to the persons of the Trinity, and where a corrective supplementation by Hardy seems apposite. For Kelsey's phrase, with its implication of meaningful directedness ('ordered to wisdom'), unavoidably suggests that this Spirit is not just between us (let alone just 'at the back of' our behaviour), but ahead of us too; this Spirit is both circumambient and also pioneering, as D. H. Lawrence's image of 'the dark hound of Heaven, whose baying we ought to listen to' as he 'runs ahead into the unknown' proposed to us at the very beginning of this book. The 'to' which marks the radical act of creating a distinct other, and thus helps us to see what is most properly the Father's story in relation to his creation, is here added to by another 'to' – or, rather, the 'towards' so important to Hardy – which is the responsive advance of that creation into the ever-more-glorious fullness of God's life (and is *also* the work of God in us). As Traherne might have put it, and as we have emphasized already, all things (insects included) come from God, but they also *go to* God. In other words, 'towards' needs to take its place alongside 'between' as a properly pneumatological preposition. Indeed, it might be said – without contradicting Kelsey's argument in any significant way – that the betweenness (or what

---

[44]Kelsey 2009, 124.

we have elsewhere called the connectedness) of creatures in the creation's movement towards glory is bestowed on them all the more precisely by the fact that they have a shared towardness.

This, I hope, will make clear how Kelsey's and Hardy's approaches have things to say to one another in respect of their pneumatologies – and justify the point of this sortie into Kelsey's theological anthropology. Because, as we have seen, for Hardy:

> The very nature of things *is* towardness. One cannot expunge towardness from the condition of things.[45]

In both Kelsey's and Hardy's thought, we can see versions of how the ultimate at-homeness of created things with one another is the consequence of their shared, vertiginous advance towards a divine consummation that is, disconcertingly but headily, *more* than they previously knew.[46]

It is into just such disconcerting, heady unknownness that Nicodemus is invited in John 3. He is asked if he will be born again – born 'of the Spirit', which is also described by Jesus as being 'born from above' (Jn 3.3-8). It is a condition of being able to 'see the Kingdom of God'; to peep into glory, and see that to which all creaturely 'towardness' must be oriented if it is to find its eschatological felicity. Kelsey describes the Spirit who gives this transformative insight both 'trustworthy' and 'unmanipulable'. Like an extreme-case abduction, or A-reasoning (Peirce's language), or like the profoundest operative condition of our life and flourishing (Hardy's language), this Spirit is not something we can straightforwardly examine and dissect. The Spirit is known by the Spirit's fruits. And as Nicodemus may have felt, the unmanipulability of the Spirit makes living by its lights, entrusting oneself to it, vertiginously unsettling.[47] But the Spirit's trustworthiness at the same time confirms the virtues of this surrender to a second birth by delivering one into a new sense of home.

---

[45]Hardy et al. 2010, 47.

[46]The main difference between Hardy and Kelsey here is that Hardy does not make Kelsey's sharp distinction between the state of creation, which has its own proper integrity and goodness, and the state of eschatological consummation, which has an additional but quite non-necessary ('enhanced') goodness. He tends more to suggest that the former must always be tending towards the latter; indeed, that the desire for eschatological consummation is actually an operative condition of creation.

[47] [U]ncontrollable and unpredictable as wind . . . utterly ad hoc, unpredictable, unmanipulable, uncontrollable, occasion-specific. . . . (Kelsey 2009, 618)

Towardness and imagination

There is a further and very striking idea latent within Kelsey's thought that I note before we move on. It appears only as a sort of indirect implication of reading two of his claims in conjunction with one another: first, his insistence (as outlined earlier) on the logical independence of the story of eschatological consummation from the story of reconciliation; and second, his suggestion that the three stories of how God relates to creation tend to suit different literary forms. So, for example, Kelsey writes:

> Some [types of narrative], mostly about God relating to deliver and to reconcile, are remarkably realistic. Some, mostly about God drawing to eschatological consummation, are more nearly fantastical narratives.[48]

(He adds that stories of God relating to us in creation – in our quotidian, proximate contexts – suit the forms of *Wisdom literature*: proverbial saws being a classic instance of these.)

But if, as we have seen Kelsey argue so persuasively, '[s]tories about God delivering and reconciling generally presuppose stories about God drawing to eschatological consummation'[49] (while the converse does not hold), then a remarkable possibility comes into view. The 'nearly fantastical' stories can be seen to function as the 'presupposition' of the 'realistic' ones (these latter being the history-like accounts in the Gospels and Acts of the works of the incarnate Christ and of responses to his teaching and ministry).

In fact, many of the 'nearly fantastical' stories Kelsey is thinking of are precisely embedded *within* the realistic narratives, mainly in Jesus's teaching about the Kingdom of God; they are not just in apocalyptic-type literature, or prophetic visions. Jesus's parables work upon the imagination, by conjuring up startling pictures of what eschatological consummation might look like, and these pictures in turn make it difficult to look at (or act in) the present in the same way again. The fantastical actually affects and directs the historical (or 'realistic'). Jesus's disciples are transformed by his pictures and stories, as – in history – the members of his Church have repeatedly been transformed by them too.

---

[48]Kelsey 2009, 187.
[49]Ibid.

There is a risk of overstating the primacy of imaginative insight
over historical evidence: the risk, perhaps, of using the claim that
the worlds conjured by our imaginative powers are *truer* than
the givenness of our day-to-day world to justify a certain naïve
escapism from the intractabilities of material and social life[50]; or the
forfeiting of an ability to judge between imagined possibilities, such
that anything imagined is allowed to command uncritical credulity
simply by virtue of being imagined.[51] But caution in relation to these
dangers ought not to disregard the theologically compelling fact –
in a Christian perspective – that the imagined worlds of parables,
apocalypses and prophetic speech are offered to be trusted. They are
divinely licensed, and (like well-worn liturgies?) they can command
assent because they seem to disclose the deep dynamics of reality
somehow authentically, even if non-literally. In the case of parables
of the Kingdom, they are revelation by the Son of what the Spirit is
doing in service of eschatological consummation. In their own way
(which interrogates our present sense of what is 'realistic', just as
Nicodemus's established sense of what is realistic was interrogated
by the idea of a second birth 'from above'), they evoke that which
all reality is moving *towards*, and without which it is quite literally
senseless. Moreover, in doing this evoking, they also (when those-
who-have-ears-to-hear do indeed hear) *elicit* that towardness, that
forward movement.

The dignity that this gives to the imagination and its activity is
of great importance to a theology that seeks to endorse but also
critically challenge artistic practice. Pneumatology, as the sphere of
Christian theology concerned most properly with eschatological
consummation, is encouraged to recognize here the role that imagination can play in Spirit-led conceptions of that which alone can
give sense and direction to present life. The imagination becomes
a key instrument of *finding* that which is able to draw us forward
from our given state. The imagination works by attraction: it is

---

[50]J. R. R. Tolkien perhaps comes near to this in his idea of the 'eucatastrophe' in the
essay 'On Fairy-Stories' in *Tree and Leaf*. Tolkien 1964.
[51]It is this that various nineteenth-century writers – and perhaps most notably
Coleridge and George MacDonald – sought to address by making a distinction
between 'imagination' and 'fancy'; the latter having an air of whimsy and personal
caprice, while the former remained penetratively in touch with profounder laws
(operative conditions?) of the universe. S. T. Coleridge 1817; MacDonald 1871.

attracted by those (God-given) things that seek to conceive themselves in it, and it in turn attracts our practices and forms of 'real life' by giving body to such conceptions.

Garrett Green's distinction between two different but interrelated capacities of the imagination is helpful here, and assists an articulation of how this final chapter (with its emphasis on the forward orientation of thought by virtue of divine attraction) relates to the first chapter (with its emphasis on the importance of an analogical and historical mode of thinking which honours particularity).[52] Green talks of the 'paradigmatic imagination', which has the power to say more than a whimsical fancy could ever say,[53] but does not rush to invent a universal and abstract concept either. The latter option takes one outside historical process and homogenizes the unique instances of things; the former remains a private vocabulary incapable of testifying to or disclosing a shared world. One key aspect of the paradigmatic imagination meanwhile, as Green explains it, is:

> the ability of human beings to recognize in accessible exemplars the constitutive organizing patterns of other, less accessible and more complex objects of investigation . . . Imagination is the means by which we are able to represent anything not directly accessible, including *both* the world of the imaginary *and* recalcitrant aspects of the real world; it is the medium of fiction as well as fact.[54]

This description of the paradigmatic imagination at work captures something of what we have suggested goes on in the exploration of otherwise 'inaccessible' realities like the divine operative conditions of the world, and how we do so through shared images in a genre like story or a medium of collective performance like liturgy. Green's working distinction in the previous paragraph is actually blurred in our account inasmuch as, with Kelsey, we have wanted to question a straightforward distinction between representations of an 'imaginary world' and representations of a 'recalcitrant-real' one.

---

[52]David Kelsey himself acknowledges the value of Green's discussion in Kelsey 2009, 143–4.
[53]This is to deploy the term 'fancy' as Coleridge and MacDonald use it.
[54]Green 1989, 66.

Imaginary worlds can be experimental approaches to the real; the key thing is that they must not be escapist or private ones; they will be dramatically (which is to say, communally and experientially) 'testable'. Green too recognizes that there is a common quality to the use of the paradigmatic imagination in both 'fiction' and 'fact', namely, that they precisely are *approaches*. They are forms of seeking. In the terms we have been developing here, we might say that the shared images they generate (neither as mere fancies nor as rarefied abstractions) make a bid to representational – even revelatory – power inasmuch as they participate in what they communicate (the divine energies at work in the world), and can command assent and elicit community as a consequence.

That is one of two aspects of the paradigmatic imagination as Green outlines it – and the one most germane to this chapter's concerns. But, as I said, it is interrelated with a second (which Green explores first – as indeed we did in Chapter 1). This is (as Kelsey summarizes it) 'the capacity to recognize the pattern in a complex whole that makes it the whole it is'.[55] It is part of the discipline of thinking historically, with which we were concerned in Chapter 1. It can be characterized as the imaginative aspect of *phronesis*.

'Enacting eschatologically hopeful practices', as Kelsey writes, 'involves cultivation of the discipline of thinking historically'.[56] In other words, the 'imagining forwards' (or, as it may be, 'upwards', towards the consummation whose attractive power is the operative condition of our historical life) requires one to be adept at taking seriously how instances relate to one another in the extended medium of time. The God towards whom we are being drawn, as we argued in Chapter 1, is a respecter of time, and of particular instances of things. He 'names cats'. And on this basis, any claim we want to make about the shape of eternal truths must work *through* and not *as an escape from* the spread-out world of particulars, whose relations to one another will be discerned in *cases*, by *analogy* (a form of reasoning that uses paradigms to assist its work). The imagination is essential in making such analogical links (which is why, as we have seen, translation is an imaginative exercise, just as much as poetry or painting is).

---

[55]Kelsey 2009, 143; see Green 1989, 49–54.
[56]Kelsey 2009, 515.

The order discerned by the imagination in historical instances is, as Kelsey says, 'localized, ad hoc, and patchy':

> It is formulated in rules of thumb or in "on balance" generali-
> zations rather than in universal and exceptionless rules.[57]

Once again, these are neither private nor universal. They are practical and revisable in the light of new findings, but they only claim to have made findings at all in the light of previous instances. Knowing how to appeal to exemplars, but knowing how to appeal to them critically, is an essential part of the power of *finding well* by which we also become 'wise in [our] actions for general well-being'.[58] Imagination (as also freedom[59]) is essential to the process: in the course of such *phronesis*, you have to be able to imagine how something you knew before can be adapted to 'fit' some new circumstance.

Kelsey displays the value of Green's two types of paradigmatic imagination for his own scheme (as also for ours). The imagination supports practical reasoning in the quotidian, historical life we must negotiate without a clear historical overview or map. It supports 'the cultivation of dispositions for measured deliberation':

> [F]air-mindedness in weighing the merits of alternative, even
> conflicting, ways in which to proceed in enactments of [any]
> practice; respect for the long-accumulated wisdom incorporated
> in received traditions about how to proceed in similar circum-
> stances; prudence in assessing how far circumstances are and are
> not similar to the past; honesty about ways in which received
> wisdom have failed [sic]; humility in the face of the challenges
> confronting the practice in new circumstances; critical self-
> knowledge to counter tendencies to self-deception; decisiveness
> in judging; and so on.[60]

These are qualities that serve *koinonia* in the Church, and are essential to what we might call its sustainable practices: a distillation

---

[57]Ibid., 173.
[58]Ibid.
[59]See Kelsey 2009, 520, and his discussion of Ulrich Luz on the Sermon on the Mount, 783.
[60]Kelsey 2009, 142.

of them into a list (fair-mindedness, respect, prudence, honesty, humility, knowledge, judgement) shows how very similar they are to a Pauline list of moral virtues, offered to the churches (and underwritten – often – pneumatologically) for the good of their common life. So, for instance, in Galatians 5 (and having itemized a series of 'works of the flesh' that destroy human betweenness) Paul specifies those positive social virtues that are 'the fruit of the Spirit':

> [L]ove, joy, peace, patience, kindness, generosity, faithfulness, gentleness, and self-control. (Gal. 5.22-23a)

To embrace these is to be 'guided by the Spirit', the one who led Jesus Christ forwards in his earthly ministry, and the one who now leads Jesus's followers forwards into Christ-likeness, managing by this very forward movement to intensify and enhance the quality of relationships in the present as well.

But imagination also serves sanctification at another level: it serves a greater movement towards eschatological consummation; it helps adumbrate another sort of 'appropriateness' in our practices and behaviour that might initially look nearly fantastical. This too requires an education of our 'personal bodies' imaginative powers', as Kelsey puts it:

> [I]t requires personal bodies' imaginative powers to be so formed and disciplined, perhaps above all by Jesus' parables of the eschatological "kingdom of God," that they are capacitated to discern when and where changes over time in their lived worlds might, for all of their ambiguity, count as additional ad hoc parables of God drawing those contexts to eschatological blessing.[61]

In both of these exercises of the paradigmatic imagination, it is possible to see the Holy Spirit at work *fitting us to our environment*.[62]

---

[61]Ibid., 517.

[62]For what it is worth, Peirce's account of how human perception is always also interpretation shows his outlook to be quite compatible with this model of how shaped desire can serve a fit between ourselves and our environments: a confluence (or *communion*) of desire and environment is evident in the fact that we can wake

For although, in Kelsey's terms, the story of creation (in which we are given a proximate, quotidian environment that is sufficient for our good) is most appropriately associated with God the Father, it is the Spirit who fits us to this immediate environment in our day-to-day moral lives, helping us to reason from one case to another. But the Holy Spirit also fits us through sanctifying hope to our *ultimate* environment, in which we are promised 'a radically new start and a new life'.[63] To encapsulate the point in now-familiar terms, this Holy Spirit is *both* betweenness (as the one whose '*idiōma*', as Oliver O'Donovan puts it, is 'communion'[64]), *and* towardness (attracting us towards an enhanced reality that takes hold on us through immersion in the stories of the Bible and participation in the Church's worship, as well as through other 'ad hoc' signs of transformation in our experience). Indeed, as we have argued, (i) a further level of communion (or betweenness) than the day-to-day sustainable kind is bestowed on us precisely as a consequence of our growing, Spirit-bestowed desire for eschatological fulfilment (or towardness). *Towardness, in other words, can serve betweenness.* And (ii) the particular *quality* of communion that the Spirit can permit to take shape even in day-to-day creaturely life can become a sign of 'unearned, unanticipated . . . possibilities' in the future.[65] *Betweenness, in other words, can signify towardness.* The indexing of present sanctity to future consummation, and the influence of the vision of future consummation on present sanctity, is made very clear in the concluding section of the letter to the Galatians we looked at earlier, for Paul's list of the social virtues that characterize 'life in the Spirit' is quickly followed by the statement:

> If you sow to your own flesh, you will reap corruption from the flesh; but if you sow to the Spirit, you will reap eternal life from the Spirit. So let us not grow weary in doing what is right, for we will reap at harvest time, if we do not give up. So then, whenever

---

up at the time we want to even without mechanical help, and yet – by contrast – we can fail to hear the loud striking of the clock in our home when we are getting on with some task, and are all the more likely to become aware of it when for some reason it malfunctions and strikes the wrong hour – or doesn't strike at all (Peirce 1998, 229).

[63]Kelsey 2009, 481.

[64]O'Donovan 2009, 36.

[65]Kelsey 2009, 481.

we have an opportunity, let us work for the good of all, and
especially for those of the family of faith. (Gal. 6.8-10)

'To move off one's chair is first to be able to imagine walking,'
writes Dan Hardy.[66] This is especially important in a church which is
called to be a 'walking Church', as Hardy believes his own Anglican
Church to be. A walking church is a church attentive to historical
circumstance as potentially having an educative role; as potentially
a source of blessing. It is, we might say, a church that engages in
Found Theology:

> [T]heologians of a walking Church wander first and then think
> theologically and practically in response to what they have found.
> Whoever or whatever turns up as they walk, whatever they find
> as they go along, these become the found realities in response to
> which they think and act.[67]

The crucial importance of the imagination in 'getting one off one's
chair' is that it can connect one to a *telos* for that walking. It can
give an eschatological context to the proximate tasks of mundane

---

[66]As told to Peter Ochs; see Hardy et al. 2010, 86.

[67]Hardy et al. 2010, 86. As we have acknowledged before, this does not entail the
consequence – against which Oliver O'Donovan is rightly on his guard – that 'the
common intuitions of our own time' are held up as some sort of final authority
for the Church (O'Donovan 2009, 44). Hardy does not think that 'the immediacy
of [an] insight' should ever 'make the interpretation of Scripture seem superfluous'
(O'Donovan 2009, 26); only that given interpretations of Scripture must be subject
to renewed interrogation when a given age leads to new questions and insights.
These questions and insights are themselves to be tested against Scripture, as we
argued on pp. 15–19. This is not a position with which O'Donovan would, I think,
fundamentally disagree, even if the accents are placed differently in this rendition of
it. In his own words:

> The logic of human historicity is that living in a given age means having a distinct
> set of practical questions to answer, neither wholly unlike those that faced other
> generations nor mere repetitions of them. It is to be neither superior to nor
> independent of the past; but it is to be answerable for our own space and time
> and for its peculiar possibilities of vice and virtue. (O'Donovan 2009, 45)

And again:

> [I]t is not *the commands the Bible contains* that we obey; it is *the purposes of
> God that those commands reveal*, taken in their context. (O'Donovan 2009, 75)

life, and – at times – direct one beyond them. It can alert one to the summons of what Hardy calls 'God's embrace', in which the person will discover her or his full integrity, as well as the fullest integrity of all created things with one another.

> [T]his seeking is a continual sense, born of life in the Church: there is yet a higher measure to be found. Like an attractive force, this sense pushes the pilgrim forward, in mind and affection, to the divine.[68]

Frequently, the *telos* – as a 'measure' so much higher, so 'divine' in character – will appear to the imagination that grasps it as nearly fantastical. Coleridge, in his *Opus Maximum*, called this measure, with its power to speak especially to the imagination, the 'Logos in Spirit'.

We have dealt a good deal with Hardy's thought in this chapter, but it is here – in this notion of attraction – that his debts to *Coleridgian* thought come more sharply into view than perhaps anywhere else. This signals a good moment, therefore, to turn to Coleridge – and in particular to his *Opus Maximum* – to see how he generates his own fertile account of the vertiginous at-homeness that can mark our life in the world; of how divine attraction secures the ultimate coherence of things; and of how the working of an abductive imagination is crucial to the process.

Coleridge and the true centre

Hardy's own essay, 'Harmony and Mutual Implication in the *Opus Maximum*',[69] is a deeply perceptive account of the theological aspects of Coleridge's project, and the best exemplification of how Hardy's own theological sympathies are in tune with it.

At the heart of Coleridge's discussion is an account of how the particularity of the manifold objects and forces in the world (*All Things*: things human, social, cosmic, etc.) must be honoured while at the same time related dynamically to that towards which they

---

[68]Hardy et al. 2010, 67.
[69]Hardy 2006, 33–52.

tend (and by which they are attracted). Indeed, proper attention
to their particularity (the first emphasis) *depends upon* proper
alertness to questions of their value, meaning and *telos* (the second
emphasis). We might say that in this case too 'stories of eschatological
consummation' have a sort of logical priority over the 'realistic'
narratives by which we describe and tabulate the things of our
experience, and help us not to think we have grasped them properly
simply by cataloguing them according to their external relations
(number, weight, dimensions, mechanical relations, etc.). Perhaps
this is why Coleridge could use the vivid and extraordinary images
of a poem like *The Rime of the Ancient Mariner* – not to take us
away from reality, but to explore it more deeply.[70] Perhaps he has
this in common with Carpaccio, painting another ancient sufferer in
another death-filled landscape that is, likewise, nearly fantastical.[71]
Attention to the inmost dynamic of the things we find in the world
is what allows a fuller and more adequate explanation of them,
and *also* of their relations to other things – and this may invite
surprising and unconventional descriptions of them, best achieved,
sometimes, in artistic genres. Traherne, who had no issue with the
idea of a doxological encyclopedia in which prose verges constantly
on poetry, would have understood.

---

[70]Wordsworth's introduction to the *Lyrical Ballads* – that revolutionary collection of
works by both poets, first published in 1798, which opened with the *Rime* – famously
said that one of its aims was 'to choose incidents and situations from common life,
and to relate or describe them, throughout, as far as was possible in a selection of
language really used by men, and, at the same time, to throw over them a certain
colouring of imagination, whereby ordinary things should be presented to the mind
in an unusual aspect' (Wordsworth 1900–14, §5) – and this is indeed evident in
a great many of the poems. But what Coleridge does in the *Rime* is different and
complementary to this aim, for the 'incidents and situations' he conjures up are in
the main very far from 'common life'. Yet they speak profound (even eschatological)
truths. So, it is perhaps better to see the great experiment of the *Lyrical Ballads* as a
double exploration of how the over-familiar 'real' (with which we are all too much
at home) can be made vertiginous again, while the imaginatively wild can be proven
to give even deeper insight into the world we actually inhabit.
[71]Like the authors of the *Lyrical Ballads*, though nearly three centuries prior to them,
Carpaccio 'throws over real events [and places] a certain colouring of imagination',
as well as letting fantasy operate in his paintings to excite a heightened attention
to the meticulously observed – almost scientific – material details he shows us. He
makes us visionaries. It is, as one commentator puts it, 'a vision of things *sub specie
aeternitatis* . . . a true metaphysics grown on the enemy soil of the phenomenal'
(Sgarbi 1994, 33). This could almost be a description of Coleridge.

Hardy writes of how the issue for Coleridge was 'how realities *are constituted* and, while remaining fully themselves, are also *mutually implicated*'.[72] This means addressing 'all their actual differentiation and complexity', in the simultaneous act of giving 'full attention to the *intensity* of God's identity in God's creation of, and love for, the world'.[73] Only when both of these tasks are undertaken can one hope to '*discover the order of all things in relation to their source in God*' and thereby to '*recover what it is for them to be formed in their fullness by reference to the purposes of God*'.[74] Realities are related to one another proximately, but they are only fully (ultimately) related to one another by reference to God.

Importing some rather more obviously Christian theological language, we might say that, for Coleridge, the fundamental unity of things is their 'communion in hope'. Created things' shared attraction to God (their shared towardness) underwrites in them a mysterious sharing and bonding with one another. Indeed, in Coleridge's view, part of what we name when we call something *beautiful* is just this mysterious bonding. In other words, among the various faculties that are awoken in us as things display to us their communion-in-hope with one another, and elicit at the same time a recognition of how we belong to them and they to us, our *aesthetic* sensibility is a central one. The affirmation that reality is participative – that light and shadow, abstraction and figuration, depth and surface, fantasy and verisimilitude may all combine in praise of their Creator – is an affirmation of beauty.[75]

Coleridge saw nature as a set of dynamic processes based on polarities of attraction and repulsion, and celebrated the aesthetic faculty because it could discern the deep unity at work in this dynamism. But the unity itself demands a theological explanation, for it is a divinely given unity. The polarities are always mediated

---

[72]Hardy 2006, 38.

[73]Ibid., 39.

[74]Ibid., 35.

[75]We see such beauty in, for example, the amazing forms woven into the structure of the twelfth-century Kilpeck Church in Herefordshire. They are all fully themselves – wonderfully individuated – but also fully *related* to each other. And they are fully individual-and-related in this way by an act of aesthetic unification which refers them all to God, their deep source. The 'deep' here is a good 'deep'; a trustworthy 'deep', and a 'deep' that loves the individual forms whose being it supports, and that wants to preserve such forms in all their diversity.

ones, and – as the *Opus Maximum* argues – the mediation is trinitarian.

Coleridge deploys a particular symbol – }{ – as a sort of short-hand to help him in talking about the different levels at which this mediation takes place; the symbol means 'as distinct from but in continuity with'. The sort of reasoning whose processes it summarizes is, of course, analogical.

In densely compressed form, Coleridge outlines how the Self, with its acknowledged (in theological terms, sinful) proclivities to turn in on itself and seek a centre within itself, is engaged in a movement that is 'distinct from but in continuity with' what he calls 'the being drawn toward the true center'. In other words, the false movement is not the simple opposite of the true movement; it is a distorted form of it. What is the 'true center' to which Coleridge refers? Coleridge discloses his answer to this in describing another sort of movement, this time a divine one:

> The influx from the Light, with the Spirit[,] as }{ by the creaturely: Conjunction: Offspring or realized Poles, Particularization, Contraction as }{ Omneity, Dilation.[76]

The Logos (or 'Light') and the Spirit emerge here as the 'true center' of which Coleridge speaks. Logos and Spirit are distinct from, yet in continuity with, the creaturely realms, and the 'poles' in creaturely life can only be 'realized poles' when they are conformed in some way to the realized relation between the particularized (contracted to a span) incarnate one and the all-encompassing (dilating) Holy Spirit. The influx of this Light and this Spirit in their interrelation offers a corrective to sin by giving to humanity its true centre. And their approach elicits a responsive movement from creatures (individually and collectively) that corrects the fundamental distortedness of creaturely life. As fundamental, redemptive, consummative attraction, it has something of the character of worship.

'In these few sentences, therefore', writes Hardy, 'we find a compressed statement of the whole scheme of creation and salvation':

> [The Light and the Spirit] are transformatively conjoined to the creaturely, both in particularity (Christ) and in its dilation into

---

[76]S. T. Coleridge 2002, 327–8.

universality (the Holy Spirit).[77] . . . In other words, the *source and end* to which, in the "Schema of the Whole Man," [one sees] Coleridge tracing the movement by which human beings [are] illuminated in Reason and directed in love is also the "true center of all" upon which all else depends.[78]

Significantly for our purposes, the creaturely movement 'towards the true center' – in other words, the movement of attraction so fundamental to Coleridge's scheme of creation and salvation – is described by Coleridge as '*Abduction* from the Self' (my emphasis).[79] Here, we meet from Coleridge's pen the term that we have been allowing Peirce to make familiar to us. Although, as Ochs points out, 'Peirce must have adopted the term *abduction* from Coleridge, for whom it also referred to the product of musement', the term is used here in a less well-defined, though also less narrow, way than it is by Peirce.[80] Coleridge here in the *Opus Maximum* makes abduction a great deal more than a mode of inference; it is close to an event of salvation by the working of divine grace. Its theological implications are central and unavoidable (though as we have noted – more in agreement with Ochs than with Hardy – Peirce's theories of abduction are not without theological content, or intent). In Coleridgian abduction not just the mind but the whole *self* is attracted towards God. Hardy himself summarizes three ways in which we can see that a great deal more than logic is at stake here. The first, to reiterate, is the simple but overwhelming fact that the whole movement of abduction is premised on the Logos and the Spirit. The second is that:

[T]his "being drawn" incorporates both ontological and temporal elements of the created world, including differentiation and continuity, and also the enduring and the progressive, as mutually complementary.

---

[77]Hardy, perhaps unfortunately, uses the word 'universality' here to characterize the Spirit, whereas one of the arguments of this book is that the Spirit's work is better described in terms like generality, indefinite reach, relevance to 'All Things' – which is why Coleridge's own term 'omneity' works rather well. I am confident that what Hardy means by universality in this instance is actually what elsewhere he describes in terms of the simultaneous extensity and intensity of the Spirit's work.
[78]Hardy 2006, 51.
[79]S. T. Coleridge 2002, 327.
[80]Ochs 2011, 193.

And the third is that:

> [I]t is applicable both to the individual (as in *Aids to Reflection*) and also to society (as in *On the Constitution of the Church and State*), as that which serves "both for the permanence and the progressive advance of whatever . . . constitute the public weal."[81]

And what is true of Coleridge's account of abduction is echoed in Hardy's theology as he admires and appropriates it:

> In Hardy's pneumatology, abduction discloses God's capacity to attract all worldly and social institutions toward the eschatological direction enacted in his triune work.[82]

'Reference to God' may only be apprehended in acts of abductive thought (to which imagination is central, if we are ever to 'get off our chairs' in the first place) which are part of the far greater, transformative movement of the entire created order towards fulfilment in God.

Coleridge's *Opus Maximum* – like much of *Hardy*'s work, it has to be said – is written densely and at a high level of abstraction. A way in which we may better see the implications of his ideas fleshed out is by turning to his poetry. Certain passages of his poetry exemplify his sense of how particularity and omneity, contraction and dilation, can be 'realized poles' in relation to one another, and thereby the bringers of grace to the world. A turn to his poetry will also serve my own argument by offering a powerful affirmation of the proper place of imagination in a pneumatologically informed account of how Christian theology is to do its work, and with that I want to close this chapter.

In what follows, I will look at Coleridge's poem *Frost at Midnight*, and I am greatly helped in doing so by the literary scholar Graham Pechey's reading of it.[83] Although the first version of the poem was written some 20 years before the *Opus Maximum*, the continuity in some of the essential themes is strong.

---

[81]Hardy 2006, 51–2.
[82]Ochs 2011, 193.
[83]See Pechey 2012, 229–44.

As Pechey points out, the poem as a whole is marked by an extraordinary rhythm of expansion and contraction, almost like the quiet inhalation and exhalation of Coleridge's sleeping child, who lies next to him. The poem first moves inwards from the wintry exterior (where 'The Frost performs its secret ministry' and the owlet cries) to the parlour of the little cottage; then outward again to village, sea, hill and wood; then inward again – this time right to the hearth where the fire flickers within the bars of the grate. From this first series of rhythms, we are propelled into a second, in the second and third paragraphs of the poem, in which we are carried backwards in time to Coleridge's schooldays and then forwards to 'what turns out to be the widest spatial expansion of the whole, taking in no less than "all things"' (l. 63). Memory of his own childhood and anticipation of the future of his son interplay, before in the fourth and final paragraph of the poem we are returned to the thatched cottage and the frost once again:

> [T]he distant and the intimate are at one; contraction and expansion are reconciled [as "realized poles", we might say] in a quiet vortex of self-circling energy. The reconciling power of the Imagination, laconically adumbrated in the first sentence of the poem, is now comprehensively on show.[84]

How was the power of imagination adumbrated in the first sentence of the poem? We can only answer this question by saying something – first – about Coleridge's view of imagination as an operation of divine grace in the human being, and then – second – about how he uses a concrete image from nature to symbolize this grace.

First: how, for Coleridge, may imagination be seen as an operation of divine grace? In answering this, we can assume that for him, as eventually for Peirce, imagination is a faculty essential to abduction. And Coleridgian abduction, as we saw in our discussion of the *Opus Maximum*, is a consequence of the influx of the Holy Spirit (along with the 'Light', which is the Logos). So (i) imagination is a mode of relationship to God founded on the intrinsic, inexhaustible attractiveness of God, mediated through the depth and variety of created things (founded, in other words, upon grace). Moreover, (ii) imagination expresses the full, creative responsiveness of human

---

[84]Pechey 2012, 239.

beings to God in their engagement with those created things (it is, like faith, a *response* to grace; and as such it is also grace in action). Revealed here are the thoroughly pneumatological dimensions of Coleridge's promotion of the venturesome imagination. As Pechey puts it:

> [Coleridge] produces a theory of the imagination the terms of which are translatable into a theory of the working of faith, such that faith and imagination for him are in fact figures for one another.[85]

Second: how may a concrete symbol from nature symbolize this grace? Well, the subject of the poem's first sentence, as also of its title, is 'Frost'; a subject which (as we have just noted) returns again at the end of the poem. The opening sentence runs as follows:

> The Frost performs its secret ministry,
> Unhelped by any wind.[86]

There is special interest in this choice of frost, as Pechey points out, in that:

> [F]*rost* is a Middle English word of past-participial formation: *froze(n)* plus the abstract suffix *–t* or *–th* (as in *trust* and *health*). At its semantic core is a verb, making it into one of that class of deverbative nouns in which action and state, cause and effect, coincide. For Coleridge the verb *to be* as exemplified in God's *I am* is the supreme form of this hybridity and the transcendental root of all words.[87]

For Coleridge, who would almost certainly have known this etymology, frost is not adequately described simply as an *effect* of cold. It is the verb (freeze) exercising its own agency, so to speak; being its own cause. So we are invited to imagine it as free of the usual chains of cause and effect by which one thing causes a change in another. It is, as the poem puts it, 'unhelped', and it may therefore

---

[85]Pechey 2007, 13.
[86]E. H. Coleridge 1975, 240–2.
[87]Pechey 2012, 231.

stimulate us to imagine other things which are not part of such causal chains – like grace; like the poetic imagination with which Coleridge associates grace (for the working of both is 'secret' and 'unhelped' by chains of 'manifest cause and effect'); and even like God's very self. As Pechey goes on:

> [W]ith the help of a "dummy subject" (*it*), *freeze* can function almost as an intransitive verb, reflexively at once subject and object of its own activity. It might on this basis be said that [the poem's opening sentence] is a circumlocution whereby the nature of the verb *to be* – intransitive *is*, which *is* not the copula, absolute *is* – is revealed; and this *is* has only one possible subject: God. Only God *is*. Frost is, in short, the agent of a theophany . . .[88]

The God revealed in this theophany is the infinite 'I AM', who is also the gracious God at work in the betweenness and towardness of creation: God the Holy Spirit, the deliverer of grace; the sustainer of faith; and (in Coleridge's terms) also and as such the awakener of imagination. Rather as wind is an image of the 'secret ministry' of the Spirit in Jesus's midnight conversation with Nicodemus in John 3, frost images that secret ministry in this poem. Moreover, as Pechey points out, if one is inclined to say that the frost in *Frost at Midnight* 'stands for' God at work in grace or in the poetic imagination, one must allow 'stands for' to mean a great deal more than it usually does in order to appreciate Coleridge's full intention. It will only be a satisfactory statement 'if "stands for" implie[s] not the analogy of two ontologically distinct entities but that frost is *in the world* as grace is: it is the being of grace under another form, adapted to the "finite mind"'.[89]

---

[88]Ibid., 232.

[89]Ibid., 231. The insistence that 'stands for' has a strong rather than a weak meaning here is wholly in line with Coleridge's strong account of what a *symbol* is. Here, too, we see the sacramentality of his thought, as well as a characteristically particularist-and-social (and therefore *dramatic*) account of reality. As Pechey points out, his observations of the frost are offered neither as 'aphorisms' (which pretend to a sort of universality) nor merely a 'perception' (in the specific sense of a private reading valid only for the reader). Neither *epic* nor *lyric*, they are also, says Pechey, 'neither abstraction nor personification, but that alternative to both, beyond Understanding and Fancy, for which Coleridge reserves the term *symbol*' (Pechey 2012, 230). That faculty 'beyond Understanding and Fancy' which deals in symbols is, of course, 'Imagination'.

Thus, while Coleridge does indeed see sacramental significance in the action of frost (as Vaughan and Traherne see it in waterfalls, flies and a host of other natural phenomena[90]), he does something even more bold than this. He allows the possibility of some sort of equation of frost and grace – or at least, a continuity between them even where there must also be a distinction (⊬).

At the close of the third paragraph of the poem, Coleridge's future-turned imaginings take the form of a direct address to his sleeping infant son, and in these lines he confirms the idea that not only frost, but a great many other created things may be sacramental symbols of this grace to an imaginatively active (abductive) mind:

> But *thou*, my babe! shalt wander like a breeze
> By lakes and sandy shores, beneath the crags
> Of ancient mountain, and beneath the clouds,
> Which image in their bulk both lakes and shores
> And mountain crags: so shalt thou see and hear
> The lovely shapes and sounds intelligible
> Of that eternal language, which thy God
> Utters, who from eternity doth teach
> Himself in all, and all things in himself.
> Great universal Teacher! he shall mould
> Thy spirit, and by giving make it ask.[91]

(*Frost at Midnight*, ll. 54–64)

And in this affirmation of imagination's calling, he also consecrates himself to a theology, as well as a poetry, of finding. He is a

---

[90]It can plausibly be argued that Henry Vaughan is one key figure in establishing the terms for a later tradition of 'nature mysticism' in English poetry and prose, to which Coleridge and Wordsworth are central. There are many risks of anachronism here – to which Traherne too has been victim in claims that he is a 'proto-Romantic' in his love of nature and his celebration of childhood innocence (see the careful work of Elizabeth S. Dodd in debunking this idea [E. S. Dodd 2012]). Vaughan is genuinely a product of his own time and ought not to be dressed up in the clothes of another. But – to reiterate a point we made in Chapter 6 – 'found things' can found things, even at some considerably later time and in ways unforeseen by their original authors, and at the very least Vaughan helps to create the conditions in which Wordsworth and Coleridge will make a new sense of their world with a sense of the sacramentality of extra-ecclesial, natural phenomena.

[91]E. H. Coleridge 1975, 240–2.

theologian-and-a-poet of what is yet to be found, the thirst for which is awoken precisely by what has already been given. 'By giving', says Coleridge, God 'makes our spirit ask':

> [A]sk plays the part of an intransitive verb for the nonce, becoming thereby a description of the activity of the receptive self, the spirit appreciative of whatever good might come its way. Imagination then itemises in progressively incarnated images the varied goods of the created world to which this receptive self will be exposed. The spirit that has been taught by God to *ask* (no object specified) will not be applying a mental faculty to phenomena so much as standing in a place lit by Reason, a place from which those goods are seen to abound infinitely.[92]

We are returned here, in the company of Coleridge (who beautifully models the disposition) to the searching openness, the 'proneness to finding', which in Chapter 2 we explored in relation to Moses, the man who first turned aside to look more deeply, and heard as a consequence the infinite I AM self-declare.

What have we found of the Spirit?

'*By giving make it ask*'. God, in the Holy Spirit, promises to our spirits – as also to our bodies – 'abundantly far more than all we can ask or imagine' (Eph. 3.20). Yet, in promising us more than we even know *how* to ask for, we are drawn into a dynamic of asking nonetheless, which (paradoxically) relates us better to our present and our past, as well as to our future. We may read our past not as complete and sealed off, but as having its own openness that presses for new receptions, new translations, in the present. We may read the detailed particularities of our present as sites where 'God truly is, though we did not know it', inviting our discernment of the analogical threads that bind what we *now encounter* to what we *have known*, and engaging us in desire and responsibility (in our 'wills' and 'shalls', our 'mays' and 'lets') for future pilgrimage. The dynamic of giving, leading to asking, leading to giving (and so on)

---

[92]Pechey 2012, 240.

can be mapped onto the dynamic of finding, leading to searching, leading to finding. We are made into people for whom asking (being prone to find) is a fundamental orientation of being, a way of life enshrined in a whole set of communal and individual virtues, many of them learnt best in worship. The prevenient work of the Spirit who first gives (or makes God findable) establishes the life of asking and imagining, and rewards it continually with *more*; 'abundantly far more': in other words, with a transformative excess that arrives like the first fruits of an unimaginable harvest, or a wind that carries the sounds and scents of the Kingdom.

As we draw to the close of this final chapter of the book, it seems appropriate to draw together some of the threads of the various claims that have been made about the Holy Spirit along the way – and especially the more exegetical claims.

The texts that speak of the Spirit in the New Testament are diverse in their emphasis and in their apparent intention. There could easily be an artificiality in forcing some sort of coherence out of them. This book has aimed to avoid that artificiality, and instead to make its forays into history, art history, literary criticism, philosophy and theology serve a vision of human historical life in the world, under God, in which the scriptural testimony to the Spirit will also hang together intelligibly. At the same time, it has aimed to let the scriptural testimony to the Spirit 'prove itself' by the way that it positively resources this vision of human historical life which is at once historical, art historical, literary critical, etc.

The Holy Spirit whom Christians worship as part of the triune Godhead is witnessed to in Scripture as one who underwrites what we might call a non-futile anti-universalism. In other words, the Spirit works particularly, making things more what they are, concretizing them rather than homogenizing them. This is the anti-universalism of the Spirit. But the Spirit also gathers and relates things more intensively than any ingenious human scheme – whether of thought or of action – could do on its own. The radical particularization achieved by the Spirit is not atomization (the multiplication of arbitrary units) but generates the basis of communion. This is its non-futility.[93]

We have seen this in texts that show the Spirit embedding people more fully in their shared history, and helping them find themselves,

---

[93]A winning celebration of this non-futility of particulars, and our need for analogical thought and artistic practice (rather than universal concepts) in order to do justice to them, comes from Dorothy L. Sayers in 'The Poetry of Search and

one another and God in the context of that history. The Spirit is one who 'leads' creatures *into* and *through* (not *out of* history). Jesus Christ was led by the Spirit to the banks of the Jordan; to Simon Peter's mother-in-law; to those first disciples to whom (sometimes literally) he would give 'names'; to the wilderness; to town after town; to the mountain or the sea to pray; to Jerusalem; to Gethsemane; to the Cross. And as Jesus Christ was led by the Spirit, so are his followers. Peter is led to the particular Gentile individual Cornelius by the speaking of the Spirit; and his mould-breaking finding is that the Spirit is not only propelling him there but also waiting for him there, presenting him with a fact that he cannot deny: 'the gift of the Holy Spirit had been poured out even on the Gentiles' (Acts 10.45-46). Nicodemus is led to Jesus by night, and on to a new baptism by the Spirit that transforms his life, giving him a new mission. The disciples to whom Jesus says farewell on the night of his betrayal go on to receive what was promised to them then: a Spirit who will lead them from moment to moment of the difficult challenges that lie ahead. This Spirit does not deliver a single, all-purpose message for them to pack up and take with them on their various missions as they proclaim the good news. On the contrary, the Spirit waits for them up ahead, in the many different contexts to which they will go; their job is to be ready to find the Spirit there with just what that moment requires:

> When they bring you to trial and hand you over, do not worry beforehand about what you are to say; but say whatever is given you at that time, for it is not you who speak, but the Holy Spirit. (Mk 13.11)

---

the Poetry of Statement'. Her sentiments capture a great deal of what this book is about:

> Poetry, history, and theology are alike in this: that they involve a philosophy of singleness, because their chief concern is with unique events. They are therefore never wholly amenable to analysis by statistical methods, neither can their crucial experiments be reproduced in the laboratory. Wars, love-affairs, myths may bear a general resemblance to one another; but only once does Frankie Drake gun the Armada up the Channel; only once does Dante meet Beatrice in Florence; only once does the only God irrupt into terrestrial history, at Bethlehem in Jewry, in the reign of Caesar Augustus. All assessment of such events must depend, perilously, on the evidence of human witnesses and on argument by analogy; and since poetry is the language of analogy, there hangs about all such events a disconcerting aura of poetry. (Sayers 1963, 280–1)

Not 'this for all times' (a given) but 'whatever at that time' (a found thing): this is what is to be looked for. Not a final word, but a series of 'words' (potentially as abundant as the languages of the earth through which the animating Spirit romped ecstatically at Pentecost), whose faithfulness to one another can only be analogically displayed, as translations between languages are, and whose multiplicity is celebrated by the Spirit as additive not diluting.

The Holy Spirit particularizes in history, and fosters communion in particularity, but also, crucially, orients the present to the eschatological future, and (which is to make a closely related point) the surface of things to their infinite depths: their operative conditions. This Spirit searches our depths as the Spirit searches God's depths (1 Cor. 2.9-13), and brings them into the deepest relation. Human understanding is transformed in this process, losing its conventional moorings and having to abandon its normal strategies of comprehension and mental containment. This is, once again, the Spirit of 'moreness', a Spirit poured out 'without measure' (Jn 3.34). The level of vertiginous dazzlement that is awoken in the human searcher by the unmeasurable Spirit becomes a sort of evidence that it is really God with whom she or he has to do. The imagination seems better equipped to step in here when understanding fails (and when fancy remains playing with its own inventions), but even here the Spirit will continue to exceed our capacities. Paradoxically, it is only through the exercise of our imaginations that Christians learn that what we look for is 'abundantly far more than all we can . . . imagine'.

The dazzlement awoken by the vision of the divine operative conditions of our world, vouchsafed to those who ask in the Spirit, is inseparable from an 'inarticulate aspiration', which is 'the deepest form of prayer' (see Rom. 8.15-27).[94] This is because the God who made us (i.e. who is the most profound operative condition of our creation) is also the God who destines us for eternal life with Godself (i.e. who is the most profound operative condition of our eschatological consummation). '[T]he Spirit comes to us from that new world, the world waiting to be born,' as N. T. Wright puts it.[95] The Spirit yields to us a perspective in which consummation can

---

[94]Dodd 1932, 135.
[95]Wright 2005.

be hoped for and imagined, even if, at times, the hope seems nearly fantastical.

But, to reiterate, this future vision is intimated to us in such a way that our appreciation and commitment to present reality is enhanced, for although the 'stories' of creation and of eschatological consummation may be capable of distinction from one another, the God who is the operative condition of one is the God who is the operative condition of the other. We belong less fully to God if our anticipation of the future leads us to belong less fully to the world (though the deeper our belonging to God and world, the more critical we are likely to be in our relation to that world). We become part of the transformation we hope for as our imaginations are resourced by the Spirit, and in our transformation we draw forward and transform the reality around us. Our imagination of future consummation is resourced in such a way that we live differently *now*. Given a taste for that consummation (in a mode, as Jesus's provocative images of the Kingdom show, that engages our imaginations just as much as our search for the depths of the created world does), our principle task is 'not to fall backwards' (Rom. 8.15).

In all these diverse passages, Scripture delivers abundant resources for a pneumatology of finding. And a pneumatology of finding reminds theology that it is itself historically discovered ('found'), and will always be so.

Inconclusion

I will be found by you, says the LORD

(JER. 29.14)[1]

I want to end in a junk shop. The British artist Anna M. R. Freeman, whose work appears on the cover of this book, has used her paintings to explore with moving intensity the odd ways in which disparate objects find themselves connected to one another. She is fascinated by the jumbled mélange of furniture, lamps, lumber, fabric, mirrors, crockery and glass that is typically found in junk shops. Things have been deracinated from a former environment where they once were at home, and await some new home, which is as yet undisclosed. Some are grandiose and baroque, and some humbly functional. Thrown together by circumstance, they seem also bound together by expectation. Though her paintings do not have human figures in them explicitly, they are deeply human: the objects she paints have been made for, and used in, human environments. They carry the traces – the smell, the imprint, the warmth – of their previous use. Eloquently, they are like signs of the human situation itself; they are *like* the humans who made and used them. We humans, too, as Freeman understands us, are marked by a sense of transition and longing:

> The making of my work is motivated by an investigation of different structural environments that provoke a sense of longing, a strange remembering of times past and a hopeful looking forward into eternity. . . . [M]y work is not only about

---

[1] I here use the Revised Standard Version rather than the New Revised Standard Version used in most biblical quotations in this book.

a particular longing for a permanent space but also [the] deep
human desire for permanence in a world that shows so many
signs of decay.[2]

We, like the objects found and painted by Freeman in junk shops,
wait in hope for a consummation that we cannot yet see.[3] For this
reason, it seems, many of her paintings have titles (and sometimes
deliberately biblically resonant ones) that express human 'towardness': 'Anticipate', 'Waiting Silently', 'Waiting Hopefully', 'Assurance about what we do not see' and so on.

While they wait, however, Freeman's paintings allow these
familiar, 'humanly warm' objects to slip the leash in some way. They
are presented to us in a way that also subverts the perspectives we
usually use to place and explain and account for them. The old
hierarchies which make a chandelier distinguishable from an oil can
are suspended, and we do not easily see, at all times, whether we
are seeing a small thing close up or a large thing far away, a surface
or a depth, a detail or a whole, a joined thing or merely an adjacent
thing. In this way, her painting works not only to accentuate the
lack of control we exercise over 'what is coming' (because the
transformations that may happen are not ones we may be able to
predict at all, with any specificity) but also 'what is now' (because
there is more to these objects and their relations with one another
than what some conscious human design has made of them). In other
words, although the denizens of the junk shops Freeman paints are
in a condition of expectation, they are also purveyors of an intense
sense of the surprising possibilities of the present moment. Partly by
means of their odd juxtapositions, they work to make one another

---

[2]Freeman 2012. The quotation comes from an unpublished paper delivered at
Biola University on 3 March 2012. Freeman's website can be visited at http://www.
annamrfreeman.com (accessed 25 July 2013).
[3]In doing so, incidentally, they expose some of the pretensions of the baroque, which
so dislikes emptiness that it seeks to fill every space; to satisfy every longing in the
here and now, with extravagant decorative flourishes. It is a language of fullness,
which can end up seeming like a sort of denial of what we know we do not (yet)
have; the satisfaction of misplaced desire; a surfeit that leaves us still hungry. The
junk shops (which themselves include now-dislocated baroque objects, and which
ironically are often – in literal terms – as 'full' as an orchestrated baroque space)
more honestly express the unfilled needs of creaturely existence.

more intensely, more richly present to our gaze than they would be if they were in an environment that we took for granted. The artist contributes to this process by joining in with what the objects are already doing to one another: framing, heightening, intensifying one another. And she can do this because even in deracination, and even in anticipation, they are also in communion: a communion she finds and does not impose. They share across – even deconstruct – their boundaries. They thrill with a special quality of 'betweenness'. The objects in the junk shops become an image of being itself as mutually participative because its source is in God and is going to God, and in this light, it is possible to look at a Freeman painting with the words of Pseudo-Dionysius in one's ears, and find that both mean more as a consequence:

> [From God] comes the bare existence of all things, and hence their unions, their differentiations, their identities, their differences, their similarities, their dissimilarities, their communions of opposite things, unconfused distinctions of their interpenetrating elements; the providences of the Superiors, the interdependence of the Co-ordinates, the responses of the Inferiors, the states of permanence wherein all keep their own identity. And hence again the intercommunion of all things according to the power of each; their harmonies and sympathies (which do not merge them) and the co-ordinations of the whole universe; the mixture of elements therein and the indestructible ligaments of things; the ceaseless succession of the recreative process in Minds and Souls and in Bodies; for all have rest and movement in That Which, above all rest and all movement, grounds each one in its own natural laws and moves each one to its own proper movement.[4]

In light of all that has been said in the preceding chapters about the continual call to finding which is generally the task of creatures and specifically the task of Christian theology, these closing remarks cannot in good conscience call themselves a Conclusion – not, at least, if a Conclusion implies a final word.

---

[4]Dionysius the Areopagite 1920, 97–8.

Sometimes at their own instigation, the protagonists of this book (or, at least, of its case studies) have been helpfully interpreted by analogy with figures from the Old Testament. The tasks that faced the translators of the King James Bible have been illuminated by an examination of Ezra's work to make the maculations of the Torah productive for his people. The radically receptive experimentation of Carpaccio, who looked on death in the hope that God's promises could ultimately give an assurance of life, was shown to have a productive fascination with the figure of Job. And Henry Vaughan, in a wilderness condition, was seen sustaining himself with the example of Ishmael. Ezra, Job and Ishmael have emerged as three – perhaps unexpected – models for a Found Theology that lives in the expectation of what the Jewish philosopher Robert Gibbs calls 'renewing and renewed instruction'.[5] They are figures who 'set out' in various ways, with a sense of God's promises providing a condition (even if, as in Ishmael's case, a condition of lament) for calling out to the future. None of them can claim his given present moment as complete, fulfilled, consummated.

Christian theology, so this book has argued, ought not to suppose that this marks a straightforward point of contrast between Christian pilgrims and Old Testament ones. Canons, like doctrines, are fixed 'in order to bear multiple meanings'.[6] Their givenness is best related to, in other words, when seen as a resource for finding, rather than as an end to searching. The problem is when their givenness becomes an occasion for idolatry; when particular exegeses themselves become idolized. Gibbs writes:

> By renewing the text, exegesis prevents idolatry. The premise of exegesis is that it does not unearth the final meaning but that reading will continue. Indeed, to stop the exegesis would be to idolize a final interpretation. Hence, there must be not only anti-idolizing interpretation of the text but also an exegesis of the exegesis, preventing the most recent exegesis itself from becoming an idol. The overflowing of meaning itself overflows the vessels in which it is received. They too become fountains of meaning, not merely because there is always more there but because to not seek that more is to reduce first the scripture and then the

---

[5]Gibbs 2010, 43.
[6]Ibid., 40.

tradition of interpretation to idols. There is an ethical need here to keep going.[7]

Gibbs calls this approach a 'pneumatological' one. It chimes well with the vision of the Catholic theologian Jean-Yves Lacoste, who articulates a principled suspicion of the idea of the hermeneutic circle in Christian thought:

> The image of the hermeneutic "circle" is less illuminating than it seems. We can learn only to the extent that we can let the unanticipated put our expectations and our prejudices in question. Authentic discovery punches a hole in the circle, since only pseudo-questions carry their own answers ready and waiting in their bosoms. Pre-understanding without honest admission of non-understanding will hardly invite more than the most meager discoveries.[8]

Coleridge has been an ally in this book's endeavour, but even Coleridge's evocation of the steady attraction of all things towards their true centre has, perhaps, not enough of a note of the uncertain and the open-ended about it.

Dan Hardy, on his final pilgrimage to the Holy Land, observed that in 'Israel's life' there was something that was neither 'discretely

---

[7]Ibid., 42. I hope that in some measure the work of the present book will contribute a response to Gibbs's challenge to Christian theology at the close of his essay, even though he thinks the cost to Christianity of responding fully will be 'exorbitant'. What Christian theology may need to learn, he says, is 'a focus on disincarnation, a trace replacing full presence, a recognition that Christianity is singular and not the totality, a heightened attention to scripture and commentary as traces of God – with a plurality of voices and acknowledgment that there is no final interpretation – an infinite that is social and not held in the mind, and a radical ethics of responsibility for others' (Gibbs 2010, 51). 'Disincarnation' is not a concept I favour in the context of this book's emphasis on multiple concretizations of God's purpose in history, but I take the overall challenge seriously.

[8]Lacoste 2007, 272; cited in O'Donovan 2009, 62. O'Donovan quotes Lacoste approvingly in service of his own very specific expectation that the 'puncher of holes' in our self-ratifying hermeneutic circles will always be *Scripture*. My point here, with Gibbs, is that Scripture can itself all too easily become confused with the exegeses it is used to endorse, and that sometimes holes are punched in our *exegeses* by encounters with the Spirit in Church and world as well as in scriptural study (though they will then need exploring in the context of the study of Scripture).

predetermined' nor simply 'haphazard', and felt able to affirm this of his own life too. What God's people do is not explicitly preplanned by God, nor is it just 'unguided wandering'. The wandering genuinely involves our own decisions and mistakes, and yet it takes place within what Hardy calls a divine 'pre-estimation', which grounds and accommodates the wandering in such a way that the wanderers can come to genuine new insights and move forward. A divine pre-estimation, for Hardy, is 'some prior assignation of values, a prior judgement that this place to and through which [God's people] were wandering was useful for God's purposes'.[9] The movement may not be linear, it will not always be progress, and it will not always be at the same speed, but it can be an advance (even, perhaps, 'from one degree of glory to another' when the movement 'comes from the Lord, the Spirit' [2 Cor. 3.18]):

> [A] pilgrimage, or a journeying to the Promised Land, is a kind of wandering, open to the contingencies of space and time, which is at the same time a gradual discovery of purpose. A significant stage of that discovery is to find that we are not wandering on mere barren lands but on places that have already served the purposes of those who came before us, and, moreover, that those places too were built on relics of prior estimations.[10]

The better our historical sensibility (the more developed our awareness of 'the purposes of those who came before us'), the better our decisions about future directions will be served.

In the first chapter of this book, I recognized two major challenges to my model of Found Theology, and the first of these was relativism: the risk that wandering is mere meandering, and that there is no goal to any of it. Hardy's model whereby the wandering itself is not predetermined, but the space in which we wander is pre-estimated, seems to me to offer good resources for answering the worry – without going to the other extreme and claiming that there is no

---

[9]Hardy et al. 2010, 58. Hardy sees this idea of divine pre-estimation, or the preparation of places and environments for human discovery in history, acknowledged in Psalm 108's words: 'I will divide up Shechem, and portion out the Vale of Succoth' (Ps. 108.7). He also reads Jesus Christ's journeys on foot as a sort of measuring out of the land, a manifestation in human footfalls of the divine 'portioning out'.
[10]Hardy et al. 2010, 58–9.

such thing as a misstep. It is possible to say, as Hardy does, that 'this entire creation' is a pre-estimated space. Oliver O'Donovan would concur, in his insistence that 'Christians . . . have encountered a God who has made himself known as Beginning and End, Alpha and Omega, whose beginnings are a faithful token of his endings'. It is on the basis of this confidence in divine pre-estimation that they may speak 'not only of a good to be loved in action here and now, but of a good to be looked for in the future'.[11] David Kelsey would concur too, in that for him there is a measure ('the Son's life') that 'defines the life into which the Spirit draws creatures':

> Eschatological life is nothing other than the life the Son has with the Father in the power of the Spirit.[12]

So relativism need not be disablingly feared – but a complacent confidence in the courses we plot in history, and their rightness, ought not to come marching through the back door either. In Hardy's words:

> [W]e must also bear in mind the indeterminacy present in each estimation, so that what we do in this world leaves room for other ways of enacting what we do – and other ways of making use of what we have done. Searching out those other ways is part of a pilgrimage; the movement of that pilgrimage is to uncover traces of God's purposes through all these possibilities; and the end of the pilgrimage is to have found one's place fully within God's purposes.[13]

The other challenge to my model of Found Theology that I identified in Chapter 1 was quietism, by which I meant the inability to name or resist evil. This often takes the form of a belief that what *is* is what *must be*.

---

[11]O'Donovan 2009, 99.

[12]Kelsey 2009, 127. He adds later that:

> [T]he concrete ways in which God goes about actualizing [eschatological] blessing [are] always consistent with the concrete particularity of Jesus Christ. "Son" norms the radical freedom of "Spirit". (Kelsey 2009, 451)

[13]Hardy et al. 2010, 59.

My response on this front is that the histories that I have traced with some care in the various case studies in this book have, I hope, been respected in their integrity rather than cynically raided for the ways in which they will neatly underwrite a prior theology of providence. They are histories that show plenty of evidence of missteps, and the marks of violence and of error. My view is that no doctrine of the Holy Spirit, and no Christian theological account of history, that cannot survive exposure to actual cases is worthy of the name. Christians must live with the fact that history is both the condition of original sin, *and* the medium through which redemption comes. Many of the found things in the world, many of its particularities, are sinful or sin-affected. My argument in this book for taking the 'found' seriously has not been that every sinful act or effect we may encounter is God-given; it has been that all God-givenness comes to us in the form of history.

In a number of the foregoing chapters, we have looked at the perennial challenge that Christian theology faces in giving an account of history that is neither too panoptic nor too despairingly relativist. It has been proposed that a theological account of history may want to begin with the idea of covenant, and that theology is in a position to read history as punctuated by a series of covenantal moments in which some sense of 'significant form' in historical process is affirmed, without that entailing a grand narrative of progress, or some hubristic claim to know the big picture. The revelation of God takes place not in the 'whole temporal series' (to echo C. H. Dodd, at whose thought we looked in Chapter 5), but through an intensive disclosure of presence at certain points in that series. Covenants themselves are about moments of intensive encounter, which may offer insight into the deeper meaning of the temporal order. This is not to suppose that the covenants in which God's hand has been discerned by the faithful in history will bring into intelligible focus – exhaustively – all the other events that they are ever likely to have to make sense of. It is to say that they disclose some of the character of God who relates to and sustains that temporal order, giving it its origin and its end. In addition to which, these covenants also have the effect of shaping possibilities in time (in that sense, making their own contribution to the patterning of history from within the temporal order).

Kelsey recognizes that the Christian doctrine of providence – though it must be deployed tentatively – does make a difference to how history is read. Special, intensive moments like covenants, or moments when the righteous appear to be rewarded and the wicked punished, when considered apart from a doctrine of providence, 'can be construed with equal probability as happenstances':

> They function as signs only when they are described using the conceptual framework of a doctrine of providence . . . taken in the context of Wisdom's creation theology [they are] signs (not "evidence") of God's moral rule . . .[14]

There is no decisive evidence for a divine purpose to be gained by the simple acquisition of more historical information. God's ordering of creation, as Kelsey puts it, is 'a quasi-personal, socially teleological ordering of events that, when detectable, is always ad hoc and situation-specific':

> This ordering of creaturely proximate contexts by God's creating them makes such reality intelligible, but only in terms of stories of what God is up to, what God's intentions are in concrete social circumstances.[15]

In such stories, Christians do nevertheless come to learn that they have a promise to go on.

We might say that covenants with the God of Abraham, Isaac and Jacob (and the God of Jesus Christ) are like 'Amens'. Amen derives from a Hebrew root which signifies *reliability*. This is a concept that may also find itself translated as 'truth', to be sure, but truth in a very particular sense. Truth as reliability is truth understood in the context of a relationship of trust. Such truth, to be affirmed, requires in its advocate a degree of appropriate understanding and experience (for as Paul says about the Corinthian *glossolalia*, no one can 'say the "Amen" to your thanksgiving when he does not know what you are saying'[16]), but it does not require some sort of total grasp of things. It can be uttered while our understanding still remains incomplete; it can be said while the 'labour of

---

[14]Kelsey 2009, 212.
[15]Ibid., 241.
[16]1 Cor. 14.16; Nicholas Lash makes the same point in his beautiful opening chapter on 'Amen' in Lash 1992, 2.

interpretation' still goes on.[17] What is being expressed in an Amen is precisely that recognition of God's integrity and truth which the Abrahamic covenant signals, and which is, as Nicholas Lash eloquently puts it, so central to Judaism's faith that '"Amen" may almost be taken as a name for God'.[18] Those who confess 'Amen' are those who 'conclude that, in the end, all shall be well, because, from the beginning, there is only "Yes" in God'.[19] So Amen is something which people affirm – or take to themselves – because they have grasped something about the reliability of God. '[Saying Amen] is a people-binding act,' says Lash, 'a pledge of solidarity with the purposes and promises of God.'[20] And as such a pledge, it becomes something that has historical effects. In this sense too an Amen and a covenant can be compared. And, like the covenant with Abraham in its various reaffirmations, Amens are strung out through history as points of intensity and recognition – mutually related and mutually conditioning although always utterly specific to their individual context of utterance. Even if it may sound like a conclusion, Amen is never just said *once* – not, at least, by us creatures in history. And yet, it points to a conclusive truth: that God is faithful.

This claim offers the key to understanding how *we* are to be conformed to God's faithfulness by our relationship to the historical process. We are to enter the covenant, as Abram did. We are to tread the 'covenant corridor', even though the guaranteeing of its trustworthiness is God's work alone. This is perhaps the moment to recall the fact that the New Testament's greatest debt to Genesis 15 is Paul's use of the line '[Abraham] believed God, and it was reckoned to him as righteousness' (Gal. 3.6). Too often – and especially in Protestant traditions of interpretation – this 'reckoning as righteous' is treated without any reference to history. On the contrary, it is read in an assertively *non*-historical way, as a forensic event – a change of status in some technical sense. Even when the link is preserved between the belief that Abraham manifests (on the one hand) and the establishing of a covenant (on the other), a frequent move is to weaken this historicity of the *covenant itself*.

---

[17]Lash 1992, 2.
[18]Lash 1992.
[19]Ibid., 3.
[20]Ibid., 1.

We may think here of Karl Barth's theology of covenant, and of Colin Gunton's nervousness about it (along with his wariness about forthright doctrines of the eternal Sonship of Jesus Christ) because it seemed to say that everything important had already been sorted out before the foundation of the world.[21] Gunton saw such a theology as a threat to the here-and-now decision of freedom. He sought to counter Barth's insertion of a divine purposing into history (to which human beings *must* conform) by a fairly strong account of the autonomy of human reason (this also acting as an apologetic strategy in relation to Kantian strands in modernity). But it may be that a better defence than autonomy against the 'insertion model' of righteousness is a different and more involving sort of 'must': the requirement to follow; to shape one's living with modal auxiliaries that both bind and open one to God in history. The righteousness of Abram is a form of discipleship (even in his simple readiness to follow God outdoors to have a look at the stars [Gen. 15.5]!). Like Ezra, Job and Ishmael, he is a figure informed by the past but radically open to the future. He is a figure who 'sets out'.

The Amen is not a pattern imposed on history, it is something both encountered and said (and re-said) *within* it. If the 'truth' that Jesus speaks about when he says that he is 'the way, the truth and the life' (Jn 14.6) is 'Amen-type' truth, then it is reliability that he is offering, and its close approximation in this saying with the idea of the 'way' (which is, in Hebrew, '*halakah*') can be read as a suggestion that the manner in which his followers will find truth in history is by living out their relation to his reliability – his Amen – in the twists and turns of history. Seeking the truth by striving for a God's eye view, we may say, leads to *spectatorship*; seeking the truth in intensive encounter leads to *discipleship*. The God who accompanies history asks us to follow him – in reliability, in abiding. It is as a 'way' that God in Christ is a 'truth'.

> For this reason it is through him that we say the "Amen", to the glory of God. (2 Cor. 1.21)

And to be established in him (with others) so as to say this Amen at all, we must first – and continually – be anointed by the Spirit whose coming is also and always promise.

---

[21]See Gunton 1998, 162–5; see also Chapter 16 of Gunton 2007.

BIBLIOGRAPHY

Adams, N. (2008). 'Reparative Reasoning'. *Modern Theology*, 24(3), 447–57.

Allison Jr., D. C. (2005). *Studies in Matthew: Interpretation Past and Present*. Grand Rapids, MI: Baker.

Andrewes, L. (1629). Easter Sermon, No. 15 (Whitehall, 1 April 1621), *XCVI Sermons*. London: George Miller for Richard Badger.

Bacon, F. (2004). 'Franciscus de Verulamio sic cogitavit' (G. Rees and K. Murphy, trans.). In G. Rees (ed.), *Novum Organum*. Oxford: Clarendon Press.

von Balthasar, H. U. (1992). *Theo-Drama: Theological Dramatic Theory, Dramatis Personae: Persons in Christ* (vol. 3). San Francisco: Ignatius Press.

—(1993). *Razing the Bastions: On the Church in this Age* (B. McNeil, trans.). San Francisco: Ignatius Press.

—(2000). *Theo-Logic: Theological Logical Theory* (vol. 1). San Francisco: Ignatius Press.

Barth, K. (1961). *Church Dogmatics* (G. T. Thompson, trans.; G. W. Bromiley and T. F. Torrance, eds; vol. 4, 3.1). Edinburgh: T&T Clark.

Belting, H. (1980/81). 'An Image and its Function in the Liturgy: The Man of Sorrows in Byzantium'. *Dumbarton Oaks Papers*, 34/35, 1–16.

Bentley Hart, D. (2003). *The Beauty of the Infinite, the Aesthetics of Christian Truth*. Grand Rapids and Cambridge: William B. Eerdmans Publishing Company.

Berlin, A. (ed.) (2011). *The Oxford Dictionary of Jewish Religion* (2nd edn). Oxford: Oxford University Press.

Bernard of Clairvaux. (1937). *On the Love of God and Fragments from Sermons on the Canticle of Canticles* (T. L. Connolly, trans.). London: Burns, Oates and Washbourne.

Bethell, S. L. (1951). *The Cultural Revolution of the Seventeenth-Century*. London: D. Dobson.

Beza, T. (1587). *Master Bezaes Sermons Upon the Three First Chapters of the Canticle of Canticles* (I. Harmar, trans.). Oxford: Joseph Barnes.

Bonhoeffer, D. (1996). *Act and Being: Dietrich Bonhoeffer Works* (vol. 2). Minneapolis: Fortress Press.

Brueggemann, W. (1992). *The Prophetic Imagination*. London: SCM Press.

Butterfield, H. (1950). *Christianity and History*. New York: Charles Scribner's Sons.

Calvin, J. (1960). *Institutes of the Christian Religion* (F. L. Battles, trans.; vol. 1). London: SCM Press.

Chambers, D., Pullan, B., and Fletcher, J. (eds) (1992). *Venice: A Documentary History, 1450-1630*. Oxford: Blackwell.

Cohen, M. R. (ed.) (1988). *The Autobiography of a Seventeenth-Century Venetian Rabbi: Leon Modena's Life of Judah*. Princeton: Princeton University Press.

Coleridge, E. H. (ed.) (1975). *The Complete Poetical Works of Samuel Taylor Coleridge* (vol. 1). Oxford: Clarendon Press.

Coleridge, S. T. (1817). *Biographia Literaria*. London: Rest Fenner.

—(2002). In T. McFarland and N. Nalmi (eds), *Opus Maximum* (vol. 15). Princeton: Princeton University Press.

Collingwood, R. G. (2005). *The Idea of History, revised edition, with Lectures 1926-1928, edited with an introduction by Jan van der Dussen* (Revised edn). Oxford: Oxford University Press.

Collins, J. J. (2005). *The Bible After Babel, Historical Criticism in a Postmodern Age*. Grand Rapids, MI: William B. Eerdmans Publishing Company.

Croce, B. (1921). *Theory and History of Historiography* (D. Ainslie, trans.). London: Harrap.

Cummings, B. (2002). *The Literary Culture of the Reformation: Grammar and Grace*. Oxford: Oxford University Press.

Dawson, J. D. (2002). *Christian Figural Reading and the Fashioning of Identity*. Berkeley and Los Angeles: University of California Press.

Demus, O. (1970). *Byzantine Art and the West*. London: Weidenfeld and Nicholson.

Dionysius the Areopagite. (1920). *On the Divine Names and The Mystical Theology* (C. E. Rolt, trans.). London: SPCK.

Dodd, C. H. (1932). *The Epistle of Paul to the Romans*. London: Hodder and Stoughton.

—(1938). *History and the Gospel*. London: Nisbet & Co.

Donne, J. (1839). *The Works of John Donne D.D., with a Memoir of His Life* (vol. 5; Henry Alford, ed.). London: John W. Parker.

Eliot, T. S. (1974). *Old Possum's Book of Practical Cats*. London: Faber and Faber.

Fenner, D. (1594). *Song of Songs*. Middelburgh: Richard Schilders.

Finberg, A. J. (ed.) (1927). *John Ruskin, Modern Painters*. London: G. Bell and Sons Ltd.

Fish, S. (1980). *Is There a Text in This Class?* Cambridge, MA: Harvard University Press.

Fowl, S. E. (2000). *Engaging Scripture, A Model for Theological Interpretation*. London: Blackwell.

Freeman, A. M. R. (2012). Exploring Structural Space: Evocations of Longing, Memory and Eternity (unpublished paper delivered at Biola University on 3rd March 2012).

Frei, H. (1974). *The Eclipse of Biblical Narrative, A Study in Eighteenth and Nineteenth Century Hermeneutics*. New Haven: Yale University Press.

Fry, P. H. (ed.) (1999). *Samuel Taylor Coleridge The Rime of the Ancient Mariner: Complete, Authoritative Texts of the 1798 and 1817 Versions with Biographical and Historical Contexts, Critical History, and Essays from Contemporary Critical Perspectives*. Boston: Bedford St Martin's.

Fry, R. (1908). 'A Genre Painter and His Critics'. *The Quarterly Review*, 208, 491ff.

Fulford, B. (2007). 'Biblical Interpretation in Gregory of Nazianzus and Hans Frei'. (PhD), Cambridge.

—(2013). *Divine Eloquence and Human Transformation: Rethinking Scripture and History through Gregory of Nazianzus and Hans Frei*. Minneapolis: Fortress Press.

Gadamer, H.-G. (1989). *Truth and Method* (2nd edn). London: Sheed and Ward.

Gibbs, R. (2010). 'The Disincarnation of the Word: The Trace of God in Reading Scripture'. In K. Hart and M. A. Signer (eds), *The Exorbitant: Emmanuel Levinas Between Jews and Christians*. New York: Fordham University Press.

Green, G. (1989). *Imagining God: Theology and the Religious Imagination*. San Francisco: Harper and Row.

Gregory Nazianzen. (1995). 'Select Orations of Saint Gregory Nazianzen' (E. H. Gifford and C. G. Browne, trans.). In P. Schaff and H. Wace (eds), *A Select Library of the Christian Church Nicene and Post-Nicene Fathers: Cyril of Jerusalem, Gregory Nazianzen* (series II, vol. 7). Peabody, MA: Hendrickson Publishers.

Gregory of Nyssa. (1978). 'The Life of Moses'. In A. J. Malherbe (ed.), *The Life of Moses by Gregory of Nyssa*. New York: Paulist Press.

Gunton, C. E. (1998). *The Triune Creator: A Historical and Systematic Study*. Grand Rapids, MI: William B. Eerdmans Publishing Company.

—(2007). 'Barth on Creation'. In P. Brazier (ed.), *The Barth Lectures*. London: T&T Clark International, pp. 239–54.

Halivni, D. W. (1997). *Revelation restored: Divine Writ and Critical Responses*. Oxford: Westview Press.

Hardy, D. W. (2001). *Finding the Church: The Dynamic Truth of Anglicanism*. London: SCM Press.

—(2005). 'Karl Barth'. In D. F. Ford and R. Muers (eds), *The Modern Theologians: An Introduction to Christian Theology since 1918* (3rd edn). Oxford: Blackwell.

—(2006). 'Harmony and Mutual Implication in the Opus Maximum'.
In J. W. Barbeau (ed.), *Coleridge's Assertion of Religion: Essays on the
Opus Maximum*. Leuven: Peeters.

Hardy, D. W., Hardy Ford, D., Ochs, P., and Ford, D. F. (2010). *Wording
a Radiance: Parting Conversations on God and the Church*. London:
SCM Press.

Hartshorne, C., Weiss, P., and Burks, A. (eds) (1958). *Collected Papers of
Charles Sanders Peirce* (vol. 2). Cambridge, MA: Harvard University
Press.

Hartt, F. (1940). 'Carpaccio's Meditation on the Passion'. *The Art Bulletin*,
22, 25–35.

Hauerwas, S. (1991). Why there is No Salvation Outside the Church *After
Christendom? How the Church is to Behave if Freedom, Justice, and a
Christian Nation are Bad Ideas*. Nashville: Abingdon Press.

Herbert, G. (2004). In J. Tobin (ed.), *George Herbert, The Complete English
Poems*. London: Penguin Books.

Higton, M. (2003). 'Boldness and Reserve: A Lesson from St Augustine'.
Anglican Theological Review, 85(3), 447–56.

Higton, M. and Muers, R. (2012). Whose Psalm is it Anyway? Why
Christians Cannot Read Alone *The Text in Play: Experiments in
Reading Scripture*. Eugene, OR: Cascade.

Hopkins, G. M. (1994). The Wreck of the Deutschland *The Works of
Gerard Manley Hopkins*. Hertfordshire: Wordsworth Editions Ltd.

Howard, D. (2000). *Venice and the East: The Impact of the Islamic World
on Venetian Architecture*. New Haven: Yale University Press.

Jauss, H. R. (1982). *Toward an Aesthetic of Reception* (T. Bahti, trans.).
Minneapolis: University of Minnesota Press.

—(1990). 'The Theory of Reception: A Retrospective of its Unrecognised
Prehistory' (J. Whitlam, trans.). In P. Collier and H. Geyer-Ryan (eds),
Literary Theory Today. Cambridge: Polity Press.

Jenkins, T. (2006). *An Experiment in Providence: How Faith Engages
with the World*. London: SPCK.

Jenkins, T. and Quash, B. (2009). The Cambridge Inter-Faith Programme
Academic Profile. Retrieved November 2012, from http://www.
interfaith.cam.ac.uk/en/resources/papers/cip-academic-profile

Jerome, S. (1989). 'St Jerome: Letters and Select Works' (W. H. Freemantle,
trans.). In P. Schaff and H. Wace (eds), *A Select Library of Nicene and
Post-Nicene Fathers of the Christian Church* (vol. VI). Edinburgh:
T&T Clark. (Reprinted from: 1989).

Katz, D. E. (2011). 'The Ghetto and the Gaze in Early Modern Venice'.
In H. L. Kessler and D. Nirenberg (eds), *Judaism and Christian
Art: Aesthetic Anxieties from the Catacombs to Colonialism*.
Philadelphia: University of Pennsylvania Press.

Kelsey, D. H. (2009). *Eccentric Existence: A Theological Anthropology.* Louisville, KY: Westminster John Knox Press.

Kermode, F. (1979). *The Genesis of Secrecy, on the Interpretation of Narrative.* Cambridge, MA: Harvard University Press.

Kinser, S. (ed.) (1973). *The Memoirs of Philippe de Commynes* (vol. 2). South Carolina: University of South Carolina Press.

Klessmann, R. (1971). *The Berlin Gallery* (D. J. S. Thomson, trans.). London: Thames and Hudson.

Kosík, K. (1967). *Die Dialektik des Konkreten.* Frankfurt a.M: Suhrkamp.

—(1976). *Dialectics of the Concrete, A Study on Problems of Man and World.* Dordrecht: D. Reidel Publishing Company.

Kristeva, J. (1989). *Black Sun: Depression and Melancholia* (S. L. Roudiez, trans.). New York: Columbia University Press.

Kueh, R. (2012). *Reception History and the Hermeneutics of Wirkungs-geschichte.* (PhD), Cambridge.

Lacoste, J.-Y. (2007). 'More Haste, Less Speed in Theology'. *International Journal of Systematic Theology,* 9, 263–82.

The Lambeth Conference (1958). *The Lambeth Conference 1958: The Encyclical Letter from the Bishops together with the Resolutions and Reports.* London: SPCK.

Lash, N. (1992). *Believing Three Ways in One God, A Reading of the Apostles' Creed.* London: SCM Press.

Lauterbach, J. Z. (ed.) (2004). *Mekhilta de-Rabbi Ishmael* (vol. 1). Philadelphia: The Jewish Publication Society.

Lauts, J. (1962). *Carpaccio: Paintings and Drawings: Complete Edition* (E. Milman and M. Kay, trans.). London: Phaidon.

Lawrence, D. H. (1988). 'On Being Religious'. In M. Herbert (ed.), *Reflections on the Death of a Porcupine and Other Essays.* Cambridge: Cambridge University Press.

Lewalski, B. (1979). *Protestant Poetics and the Seventeenth-Century Religious Lyric.* Princeton: Princeton University Press.

Lewis, C. S. (1970). *God in the Dock.* Grand Rapids, MI: Eerdmans.

Lily, W. (1970). *A Shorte Introduction of Grammar, Generally to be vsed in the Kynges Maiesties dominions.* Menston: Scolar Press.

Lipton, D. (1999). *Revisions of the Night: Politics and Promises in the Patriarchal Dreams of Genesis.* Sheffield: Sheffield Academic Press.

Ludwig, G. and Molmenti, P. (1907). *Life and Works of Vittorio Carpaccio* (R. H. Hobart Cust, trans.). London: Murray.

MacDonald, G. (1871). *Works of Fancy and Imagination.* London: Strahan & Co.

Maritain, J. (1953). *Creative Intuition in Art and Poetry: The A.W. Mellon Lectures in the Fine Arts National Gallery of Washington.* New York: Pantheon Books.

Martz, L. (1954). *Poetry of Meditation, A Study in English Religious Literature of the Seventeenth Century*. New Haven: Yale University Press.

Mason, S. (2000). *Carpaccio: The Major Pictorial Cycles* (A. Ellis, trans.). Milan: Skiro.

Mateo-Seco, L. F. and Maspero, G. (eds) (2010). *The Brill Dictionary of Gregory of Nyssa*. Leiden: Brill.

Milbank, J. (1997). *The Word Made Strange: Theology, Language, Culture*. Oxford: Blackwell.

—(2010). *Culture, nature, and mediation*, The Immanent Frame. Retrieved 13 August 2013, from http://blogs.ssrc.org/tif/2010/12/01/culture-nature-mediation/

More, T. (1981 [1531]). *A Dialogue Concerning Heresies*. Vol. 6 of Thomas M. C. Lawler, Germain Marc'hadour and Richard C. Marius (eds), *The Complete Works of St. Thomas More*. New Haven and London: Yale University Press.

Morgan, R. (2013). 'Spirit and Letter: Mapping Modern Biblical Interpretation'. In P. S. Fiddes and G. Bader (eds), *The Spirit and the Letter: A Tradition and a Reversal*. London: T&T Clark.

Mori, G. (1990). 'L' "iter salvationis" cristiano nel Spellimento di Cristo di Vittore Carpaccio'. *Storia Dell Arte*, 69, 164–200.

O'Donovan, O. (2009). *A Conversation Waiting to Begin: The Churches and the Gay Controversy*. London: SCM Press.

O'Reilly, J. (1992). 'The Trees of Eden in Mediaeval Iconography'. In P. Morris and D. Sawyer (eds), *A Walk in the Garden: Biblical, Iconographical and Literary Images of Eden*. Sheffield: JSOT Sheffield Academic Press.

Ochs, P. (1998). *Peirce, Pragmatism, and the Logic of Scripture*. Cambridge: Cambridge University Press.

—(2011). *Another Reformation: Postliberal Christianity and the Jews*. Grand Rapids, MI: Baker Academic.

Origen. (1989). *Commentary on the Gospel According to John, Books 1-10* (R. E. Heine, trans.). Washington, DC: Catholic University of America Press.

Osten, G. v. d. (1952). 'Christus im Elend, ein niederdeutsches Andachtsbild'. *Westfalen: Hefte für Geschichte, Kunst und Volkskunde*, 30, 185–98.

Owen, John (1674). *Pneumatologia or, a discourse concerning the Holy Spirit. Wherein an account is given of his name, nature, personality, dispensation, operations, and effects*. London: J. Darby for N. Ponder.

Parris, D. P. (2009). *Reception Theory and Biblical Hermeneutics*. Eugene, OR: Pickwick Publications.

Pechey, G. (2007). 'Pointed Remarks: Scholasticism and the Gothic in the English Counter-Enlightenment'. *Christianity and Literature*, 57(1), 3–33.

—(2012). '"Frost at Midnight" and the Poetry of Periphrasis'. *The Cambridge Quarterly*, 41(2), 229–44.

Peirce, C. S. (1992). In N. Houser and C. J. W. Kloesel (eds), *The Essential Peirce: Selected Philosophical Writings* (vol. 1). Bloomington, IN: Indiana University Press.

—(1998). In P. E. Project (ed.), *The Essential Peirce: Selected Philosophical Writings* (vol. 2). Bloomington, IN: Indiana University Press.

Perkins, W. (1591). *A Golden Chaine, or the Description of Theologie: Containing the Order of the Causes of Saluation and Damnation, According to Gods Woord. A View of the Order Wherof, is to be Seene in the Table Annexed. Written in Latine by William Perkins, and Translated by an other. Hereunto is Adioyned the Order which M. Theodore Beza vsed in Comforting Troubled Consciences* (T. de Bèze, trans.). London and Cambridge: Edward Alde and John Legate.

Phillips, C. (1911). 'An Unrecognized Carpaccio'. *The Burlington Magazine*, 19, 144–52.

Quash, B. (2005). *Theology and the Drama of History*. Cambridge: Cambridge University Press.

—(2012). *Abiding*. London: Bloomsbury.

—(2013). 'Community, Imagination and the Bible'. In N. Messer and E. Paddison (eds), *The Bible: Culture, Community, Society*. London: T&T Clark International.

Quinn, D. (1969). 'Donne and the Wane of Wonder'. *English Literary History*, 36, 626–47.

Ricoeur, P. (1980). 'Toward a Hermeneutic of the Idea of Revelation'. In L. S. Mudge (ed.), *Essays on Biblical Interpretation*. Philadelphia: Fortress Press.

Ridolfi, R. (ed.) (1957). *Prediche sopra Giobbe* (vol. 1). Rome: A. Belardetti.

Rogers Jr., E. (2005). *After the Spirit: A Constructive Pneumatology from Resources Outside the Modern West*. Grand Rapids, MI: William B. Eerdmans Publishing Company.

Rush, O. (1997). *The Reception of Doctrine: An Appropriation of Hans Robert Jauss' Reception Aesthetics and Literary Hermeneutics*. Rome: Gregorian University Press.

Sandri, M. G. and Alazraki, P. (1971). *Arte e vita ebraica a Venezia, 1516-1797*. Florence: G.C. Sansoni.

Sayers, D. L. (1963). *The Poetry of Search and the Poetry of Statement*. London: Victor Gollancz.

Scavone, D. (1999). 'Joseph of Arimathea, the Holy Grail, and the Edessa Icon'. *Arthuriana*, 9(4), 3–31.

Sgarbi, V. (1994). *Carpaccio* (J. Hyams, trans.). New York: Abbeville Press.

Smith, P. (1966). *The Historian and History*. New York: Random House.

Southwell, R. (1595). *St Peter's Complaint*. London: John Windet for John Wolfe.

Ticciati, S. (2005). *Job and the Disruption of Identity*. London: Continuum.

Tolkein, J. R. (1964). *Tree and Leaf*. London: George Allen and Unwin Ltd.

Traherne, T. (1958). In H. M. Margoliouth (ed.), *Centuries, Poems and Thanksgivings* (vol. 2). Oxford: Clarendon Press.

—(2005). In J. Ross (ed.), *The Works of Thomas Traherne* (vol. 1). Cambridge: D.S. Brewer.

—(2007). In J. Ross (ed.), *The Works of Thomas Traherne* (vol. 2). Cambridge: D.S. Brewer.

Tyndale, W. (1530). *The Obedience of a Christen Man and how Christen Rulers Ought to Governe*. Antwerp: M. de Keyser.

Valcanover, F. (1989). *Carpaccio* (L. Pelletti, trans.). Antella, Florence: Scala.

Vaughan, H. (1976). In A. Rudrum (ed.), *The Complete Poems of Henry Vaughan*. Harmondsworth: Penguin.

Vaughan, T. (1650). *Anthroposophia Theomagica*. London: T.W. for H. Bluden.

Wade, G. (ed.) (1932). *The Poetical Works of Thomas Traherne*. London: P.J. and A.E. Dobell.

Weinfeld, M. (1970). 'The Covenant of Grant in the Old Testament and in the Ancient Near East'. *Journal of the American Oriental Society*, 90, 184–203.

Weinstein, D. (2011). *Savonarola, the Rise and Fall of a Renaissance Prophet*. New Haven: Yale University Press.

White, T. (1655). *A Method and Instructions for the Art of Divine Meditation*. London: A.M. for Joseph Cranford.

Williams, R. (2000). *On Christian Theology*. Oxford: Blackwell.

—(2003). *Anglican Identities*, Plymouth: Cowley.

—(2004). 'Historical Criticism and Sacred Text'. In D. Ford and G. Stanton (eds), *Reading Texts, Seeking Wisdom*. Grand Rapids, MI: William B. Eerdmans Publishing Company, pp. 217–28.

—(2005). *Grace and Necessity*. London: Continuum.

Wordsworth, W. (1900–14). 'Preface to Lyrical Ballads'. In C. W. Eliot (ed.), *Prefaces and Prologues to Famous Books* (vol. 39). New York: P.F. Collier & Son.

Wright, N. T. (2005). The Holy Spirit in the Church. Retrieved 13 August 2013, from www.fulcrum-anglican.org.uk/events/2005/inthechurch.cfm

INDEX